The Haunted Cinema of
Pedro Costa

The Haunted Cinema of Pedro Costa

James Naremore and
Darlene J. Sadlier

INDIANA UNIVERSITY PRESS

This book is a publication of

Indiana University Press
Office of Scholarly Publishing
Herman B Wells Library 350
1320 East 10th Street
Bloomington, Indiana 47405 USA

iupress.org

© 2025 by Indiana University Press

All rights reserved
No part of this book may be reproduced or utilized in any form or by any means, electronic or mechanical, including photocopying and recording, or by any information storage and retrieval system, without permission in writing from the publisher.

First Printing 2025

Cataloging information is available from the Library of Congress.

ISBN 978-0-253-07322-8 (hdbk.)
ISBN 978-0-253-07323-5 (pbk.)
ISBN 978-0-253-07324-2 (web PDF)
ISBN 978-0-253-07325-9 (ebook)

FOR

Teolinda Gersão and Bertina Sousa Gomes,
longtime friends in Lisbon

AND

Alex, Patrick, Jay, and Amy

CONTENTS

ACKNOWLEDGMENTS

WE OWE SPECIAL THANKS to Pedro Costa, who provided material related to his films and generously spent time with us in Lisbon answering our questions. This is not an "authorized" book about him—we never submitted pages for his approval, and our critical judgments are entirely our own. But we are certain the book is better because of the help he gave us.

Thanks also to Jon Vickers, founding director of the Indiana University Cinema, who invited Costa in 2011 for a retrospective titled *The Films of Pedro Costa: The Artful Tableau of Everyday Life*. The experience of meeting Costa and seeing everything he had created up to that point generated our desire to write this book, and it never would have happened without Jon's discriminating intelligence as a programmer.

Photographer João Pina gave us permission to use his portrait of Pedro Costa, and Carmel Curtis of Indiana University's Moving Image Archive provided expert help with the book's other illustrations. We are grateful to Jonathan Rosenbaum and the second anonymous reader for their helpful comments on the manuscript. We thank our editorial project manager Carol McGillivray, and at Indiana University Press assistant acquisitions editor Sophia Herbert, designer Pamela Rude, and project editor Nancy Lightfoot. They were a wonderful team to work with on the project.

Finally, we thank one another. One reader of our manuscript asked who wrote which chapters, a question impossible to answer because everything was written by the two of us. As individuals, we took turns writing the first drafts of chapters, but everything was passed back and forth between us for rewriting. This book is the product of a long and happy marriage. There were times when we bickered with one another like Jean-Marie Straub and Danièle Huillet in Costa's documentary, but working together has been a labor of love.

The Haunted Cinema of
Pedro Costa

Pedro Costa

INTRODUCTION

Who Is He and What Is Cinema?

WHEN WE MENTIONED to friends and colleagues that we were writing a book about Portuguese film director Pedro Costa, many of them asked, "Who is he?" This reaction is not surprising, as Costa's films have never received wide distribution in the United States and he is not the sort of commercial artist who is backed by an army of technical support, A, B, and C camera crews, a bevy of producers, brand-name actors, and a publicity machine. Apart from his earliest pictures, he has chosen to work with very small budgets, minimal equipment and crew, and mostly nonprofessional actors, creating paradoxically beautiful films about unglamorous and difficult lives in impoverished locations. But although he is relatively unknown to general moviegoers, a growing number of cinephiles recognize him as one of today's most important filmmakers. We hope this book will stimulate curiosity about his work among the uninitiated and be of value for his many confirmed admirers. Probably no other living director has made such socially and artistically significant films or so often provoked viewers to ask another question, famously posed by André Bazin: "What is cinema?"

We will eventually address that question, but at the outset, some historical and biographical information will be of use. Costa's national origins have shaped his work, and his life and career have been strongly marked by his responses to Portugal's history, politics, and culture. Once a maritime empire, the small nation began its rise to global power in the early fifteenth century with the conquest of the North African port of Ceuta; by 1498, its commercial reach extended as far as India, where Vasco da Gama arrived after sailing around the Cape of Good Hope to establish a lucrative spice trade. By the mid-sixteenth century, Portugal's empire included Brazil, several Atlantic islands, Angola, Mozambique, Guinea-Bissau, Goa, Macau, and numerous costal outposts in Africa, India, China, Southeast Asia, and Japan. Its national identity was strongly tied to exploration, commercial trade, conquest, and colonialism—including periods of slavery and persisting after other European powers began to divest themselves of colonies.

Brazil became an independent nation in 1822, but after World War II, António de Oliveira Salazar's right-wing Estado Novo dictatorship (1933–1974) was criticized in the United Nations, in part because of Portugal's continued rule over diamond- and sugar-rich Angola and other African territories, where resistance movements were growing and a war of independence broke out in the early 1960s. This costly, protracted war eventually resulted in a 1974 rebellion by officers in the Portuguese military, the collapse of the Estado Novo, and the establishment of a left-wing government through what became known as the Carnation Revolution—so called because although the streets on April 25 were filled with soldiers, cheering citizens placed flowers in the barrels of their rifles. One year later, in 1975, the African territories gained their independence. With decolonization underway, those in former African colonies who had benefited from and supported the right-wing regime grew increasingly uneasy and began returning in droves to Portugal.[1]

Among the colonies that became independent after the revolution was Cape Verde, an island archipelago off the west coast of Africa that had served as a port for slave trading and was the location of the infamous Tarrafal prison, where Salazar kept political prisoners rounded up by his secret police. Beginning in the 1960s, the archipelago became important for another reason. Lisbon was initiating many new construction projects, among them the Banco de Portugal and the Calouste Gulbenkian Museum, and at the same time suffering from a labor shortage; nearby Cape Verde was a good source of low-paid immigrant labor. A generation of Black and brown men from the islands began to take jobs in the most arduous and dangerous construction sites, some sending money home to their wives and families and others never reuniting with loved ones. They settled in shantytowns, eventually building a large casbah-like community in an area of Lisbon called Fontaínhas, which gradually became notorious for its drug trade.

Beginning with his second film, *Casa de lava* (*Down to Earth*, 1991), which was shot on the island of Fogo in Cape Verde, Pedro Costa grew intensely interested in Lisbon's Cape Verdeans, developing friendships with them, learning their Creole language—which is spoken in most of his films—and making their lives the chief focus of his work. They are the displaced and disenfranchised of Portugal, and his films give them an unsentimental dignity.

Costa was born on December 30, 1958, to a middle-class family in Lisbon. His parents, who were sympathetic to communism, worked for RTV, Portugal's television network, but their marriage broke up when Costa was young. As a teenager, he was deeply affected by the 1974 revolution. He recalls that "as a kid," he was almost daily "yelling in the streets," taking part in school and factory organizations, and becoming simultaneously interested in "music, politics, films and girls."[2] This was a period of cultural as well as political revolution during which he played guitar in the first wave of Lisbon's punk scene and experienced the effects of worldwide cinephilia. A new Portuguese exhibition policy made it possible for him to view films and access music the Salazar regime had prohibited. All at once, young Costa discovered Wire, Godard, The Clash, Straub and Huillet, Ozu, and Bresson.

At university, Costa majored in history, but he soon changed direction and enrolled in Lisbon's Escola Superior de Teatro e Cinema. By his own account, he was a rebellious student, contemptuous of what he regarded as a bourgeois approach to film study. But he did encounter two filmmaker-teachers who would influence his work. One of them was Paulo Rocha (1935–2012), whose film *Mudar de vida* (*Change of Life*, 1966) was filmed in the Portuguese fishing village of Furadouro and involves a soldier returning from the war in Angola to find his life irreparably changed. The cast is made up of nonprofessionals along with a few of Portugal's major players, among them Isabel Ruth, who would appear in Costa's *Ossos* (*Bones*, 1997). Costa later supervised the restoration of Rocha's beautiful black-and-white film.

Even more important was poet, sculptor, and filmmaker António Reis (1927–1991), who as a teacher guided not only Costa but also the generation of important Portuguese directors film scholar Hayden Guest has dubbed "the school of Reis." Like Rocha, Reis worked with Portugal's most honored director, Manoel de Oliveira, who made only two feature films during the Salazar period but resumed after the revolution, producing an astounding number of features from the mid-1970s into the twenty-first century, the last released in 2012, when he was one hundred and four years old.

Reis himself was an artist of the first rank who, in collaboration with his ethnographer wife, Margarida Cordeiro, made the remarkable *Trás-os-Montes* (1976), titled after the remote region of northeastern Portugal where it was shot. A unique blend of ethnographic documentary, fiction, folklore, and myth, it was cast with residents of the village of Terra Fria and captures not only their daily lives but also their collective imagination. It has an elliptical, nonchronological narrative and an air of mystery that transforms the landscape itself into a dreaming consciousness. When the great French documentarian Jean Rouch saw *Trás-os-Montes,* he wrote a letter to Reis, saying, “For me, this film reveals a new cinematographic language.”[3] For others, it seemed to confirm a famous pronouncement supposedly made by Jean-Luc Godard: “All great fiction films tend toward documentary, just as all great documentaries tend toward fiction.”[4]

Costa was especially struck by this film. In a 2015 interview with Anabela Moutinho and Maria da Graça Lobo, he said, “For me, from the moment I watched *Trás-os-Montes,* it was finally the opportunity of starting to have a past in Portuguese cinema . . . a type of past. Of family, of identity, that gave me security. Not only with Reis but also with Paulo Rocha, at least with . . . *Mudar de vida.*”[5] Reis was equally influential in the classroom, speaking informally, encouraging oral participation, and often arranging classes in which students gathered around the editing table to study a film. He had a list of about twenty essential films he assigned, and Costa remembered them well—among them were Roberto Rossellini’s *Stromboli* (1949) and *Journey to Italy* (1954), Sergei Eisenstein’s *The General Line* (1929), F. W. Murnau’s *Faust* (1926), Orson Welles’s *The Magnificent Ambersons* (1942), Alfred Hitchcock’s *Marnie* (1964), and Jean-Luc Godard’s *Breathless* (1960) and *Pierrot le Fou* (1965). Costa added, “there was Bresson, of course; Bresson most of all.”[6]

After university, Costa’s first professional filmmaking came in the mid-1980s as codirector of twelve ten-minute 16mm episodes of a Portuguese TV series for young people entitled *As cartas da Júlia* (*Letters from Júlia*)—an intriguing title, given that so many of Costa’s later films involve letters. These films are now lost. Before directing his first film, *O sangue* (*Blood,* 1989), he worked sometimes unhappily as assistant director on films by Portuguese directors Daniel Del-Negro, João Botelho, Vítor Gonçalves, and Joaquim Leitão. As we shall see in part I of this book, his film debut was impressive, but his working methods began to change not long afterward. Reis’s instruction had centered on the shot rather than the continuity of narrative—a lesson Costa took to heart and found increasingly important. He seldom relies on montage, instead composing his films within fixed camera shots of long duration. Evocative and pictorially fascinating, each shot is linked to the next in elliptical fashion, sometimes mysteriously. As he has explained, he feels that

> The story is in the shot. And after the shot there's another shot, and what happens between these two shots is what's important. . . . In the link between shots you can merge with the characters (if there are any) or the things (the objects, the houses, the rocks, the clouds). . . . Personally I live the "filming" of a film in the sense that the whole film is *something done* with a minimal intervention on my part. . . . More and more, my films get closer to the almost pure documentary or its absolute contrary. . . . I carry out a reorganization of reality that I have come to with a great abstract perspective. I prefer to discover the stories as I film.[7]

Costa has retained his cinephilia, redolent of canons established in the period of the European new waves of 1960–1980. In 2015, he curated a three-week series of films at Lisbon's Cinemateca Portuguesa, showing his own pictures and giving interviews interspersed with screenings of over twenty other films he selected. Among the directors, in the order in which their works were shown, were Charles Chaplin, Fritz Lang, Jacques Tourneur, Jacques Tati, Robert Bresson, Paulo Rocha, Chantal Akerman, Ernst Lubitsch, Thom Andersen, Jean Eustache, Jacques Rivette, Jean-Luc Godard, Richard Fleisher, Carl Dreyer, Mikio Naruse, Alfred Hitchcock, Jean Rouch, and Howard Hawks. (The surprising contemporary outliers were Gus Van Sant's *Last Days*, 2004, and Matt Reeves's *Dawn of the Planet of the Apes*, 2014.)

In interviews and public appearances, Costa has often praised certain directors, especially Chaplin, Bresson, Ford, Ozu, and Tourneur, and he paid special tribute to Straub and Huillet by making a feature documentary about them. The influence of these figures on his work, however, is subtle and indirect. He is not a director who quotes others; he has forged his own style, most evident in the films about Fontaínhas, especially *No quarto da Vanda* (*In Vanda's Room*, 2000) and *Juventude na marcha* (*Colossal Youth*, 2006), when he began to use digital photography and minimalist production methods. Because he favors the shot, these films have the elliptical quality of Reis's *Trás-os-Montes* and many contemporary art films. They never provide expository information, narration, or intertitles as an aid to the viewer, and they have nothing in common with the typical "social problem" picture, which has a teleological plot structure (a struggle against injustice that leads to failure or success). Often one understands the narrative significance of a shot or sequence in retrospect; hence, they have been described by critic Dominic Lash as a "cinema of disorientation."[8]

The Fontaínhas films in particular were shaped by difficult circumstances over many hours of shooting from which their slender narratives were constructed. They nevertheless have a meticulous, exquisitely composed pictorial quality and a mesmerizing sense of light and color. Their strange beauty is quite different from the harshness of post–World War II neorealists or direct-cinema documentaries of the 1960s, and perhaps for that reason, some of Costa's detractors have accused him of aestheticizing poverty. But there is no reason why films about the poor should be devoid of beauty. Costa's images show great respect for his subjects and could be described as what Brecht called jewels for the poor. He himself has described them not as "protest" but as "a gift."[9]

In part because Costa sometimes uses very long takes from a fixed camera position, he has also been labeled a proponent of "slow cinema," a term associated with a putative movement in postmodern art movies. He resists this term, pointing out that some of the best classic Hollywood directors also used long takes. There are, in fact, many examples of lengthy shots in the studio era, especially in the films of Welles and Max Ophuls, but these usually involve camera movement and reframing of action. Two good unmoving examples are the legal interview between Katharine Hepburn and Judy Holiday in George Cukor's *Adam's Rib* (1949) and the riverside conversation between James Stewart and Richard Widmark in John Ford's *Two Rode Together* (1961); in these cases, however, nothing seems slow because our attention is held by clever dialogue and star performances. Several of Costa's shots of long duration have more in common with the slowness of art films such as Chantal Akerman's *Jeanne Dielman* (1975), in which Delphine Seyrig prepares a meal and chooses a spool of thread in lengthy, static shots with little or no dialogue. Costa's long takes are beautifully composed and sometimes have interesting dialogue, but of a kind that seems especially realistic because it has no clear narrative purpose and resembles *temps mort.*

The question of realism or the "reality effect" is one of several raised by Costa's work, which on multiple levels disturbs categorical distinctions used by critics and theorists of film. His films have provoked some to ask whether they are cinema. When digital cameras were first introduced (along with CGI and digital postproduction, which allow for manipulation of images), theorists argued that the new technology portended a death of cinema. It seemed to them that digital imagery destroyed what André Bazin had described as an existential realism at the basis of the medium—the celluloid film strip's ability to register the visible world like a footprint of the real, creating a bond between film and world without the intervention of a human hand. We discuss such arguments in part II, but it seems sufficient to say that enough time has passed to render these concerns obviously invalid. It is certainly true that animated films are not a record of the actual world (though no less cinema), but digital cameras can and often do record the world as directly as celluloid.

Other questions are more difficult to resolve. Some of Costa's films—*Blood, Down to Earth,* and *Ossos* (*Bones,* 1997), for example—are clearly fictional. Others—*Oú gît votre sourire enfoui?* (*Where Does Your Hidden Smile Lie?,* 2001) and *Ne change rien* (*Change Nothing,* 2009)—are, at least in our view, clearly documentaries. But is *In Vanda's Room* a documentary or fiction? The people in the film are "playing" themselves, using their own words and daily experiences. The scenes come from their lives, and the ideas for most of the scenes are theirs, but the film is not a "fly on the wall" or direct-cinema documentary. The images were artfully composed and the scenes often reshot many times, with the performers repeating lines they had created. Some dialogue had to be rerecorded for clarity in postproduction, and the soundtrack was also manipulated for bits of diegetic music and sound effects.

Throughout, the collaboration between Costa and his performers is so intense and complete that it raises other questions: If the performers did so much, what is the authorship? Should the performers be described as actors? Whatever the answer, Costa's films occupy a liminal space between narrative and nonnarrative, documentary and fiction, auteur and collective, and acting and being.

Equally important, the people depicted in Costa's films about Cape Verdeans exist in a liminal condition somewhere between life and death—they are usually wounded, drug addicted, isolated, ill, displaced, schizophrenic. In the title of this book, we have described the films as "haunted," but we should make it clear that these are not horror or fantasy pictures (although *Cavalo dinheiro* [*Horse Money,* 2014] comes close). Critics have used such terms as "unquiet," "ethereal," and "spiritual" to describe Costa's sometimes gloomy settings, nocturnal scenes, and quiet but resonant events. One could argue that his world is haunted in several respects. His characters are haunted by memories, guilt, or loss, and they tend to occupy an outsider, mysterious, or hidden world. It is significant that his first film about Cape Verdeans, *Casa de lava* (*Down to Earth*), deals with an immigrant laborer who, because of an injury, spends most of the picture in a coma—and even more significant that the film was inspired by Jacques Tourneur's poetic horror picture *I Walked with a Zombie* (1943).

As Horacio Muñoz Fernández and Iván Villarmea Álvarez have pointed out, after *Down to Earth,* the zombie "is a key figure that resonates with a clear aim" in Costa's pictures. As they explain, "the main characters of his films live in a zombie's liminal condition: they are like living dead in the hands of the system."[10] The zombified feeling is most apparent in the films about Ventura, one of Costa's major players, who is aging, tall, and slender, with a slow, deliberate pace and an elegant but relatively inexpressive face. Sometimes he wears a funereal black suit, and in one film he plays a feeble priest who officiates at burials. In *Horse Money* and the short film *Tarrafal* (2007), he has several conversations with dead men, who appear without any ghostly aura and seem to be alive.

Costa's unusual films are both soulful and realistic, haunted and politically acute. They have been discussed by many outstanding critics to whom we are indebted, among them Thom Andersen, João Bénard da Costa, Emma Fajgenbaum, Chris Fujiwara, Adrian Martin, Mark Peranson, Jacques Rancière, and Jonathan Rosenbaum, and Costa has been widely and intelligently interviewed. (His unusual generosity in giving interviews is partly, one suspects, because he does not have a publicity apparatus of the kind that supports studio productions.) Thus far, there is only one book in English about his films: *Refocus: The Films of Pedro Costa, Producing and Consuming Contemporary Art Cinema* (2020), by Nuno Barradas Jorge. It is especially useful for the study of Costa's financing and distribution and the network of festivals that has supported his work.[11] Our approach is different from Barradas Jorge's. In the following pages, we provide close readings of Costa's feature-length films in roughly chronological order, separating the fictional and quasifictional features from the documentaries, with additional commentary on his museum exhibitions and short films.

As of this writing, Costa is at work on a feature related to his recent short picture *As filhas do Fogo* (*The Daughters of Fire*, 2023), the title of which refers to the island of Fogo (fire) in Cape Verde, where he shot *Down to Earth* and began his love of Cape Verdean islanders and immigrants. It was shown in 2023 at Cannes in company with two other shorts, Wang Bing's *Man in Black* and Godard's posthumous last picture, *Film annonce du film qui n'existera jamais* (*Preview of a Film That Will Never Exist*, 2023), and packaged with those films in a Blu-ray release. We have more to say about the short and the film in progress that it inspired in our last chapter. The experience of writing about Costa's cinema has been invigorating, and we hope the following commentary will broaden and deepen interest in his unique and important work.

Notes

1. For a full account of the rise and fall of the Portuguese empire and its many effects on literature and film, see Darlene J. Sadlier, *The Portuguese-Speaking Diaspora: Seven Centuries of Literature and the Arts* (Austin: University of Texas Press, 2016).

2. Michael Guarneri, "Documentary, Realism, and Life on the Margins," interview with Pedro Costa, *BOMB* 133 (Fall 2015), https://bombmagazine.org/articles/2015/07/16/pedro-costa/.

3. Quoted in Dennis Lim, "António Reis and Margarida Cordeiro," *Artforum* 5, no. 10 (Summer 2012), https://www.artforum.com/columns/antonio-reis-and-margarida-cordeiro-200235/.

4. Jean-Luc Godard, "Africa Speaks of the End and the Means," in *Godard on Godard*, ed. Jean Narboni and Tom Milne (New York: Viking Press, 1972), 132–33.

5. Anabela Moutinho and Maria da Graça Lobo, "Conversation with Pedro Costa: The Encounter with António Reis," *Cinema Comparat/ive Cinema* III, no. 6 (2015): 19.

6. Moutinho and Lobo, "Conversation with Pedro Costa," 19. Reis also assigned the students Bresson's short book *Notes on the Cinematograph*.

7. Moutinho and Lobo, "Conversation with Pedro Costa," 20.

8. Dominic Lash, *The Cinema of Disorientation: Inviting Confusions* (Edinburgh: University of Edinburgh Press, 2020).

9. Giovanni Marchini Camia, "Pedro Costa and Wang Bing, Music and Reality," *Cinema Scope* 95 (September 2023): 48.

10. Horacio Muñoz Fernández and Iván Villarmea Álvarez, "Aesthetic Tendencies in Contemporary Portuguese Cinema," *Cinema Comparat/ive Cinema* III, no. 6 (2015): 40. José Bértolo also writes of Costa's "dead in life" characters in "Alone in the Marriage Portrait: Pedro Costa's *Vitalina Varela*," *Forma de vida*, https://formadevida.org/jbertolofdv23.

11. A book by Patrícia Sequeira Brás entitled *The Political Gesture in Pedro Costa's Films* is forthcoming from Peter Lang.

PART I

Early Films

O sangue (*Blood*, 1989)

The ambiguous title of Costa's debut feature might refer to family ties and relationships between a nameless father (Henrique Canto e Castro); his seventeen-year-old son, Vicente (Pedro Hestnes); his ten-year-old son, Nino (Nuno Ferreira); his nameless bourgeois brother (Luís Miguel Cintra); and a nameless woman (Isabel de Castro) who may or may not have been the brother's lover. Costa has been vague about the title's origin: "What I like in *Blood*," he said in 2017, "is the feeling of the long night of childhood contained in so many American films and books. . . . Probably the title comes from Flannery O'Conner."[1]

The film is about the loss of family and its reconstitution in surrogate form by a trio of young people living "long night[s] of childhood." It is the closest Costa has come to a generic movie—a nocturnal, mysterious, 35mm black-and-white picture about crime, death, and dislocation. When it was shown—almost two decades after its release—at a 2008 Canadian revival in Ontario, *Blood* was described as a mix of "fairy tale, film noir, love story, and murder mystery."[2] It was first shown at the 1989 Venice Film Festival and returned to the festival in 2022 for a special screening at the Venice Critics' Week following its digital restoration that year. It had been Portugal's entry for Hollywood's Best Foreign Film Academy Award in 1989.

The father and two sons in the film live in a small house with peeling walls and few furnishings located somewhere in a rural province near the Tagus River. (The areas where scenes were shot include the river towns of Barreiro,

Seixal, and Valada and the village of Vale de Santarém, just west of the Tagus.) Facts about the characters emerge gradually, and the pacing is deliberately, often fascinatingly slow—here and in his later films, Costa favors portrait shots of faces that are almost inexpressive but have a quiet intensity over expository dialogue. The strategy is evident in the precredit sequence, which begins with a black screen and the sounds of distant thunder, a vehicle's engine, and the footsteps of two individuals, followed by an extended close-up of a poor but handsome young man in a bleak outdoor setting, looking at the camera with an impassive expression. Suddenly, without warning, a hand from offscreen slaps his face—bewildering and unprovoked, the sound is as sharp as a gunshot. The sequence cuts to an equally extended, reverse angle close-up of the perpetrator—an older man in a matted, fur-collared coat—then back to the youth, who says: "Do with me what you will." Another close-up of the older man emphasizes the growing darkness. The camera pulls back, showing the two characters in a near silhouette as they stand facing one another on a back road where a small, three-wheeled truck is sitting. The youth says, "Come with me. . . . What will I tell Nino?" "That I died," the older man gruffly replies as he walks away with a suitcase. The youth follows slowly in the truck, its single headlight piercing the darkness.

Costa keeps the characters' relationship from us until a bit later, after shots of a sunrise and the traveling truck, two lovely close-ups of a poor boy and girl waking, and a shot of a schoolroom with unruly children. A teacher's aide named Clara (Inês de Medeiros) and the young man we have seen, whom she calls Vicente, go on a search for Nino and Rosa, two children who have fled the school and run into the woods. Only then does the film return to Vicente's father, his truculent, dour face marked by illness. Still wearing his coat, he and Vicente are back home caring for Nino, who is suffering from a cold. The child describes his father as a "loser," and a useless argument ensues about how much the tough, surly kid weighed when he was born. There is no sign of a mother in the house.

We gradually learn that the father often leaves home for what he claims are medical treatments and owes money to what seem to be gangster-creditors. Unsure that he will survive for long, he writes two lines in a farewell letter to his sons, which Vicente discovers along with a hidden cache of money. This determines much of the rest of the narrative. The plot is chronological, although the world seems almost outside diurnal time. We know Christmas is approaching from an early warehouse scene in which "Santa Claus Is Coming to Town" plays as Vicente and his friend Zeca (musician Manuel João Vieira)

A troubled son

The father

pack boxes with black-market audio tapes. On Christmas Day, Vicente and Clara decorate a small tree. The movie ends after a fireworks display on New Year's Eve in Lisbon.

Although *Blood* deals with the theme of crime and has a noir-like atmosphere, it is not a suspense film, and it lacks the melodramatic tension of a genre picture. Costa is interested in other things, mainly family, love, loneliness, and survival. Throughout the film, he slightly elides or suspends cause and effect, requiring us to speculate about actions and motivations. One of the most important examples of the technique occurs twenty minutes into the picture. Vicente sits quietly at his father's bedside, holding the unfinished farewell letter. Suddenly, we cut to shots of him running down a street, breaking into a closed pharmacy, pulling medicines from a cabinet, then pausing to watch blood ooze from a cut in the palm of his hand. Next, we see his hand locking the father's bedroom door. The film cuts to a daytime street scene, where Vicente finds Clara and pleads with her to "save me," then to late night. The young couple are riding in the truck, and after stopping, they carry a shrouded body from the truck into a cemetery, where Vicente digs a grave. Seated on the ground, a frightened Clara looks away, covering her ears with her hands to block out the shovel's sound.

We do not see how the father died, but the strange concatenation of events—the robbing of the pharmacy, the locking of the bedroom door, the recruiting of Clara, and the secret burial of the corpse—leaves open the possibility that Vicente had a hand in his father's demise. It could just as well mean that the father died naturally, without the help of stolen medication, and that Vicente wants to keep his death a secret.

Left to care for Nino, Vicente fakes an anonymous letter that says their father died penniless; he mails it to himself to cover up his role in the disappearance of the father and the cash. A new family begins to emerge that includes Clara, who cuts Nino's hair and sweeps the house. We see Vicente donning Nino's too-tight sweater in response to Nino's wish that they look more alike—which indeed they do in a beautiful close-up of their faces side by side as they peer through a window, a shot reminiscent of the child Pedro peering into a window in Luis Buñuel's *Los Olvidados* (*The Young and the Damned*, 1950).

But even in death, the father remains an issue. As Vicente scouts outdoors for a Christmas tree, two sinister creditors in black appear (Henrique Viana and Luís Santos), seizing Vicente's axe and telling him he is responsible for paying a debt. The father's brother then arrives from Lisbon for his annual

Christmas visit, accompanied by a somewhat slatternly woman (Ana Otero) whom he describes as his housekeeper. (Later we will see them in a sexual embrace.) Concerned, the uncle scorns the authenticity of Vicente's fake letter and tries to take Nino with him to Lisbon. A struggle ensues, with Vicente hitting the uncle with a brick, injuring his ear and forcing him to leave.

Other problems arise. Nino's absences from class make school authorities suspicious, and Clara worries that the boy has changed after his father's death. She and Vicente are also becoming lovers. They leave Nino home alone one evening to stroll to a riverside amusement park, where they meet Vicente's friend Zeca, have a lovers' quarrel prompted by Vicente's jealousy, and see a dead body being fished from the foggy river, the latter an unexplained, haunting, and disturbing reminder of the father and the mysterious circumstances of his death. In their absence, the uncle returns and kidnaps Nino. Vicente then goes to Lisbon to rescue Nino but is seized by the creditors we saw earlier. They take him to an apartment to rough him up, and one of the men and a nameless older woman discuss his refusal to talk.

Meanwhile, the uncle assumes the role of Nino's father, introducing him to his son Pedro (Miguel Fernandes), who is slightly younger than Nino but strangely mute and sleeping in a baby crib. The uncle has a TV set where the children can watch cartoons, and he attempts to win over Nino with new clothes, a restaurant meal, and a trip to the eerily lit Vasco da Gama Aquarium. Eventually, Nino escapes and runs away down a dark cobblestoned street, where he unexpectedly, almost magically, finds Clara looking for him. His anger at being abandoned cannot be assuaged, however, and he sets off on his own.

With the help of the older woman, Vicente escapes and goes to the uncle's apartment. Nino has gone, but Vicente and the uncle have a violent fight in the apartment hallway, where Vicente leaves his uncle unconscious on the floor. The woman then drives Vicente back to his home; the entire scene, shot from outside the car's windshield, focuses on their faces as they talk and look out. She explains the history of a criminal racket involving illicit donations solicited for a labor union fund. The men in charge of the racket, she says, are ruthless, and Vicente's father was drawn into their scheme. She believes the father is still alive and will survive his illness; she obviously loves him and has maternal concern for Vicente and Nino, but Vicente is unmoved, staring silently out the car's windshield. Arriving at his village, he runs to Clara, who lies asleep on the riverbank and awakens in his arms as if from a spell—the first time they have touched since the quarrel at the amusement park. Rising, they kiss passionately and sink to the ground off camera. The film ends with a cut to Nino, who is steering a small motorboat along the river. An offscreen voice, possibly the boat's owner, asks him if he will become lost. Nino looks resolute and responds confidently that he will not.

According to several critics, Costa wanted the cast to see three films before production on *Blood* began: Nicholas Ray's *They Live by Night* (1949), one of the most sensitive treatments of the lovers-on-the-run formula of film noir; Charles Laughton's *Night of the Hunter* (1955), about a brother and sister who travel down a river in flight from a maniacal preacher who has killed their mother and is looking for money stolen by their dead father; and Robert Bresson's *Mouchette* (1967), about a poor village girl with a bullying, alcoholic father and an ill mother who is taunted and abused at school, trapped and raped by a criminal, and determines to commit suicide by rolling down a steep hill. (Inês de Medeiros, who later became a film director, has said that the cast saw the films as well as Bresson's emotionally powerful *Au hasard Balthazar*, 1966.)[3]

Blood never alludes directly to these three films, and when we asked Costa about them, he laughed and said the story about showing them to the cast was untrue.[4] The closest references are the slap in the face in the first shot, which echoes *Mouchette*, and a fragment of a musical theme, which might be inspired by *Night of the Hunter*. If not for Medeiros's comment, one might never think of them. All three are in black and white, and although they have thematic similarities, their styles are different. One could argue that some of these qualities are absorbed into *Blood*, but never in a calculated sense. As critic Adrian Martin has pointed out, the various influences on Costa's poetics are "deeply internalized . . . too tangled, fused, and transformed to ever be completely separated."[5] In an interview published in 2016, Costa described *Blood* as "a film I obviously had to make because I had to go through all the guys before me: Fritz Lang, Nick Ray, Fuller. You only prepare to discover things in the second film. [The first is] a film that comes from cinema."[6]

Although in some ways generic, *Blood* nevertheless foreshadows Costa's more obviously unconventional work. Like nearly all his pictures, it concerns marginalized characters who live in a lonely, dangerous world and bond together in a protofamily or community. In a noncomic, unsentimental mode, the characters exemplify what Costa once described as the essence of Chaplin's Tramp: "the fear of lack of things, money, food, love."[7] *Blood* also hints at recurring themes and motifs in Costa's later films about Cape Verdeans in Lisbon, especially in the way it juxtaposes poor, half-ruined but somehow comforting domestic spaces in the village with soulless middle-class apartments in Lisbon, suggesting a critique of class conditions that emerged in the late 1980s after Portugal entered the European Union. (Nino, for example, can be read as a rebel against the materialism of a rising bourgeoise.)

Costa's later films also use letters as keepsakes and reminders of painful family separations and lost love. In *Blood,* the father's unfinished letter simply announces his departure, perhaps not in the manner he had envisioned, and he shows no concern or love for his sons—in fact, he seems almost bored, telling Vicente that "You're not an orphan yet" and that he can keep the money the father has left behind. Vicente guards his own subsequently faked letter like a keepsake, but it has nothing to do with sorrow or leave-taking—indeed, it motivates the uncle's suspicions and kidnapping of Nino.

The film is at its most powerful at the level of imagery, mood, and texture. It had a small crew, mostly from Lisbon's film and theater school, and was shot in 35mm black and white for a cost of 32,000,000 *escudos* or 115,000 euros (about $200,000).[8] Today's audiences tend to think of black and white as typical of low-budget pictures, but at the time that this film was made the industry had converted to color, and black and white was an expensive format. Whatever it might have cost, the decision to film in black and white was worth it. Costa told critic Mark Peranson that he particularly liked the "milky" whites in the film, which he associated with Fritz Lang's *The Big Heat* (1950). He went to some trouble to find a photographer for the film: "I wanted to have Stanley Cortez [photographer for Orson Welles, Samuel Fuller, and Charles Laughton] and I wrote him a letter. And then I discovered he was dead!"[9] He then tried the great Mexican cinematographer Gabriel Figueroa, who had retired. Ultimately, he contacted German photographer Martin Schäfer, who had worked with Wim Wenders and could connect Costa with the best lab technicians. Unfortunately, Schäfer died in 1988, before primary photography was completed; the remainder of the film was shot by Portuguese photographers Acácio de Almeida and Elso Roque. In 2012, Costa told critic Nuno Barradas Jorge that the 35mm camera and lighting equipment were big and heavy: "Filming at night near the river . . . during winter was complicated. . . . I was lucky. The cinematography in *Blood* ended up looking like those in old Hollywood films."[10]

Blood is one of the most mysteriously moody black-and-white films of the period, distinguished by its pellucid, high-contrast lighting, carefully controlled imagery, and impressive lateral tracking shots—some through dense woods near the river, where the ground was often swampy. The atmosphere is mostly nocturnal; daylight along the Tagus looks grey, and at one point, Nino says he hates the sun because of what it does to his skin. Most images are pervaded with deep blacks that hide areas of the screen and create an atmosphere of fear and mystery that is set off by milky, almost ghostly whites. (The simple white dress Inês de Medeiros wears in the darkness of the latter part of the film is an inspired costume, creating contrast with Vicente's dark clothing. It is as effective as the red dress she wears in Costa's 1994 film, *Down to Earth.*)

Close-ups of faces are eloquent in an inexpressive, almost Bressonian manner, and the same can be said of close-ups of hands, as when the older woman in Lisbon touches Vicente's hand, causing him to withdraw his own. Costa also likes to shoot walls and through doorways and windows.[11] Early in the film, the child Rosa looks out a window, her contemplative face lit by early morning light. Later, in an equally compelling shot, a contemplative Clara poses in front of a schoolhouse window as children jump on desks and race around her. One of the most beautifully composed and oneiric shots is of the father seated on a step outside his home, framed by an open front door; the deep focus reveals Vicente standing inside, backed by window-like glass panes that create frames within the frame. Around the open doorway, dark shadows from clustered leaves in a nearby tree loom large, like splayed hands in motion.

The sound design, supervised by Pedro Caldas, is equally effective in its use of foley effects, postrecorded ambient sound, and music. Costa has attributed this choice to the fact that he was "completely enchanted with American movies. . . . I committed some crimes, like using Stravinsky."[12] Besides bits of Stravinsky's *Firebird* and *Orpheus,* the film uses the vanguard, postpunk music of British group The The—whose song "This Is the Day" can be heard in the fairground sequence—and an original score by António Pinho Vargas. Ambient sound is important because Costa uses dialogue sparingly, often shooting takes in which characters are silent for relatively long periods or speak in near whispers. Outside Vicente's house we hear distant dogs barking, the cries of children, and indecipherable voices; at the amusement park, we are aware of the postpunk tune, motorbikes, autos, and river water.

Often, Costa creates eerie moods portending the haunting, labyrinthine passageways in subsequent Fontaínhas films. In the woods along the riverbank, Clara warns Nino not to approach a gnarled, leafless tree because it is haunted; she also tells him of an important secret she cannot remember and of her childhood fears of the woods, which only Vicente, her schoolmate, could kiss away. Later, from the edge of the riverbank, as Clara and Vicente watch the unidentified dead body fished from the foggy current, villagers arrive,

An unhappy home

their shapes shadowy and blurred like a gathering of specters in the darkness. Hanging from a branch of the nearby "haunted" tree is the drowned man's scarf, which Vicente drapes around Clara's neck from behind. His tender touch pleases her, but at the sight of the scarf, she tears it off and runs away as if from a ghost. This is the last time they touch until the end of the film.

When the uncle in Lisbon takes his son and Nino to the dimly lit aquarium, the large fish in the glass tanks are almost as surreal and disturbing as the strange creatures in the aquarium sequence in Orson Welles's *The Lady from Shanghai* (1946). The fight between Vicente and the uncle is shot with a wide-angle lens and staged in a long apartment hallway with the two characters silhouetted in the distance; they stagger and struggle in a quick, realistic battle, and at one point the camera starts to track toward them as if to get a closer view, stopping when the uncle collapses to the floor and Vicente walks back toward us.

The plot is mysterious and ambiguous, raising questions it deliberately refuses to answer. What is the secret Clara cannot remember? What does Nino mean when he speaks of "the greatest human invention"? Who is the

Vicente and Clara on the riverbank

A body fished from the river

dead body in the river? What happens to Nino's cousin, Pedro? Above all, how do we explain the death of Vicente's father? Alongside these questions and complementing them is a sense of loneliness in both the village and in Lisbon. Vicente, Nino, and Clara live in a barren house almost hidden from the villagers, and their only visitors are threatening. Before driving Vicente home, the older woman in Lisbon takes him to the balcony of the apartment where he was held by the men who captured him. The sounds of a New Year's Eve celebration can be heard in the distance, and they look out at other balconies around them. On one, an older, heavily made-up woman in pearls and an expensive dress holds a large drink, standing alone with a drunken expression; on another, two young lovers or perhaps a recently married couple, unsmiling, stand slightly apart, their faces solemn as the fireworks crackle far away; on still another, an older man in a business suit rubs his head and eyes wearily as he stares down toward the street. These are the sorts of details ordinary genre films avoid because the characters have no function in the plot. They show, however, that the city is filled with quiet desperation and urban anomie.

Nino, who is sometimes left on his own, expresses a different kind of loneliness or unhappy solitude. Resilience and aggressiveness become part of his character. He sloughs off his uncle's attempts to win him over during the aquarium visit, sitting alone and writing sums on a piece of paper. He shows no interest in the fish behind him and explains to the uncle that "When I leave, I have to pay you." When the devious uncle steps close to Nino and claims that Vicente might kill him, Nino, unmoved, keeps writing and says, "There's always hope."

Later that night, in the bedroom he shares with the silent Pedro, Nino paces back and forth, talking to himself and breaking into a series of karate moves, ending with skillful side and back kicks directed at an invisible enemy and a sudden, tough pose that shows his small muscles. Dropping to the floor in exhaustion, he momentarily acts defeated but recovers quickly—a charming, amusing performance by a child whose serious demeanor occasionally breaks into a little smile. When Vicente fails to rescue him that night, he stealthily eludes his captor-uncle and flees. Perhaps he is returning home or heading into the unknown, another question we cannot answer.

In a stroke of good luck in casting similar to his practice in later films, Costa found Nuno Ferreira, who plays Nino, at a Catholic orphanage from which many young boys had run away. Nearly feral, Ferreira was difficult to direct, but he makes a vivid impression. "Probably," Costa said, "I saw a lot of myself in this boy at his age."[13] Costa lost track of Ferreira after the film but later

Nino practices karate

Nino at the helm

found him scoring heroin in Fontaínhas. "He was wild and suicidal," Costa said, and he refused Costa's offer of work on another film.[14] Ferreira was the first of many important nonprofessional actors Costa found living in impoverished conditions who became great presences in his films. The last shot of *Blood* shows him intently looking out while steering a small motorboat. It is an echo of the close-up of Vicente that started the film, but Nino is strong and happy, apparently the master of his fate.

Casa de lava (*Down to Earth*, 1994)

In the early 1960s, soldiers, occasionally accompanied by wives and families, left Portugal for combat in the colonial wars in Africa. Economic incentives lured Portuguese workers to Angola, Brazil, the United States, and different parts of the European Union. The labor force in Lisbon grew smaller. Among the many construction projects in Lisbon at the time was the Fundação Calouste Gulbenkian, a museum-foundation to house the world-class art collection of its oil-rich patron, Calouste Sarkis Gulbenkian, an immigrant from Armenia who left a large endowment for its erection. Anthropologist Luís Batalha has written that although workers from Portugal's economically depressed interior filled some of the demand for labor in construction jobs such as the Gulbenkian museum, better-paying jobs outside Portugal had sapped the workforce.[15] In response to this growing demand and because of depressed conditions in Cape Verde, a mostly male, dark-skinned, poorly educated, unskilled workforce began arriving in Lisbon from the archipelago. Hired largely for heavy construction work, they initially lived in makeshift housing on work sites or in rooms in impoverished, low-rent areas. They also built shantytown communities where a sense of freedom, fellowship, and cultural identity began to emerge.[16]

By the mid-1990s, first and second generations of workers who had come in the 1960s and 1970s were living in these poor neighborhoods. It was at this time that Costa made *Down to Earth* (1994; a literal English translation of the Portuguese title, "House of Lava," would have been better), his first in a series of remarkable films about the Cape Verdean diaspora. One of Costa's best pictures, *Down to Earth* established him internationally as a filmmaker. Costa told interviewer Patrick McGilligan that "*Casa de lava* held the key to my life, to all the choices I've been making since."[17] While his first film had indirectly declared his relation to an important cinematic tradition (especially the American film noir), this one seems unlike almost any other filmmaker's work.

While working on a project similar to *Blood,* Costa had been invited by Portuguese producer Paulo Branco to make a television film with Rádio e Televisão de Portugal (RTP), the national radio and television network in Lisbon, as part of a dramatic series about the four classical elements: earth, wind, fire, and water. Costa's film would be devoted to fire and set on a volcanic island. But because he soon realized the subject had bigger possibilities, Costa convinced Branco to raise international funding for a theatrical film set in Cape Verde. The beautiful color film, photographed by Emmanuel Machuel, who had worked with Robert Bresson, was produced by Branco's Madragoa Filmes with coproduction assistance from Gemini Films in France and Pandora Films in Germany. It also received support from RTP, the Institute for Cinematographic Art and Audiovisuals (IPACA), and the National Center for Cinema in France (CNC). French funding meant that at least some French talent would be used; hence there are two French actors in important roles. In 1995, the film won the Grand Prize at festivals in Belfort, France, and Moscow.

In 2013, nearly twenty years after making *Down to Earth,* Costa published a scrapbook he assembled during and slightly after filming.[18] (It would be used later in one of his museum installations.) Despite its disparate, jumbled character, the scrapbook offers a window into some of Costa's preoccupations. Among its many items are postcards of Picasso's cubist works, photographs of the island of Fogo (the Portuguese word for "fire"), stills of the veteran and nonprofessional actors in the film, pictures of men with head injuries lying in hospital beds, and various images of world poverty alongside cutouts of historical figures and cinema stars. There are numerous newspaper clippings in Portuguese, English, and French about topics such as Egyptian art's funereal style, the use of the former Tarrafal concentration camp in Cape Verde, and the remarkable story of a Nigerian who survived a fall from a fourteen-story building with barely a scratch. Both handwritten and printed words appear like captions under and above images, and typed lines of dialogue in Portuguese and Creole (Kriolu), the native language spoken in Cape Verde, are pasted on several pictures. Items overlap on the pages, resulting in a collage.

The collage reproductions indicate an interest in vivid contrasts and juxtapositions, especially evident in the sound design of *Down to Earth,* which sets diegetic, indigenous Cape Verdean music, including *morna* ballads and lively local dance music, against nondiegetic classical and modernist pieces deliberately in disharmony with the images on the screen. Two pages that face each other in the scrapbook offer hints of Costa's story line. On the left is the reverse side of a postcard with the printed description "Fogo's volcano" and the name "R. Desnos" handwritten across the space reserved for messages. (The poet Robert Desnos is quoted twice in the film, and a poetic letter by him has an important function.) Two Cape Verdean postage stamps have been affixed to this card. One shows three nurses in white uniforms and headscarves seated on the island's rocky terrain with their backs to the camera. Their uniforms' large Red Cross emblems provide splashes of color against the island's dark terrain, not unlike the bright red dress of the nurse who is the film's central character. (In one of the film's scenes, a cross is painted on a red door to mark a site of disease or death.) The scrapbook's opposite page contains a newspaper clipping about dangerous vaccines introduced by Portugal's Ministry of Health and given to Cape Verde's children. In *Down to Earth,* a nurse inadvertently brings a tainted vaccine to Fogo.

The completed film has a subtle yet sharp political edge, but it is far from a typical picture about social problems. When it was shown at the 1994 Cannes Film Festival, Costa told reporters that it was an expression of "disgust" toward the Portuguese politics and society of the period.[19] The film itself, however, says nothing about the history of Fogo and the Cape Verdean diaspora. It makes clear that men who work dangerous jobs in Lisbon are being exploited, but it simply inserts us into a strange world, viewing inhabitants with startling intimacy and respect. Featuring a cast of largely nonprofessional local actors and striking color scenes shot in natural light, the film offers a new kind of social realism characterized by straightforward observation; a poetic, otherworldly atmosphere; and performances notable for their silences and lack of affect. The island of Fogo, whose pulsing, red-hot volcanic core resembles a surgically exposed beating heart, offers majestic views of high ocean cliffs and sweeping plains. But the natural beauty also has a tough, unforgiving side suggested by pounding surf, miles of hot ash road, and inky-black, rocky terrain fit only for goats.

As in *Blood,* landscape plays a central role. The film begins with color documentary footage of a 1951 volcano eruption on Fogo photographed by Orlando Ribeiro, a renowned Portuguese geographer. The scenes of fiery-red lava spewing from black volcanic rock may have inspired Costa's fondness for touches of red contrasting with darkened interiors here and in later films. The soundtrack, meanwhile, shifts from a quiet rumbling to a furious, dissonant Paul Hindemith viola solo as the camera pans across the island's mountainous expanse. The introductory landscape calls to mind António Reis's introductory scene of the mountainous terrain in *Trás-os-Montes*; Costa then cuts to close-up portraits of villagers standing outdoors—a juxtaposition of landscape and inhabitants that is again like Reis, though Costa's portraits are more unusual. Costa is elliptical, avoiding exposition and melodrama, just as in *Blood* but to a greater degree, and his close-ups and wide shots are held even longer.

The portraits are quiet, with no background music, and the subjects are quite still. All of them are girls or women (young men are scarce in Fogo). We see spiky, sun-bleached hair on the back of a girl's head and a girl's hands clasped behind her back, followed by a series of faces that have a quiet, Bresson-like intensity as they gaze past the camera with ambiguous, unchanging expressions. Not acting in the usual sense, the actors have an integrity and personality that seems a bit hidden. Each face establishes a unique, memorable character, and the portraits have the straightforward but eloquent quality of works by photographers like Walker Evans.

The film suddenly cuts without explanation to a noisy construction site in Lisbon filled with Cape Verdean workers, creating sharp contrast between quietness and noise and establishing a bridge between people who are separated geographically but share a history shaped by centuries of Portuguese imperialism and slavery. The ensuing film has a relatively slight plot but observes classical narrative in the sense that it involves change and a sort of closure. The action is initiated when a construction worker, a man named Leão (Ivorian French actor Isaach de Bankolé), is badly injured. His coworker says he "had a fall," but the film strongly suggests that he tried to commit suicide. Later in the film, Leão says he experienced vertigo, but there is no sign of it in the scene where he falls. We see him standing without his hard hat close to the ledge of an opening high atop a partly constructed edifice. A close-up shows him gazing out with a somber, meditative expression, and a jump cut takes us closer to his face as he looks down intensely. We then cut to a Lisbon hospital where he has been in a coma for two months. Little is known about him. He has no known friends or family, and according to the construction crew, he never talked much. But an anonymous letter has arrived, apparently from a woman in Cape Verde, containing a check paying for his return home.

The bleak Lisbon hospital is grey, antiseptic, and generally miserable. Veteran actors Luís Miguel Cintra and Isabel de Castro appear in nameless cameo roles as a doctor and patient, respectively. The doctor holds little hope for Leão's recovery, and the patient, who is dying, nearly strangles a young

A woman in Fogo

nurse named Mariana (Inês de Medeiros, who plays Clara in *Blood*). Looking in a bathroom mirror after the patient's death, Mariana borrows red lipstick from a coworker but then fills a basin with alcohol and rubs it off, scrubbing herself as if to avoid bacteria. The doctor summons her and assigns her the job of accompanying Leão back to his home in Cape Verde, on the island of Fogo.

Costa, a confirmed cinephile, has said that at the time he made *Down to Earth*, he was thinking a good deal about Godard's *Ici et ailleurs* (1975) and Alan Resnais's *Muriel* (1963).[20] He has also frequently expressed admiration for Hollywood director Jacques Tourneur, a poetic realist who worked mostly at the lower levels of the industry; Costa has said in interviews that *Down to Earth* was inspired by Tourneur's classic semihorror film *I Walked with a Zombie* (1943), which itself is very loosely based on Charlotte Brontë's *Jane Eyre* (1847). Both films deal with young, white nurses who leave the modern world to care for comatose patients in distant island communities marked by colonialism. Some critics have noted that *Down to Earth* also has elements in common with Roberto Rossellini's *Stromboli* (1949), which features Ingrid Bergman on a volcanic island, but the connection with *I Walked with a Zombie* is more apparent and interesting. Parallels were likely even clearer in Costa's original screenplay, much of which he abandoned because of difficulties shooting on Fogo.

Photography on the island took place over a one-month period, and traveling with heavy 35mm equipment over the terrain near the volcano was hazardous. "At one point," Costa told Peranson, "I just left the script behind, because I thought if I'm going to shoot this girl in this new place that's foreign and dangerous, then I had to shoot it from her point of view. . . . This girl didn't know what she was going to find, so she could find anything."[21] He began to improvise during production, and improvisation would figure strongly in his subsequent work. There were tensions and quarrels with de Bankolé (one of which led to a fistfight), who became angry when he discovered he would play an unconscious character for much of the film.[22]

The differences between Costa's film and Tourneur's are as important as the similarities. Cape Verde is quite different from Haiti, where the Tourneur film is set; the former's population, derived from the mixing of Portuguese colonists and African slaves, looked to Portugal for a better life. Black slaves in Haiti under the rule of France did not experience the racial mixing widely practiced in Cape Verde (also never seen in the heavily censored Hollywood pictures of Tourneur's day), and they had nowhere to go under colonial rule. They often sought solace in religious practices, including the trance-like states associated with voodoo, the "zombie curse" in Tourneur's film. For all its virtues, *I Walked with a Zombie* is a studio film with artificial sets, its cast dominated by white actors—although in it as in his other films, Tourneur gives dignity and beauty to his Black players.

In *Down to Earth*, Costa shares something of Tourneur's spiritual theme but is far more interested in documentary evidence of local geography and culture. Although two of his lead actors are white, nearly all the others are Black, and the only one who can be considered a sort of zombie is the unconscious Leão. Throughout, we see that Cape Verde suffers from gross injustices and neglect caused by centuries of colonial rule, plus more recent economic incentives from Portugal that require husbands to leave wives and children behind. (An icon of this situation is the island of São Vicente's statue of a mother and child, looking out to the sea and waving goodbye.)

We gradually learn about the people and the island through Mariana, who cares for Leão, roams Fogo, administers vaccines to children, and warns younger men about the dangers of migrating to "a rat hole" in Lisbon. The sterile environment of her life in the Lisbon hospital contrasts vividly with Fogo, where, on arriving, she and the stretcher-borne Leão are engulfed in clouds of dust stirred by an offscreen helicopter not due to return for a week. The earth clings to her like a baptism despite her frenzied attempts to brush

Mariana on the volcanic ash of Fogo

it away. She and the unconscious Leão are put aboard a dilapidated pickup truck that bumps over a gravel road made of lava, a stray dog following closely behind them. She cradles Leão's head in her hand and looks out at the barren landscape where, on the horizon, women are carrying heavy bundles of cloth. Over time, she moves closer to the firmament, sleeping outside the tiny local hospital in a low-slung hammock where an unknown person brings her baskets of apples, walking barefoot, and resting on the black volcanic rock. When Dr. Medina (João Medina), the island physician, realizes she is sleeping outdoors, he offers her a room indoors and asks whether she misses the clean sheets of her homeland. She declines and seems content in her new environment, wearing the same red garment every day and sleeping with traces of earth on her neck.

The short red summer dress Mariana wears on the island suggests an erotic vitality that comes alive like the bubbling lava in this poor yet colorful place, rich in music, extended family ties, and communal warmth. Mariana begins to feel intense sexual desire, perhaps for the first time.[23] Walking the streets and rocky hillsides, opening and closing doors, and rifling through bureau drawers, she searches for clues to the island's secrets. Linguistic and other kinds of barriers, both visible and invisible, are everywhere, and while the Cape Verdeans mostly welcome her medical expertise and vaccines, the men ignore her urgings to stay put and "not give up."

Unlike Brazilian sociologist Gilberto Freyre, who expressed reservations about Creole and its mix of Portuguese and West African languages, Costa celebrates the local speech. Virtually everyone in the film speaks it, including a white, sometimes somnambulant middle-aged widow named Edite (French actor Edith Scob, star of George Franju's celebrated horror film *Les yeux sans visage*, 1960). We learn that twenty years earlier, Edite followed her Portuguese husband, a political activist, when he was sentenced by the Salazar dictatorship to a slow death with other dissidents in the Tarrafal concentration camp on the nearby island of Santiago.[24] Living off her husband's pension, she mostly spends her days drinking alone and falling into stupors in the house she shares with her nameless, mostly silent yet vigilant adult son (Pedro Hestnes). At other times, she chats in Creole with local women as they launder clothes, plays cards, and drinks and dances with Amália (Amália Tavares), a friend and former Tarrafal cook who helped Edite and her husband during his imprisonment.[25] (While dancing, Amália shouts "Juventude em Marcha," a slogan associated with revolutionary Portugal that Costa used ironically as the title of a later film.)

Amália creates problems at the local hospital, where we see a small portrait on the wall of Amílcar Cabral, the Cape Verdean revolutionary leader. She defies Mariana's westernized treatment of Leão, opening the shutters over his bed, preparing him local foods, and hiding Mariana's medicines. Mariana becomes furious, but when she finally gains control of the situation, she decides to explore the island.

A great deal of Inês de Medeiros's performance involves little more than walking from point to point, but she is graceful and impressive to watch. The best example of her movement is an extended lateral tracking shot in which Costa keeps her at the center of the frame in her red dress (as effective a costume as the white dress Medeiros wears in *Blood*, its color making her visible in the film's most extreme wide shots). She walks briskly from the hospital through the nearby town, where we see dilapidated but colorful buildings and occasional older men sitting outdoors. At a local marketplace, a woman sells Mariana shoes that are good for walking on lava. That evening, exhausted

Mariana on her way through town

from exploration, she goes to the seashore and bathes in the turbulent waves. When she lies down to rest, she is spotted by an adolescent boy who beats her and attempts rape; he is chased off by the dog who followed her when she arrived with Leão in the pickup truck.

On another walk through the town, Mariana encounters an elderly violin player named Bassoé (musician Raul Andrade). Somewhat like the folkloric guitarist in *I Walked with a Zombie*, Bassoé wanders the area, in his case playing *mornas*, a music indigenous to Cape Verde, its lyrics speaking of island departures and *saudades* for loved ones and homeland. (At points in the nondiegetic soundtrack, a child's slender voice sings these sorrowful lyrics without musical accompaniment.) A woman's voice can be heard shouting "Go away, you old madman," but Bassoé is unperturbed. He and Mariana sit beneath a tree as stray piglets walk past in the background. Showing no concern for the woman who yelled at him, he refers to her merely as "that lady, the pale one." This may be Edite, who lives nearby and whom we have earlier seen gossiping with local women as they did laundry.

Bassoé plays for Mariana and tells her of his many voyages outside Cape Verde. They go for a walk near the volcano, where they see a girl on a white donkey. According to Bassoé, the girl is his daughter; he also claims to have more than thirty sons who never come to visit him. It is difficult to believe this

Mariana and Bassoé

claim, which resembles one made by a Cape Verdean in a later Costa film and reflects the way inhabitants of the island think of their extended community. "Music is a bitch," Bassoé says, "I worship her." He invites Mariana to a feast at his home, where he plays dance music alongside a young guitarist as a small crowd of his "children" enjoy themselves. One of them approaches Mariana and says, "We're going to Portugal. Is it nice there?" She tells him conditions are awful and that "nobody cares." He responds, "Not even the dead rest here."

Mariana begins walking around the outskirts of Fogo, administering vaccines to children. Although *Down to Earth* is very much a landscape film, here, as everywhere in his work, Costa is interested in evocative scenes photographed in intimate, domestic spaces. Consider the moment when Mariana gives an injection to the child of a woman sitting unconcerned at the right of the screen, plucking a scrawny chicken. The undecorated room has a grey stone floor and is lit by nothing but an open doorway. The lengthy shot gives us documentary evidence of quotidian life in Fogo, but the balanced composition and subtle color have the relative stillness and artistic power of a painting. Costa is frequently interested in the closed doors of the village's dim interiors—several are closed to Mariana, and in one case we hear only a child's cry within.

During another exploration, Mariana finds the drunken Edite lying on the beach dressed in a filmy nightgown, embracing the dog that followed

A home visit with vaccine

Mariana when she arrived on Fogo. The dog has been killed. Edite's son appears and leads her away while a group of mute Black men look on and Edite deliriously claims her son is the dog's killer. Mariana follows them to Edite's home, which is larger and more prosperous than any other we see in the film. Time passes, and Mariana enters, finding Edite in bed, overdressed and overheated. Her son, who has been drinking, broods guiltily about the dog, which he buried in a local cemetery of the dead from Tarrafal. Mariana tries to convince the young man to take Edite to the hospital, and when this fails, she goes into Edite's bedroom, opens a desk drawer, and examines the items she finds. Close-ups show us evidence of Edite's past: a picture of a baby; a pair of photos of a dozen men in uniform, two of them marked with an x; a photo of a boy; a photo of young Edite in Paris; a number of pension receipts and checks; an official declaration dated July 1962 indicating that Vicente Bento Águas is being sent by the government to Tarrafal; and a handwritten letter, which Mariana keeps.

When Mariana returns to Edite's son, the two sit side by side at a table, Mariana wary and the son increasingly disturbed about the dog and his meaningless life. The scene is very skillfully played, less through dialogue than through an exchange of glances that suggest a spark of eroticism. When darkness falls, the son embraces Mariana. The pair move to a couch, where we dimly see the son climb atop her. She resists, and he appears to have a premature ejaculation; "You're done," she says, "you can move now," and they roll apart, lying together on the couch.

Meanwhile, at the apparently empty hospital—one of the few times we see something away from Mariana's presence—a kind of miracle happens. A drunken, cursing young patient named Tano (Cristano Andrade Alves) approaches the unconscious Leão and touches him. Leão's eyes open, and Tano, perhaps in fear, pulls him to the floor. A brief struggle ensues, and Tano leaves. A close-up of Leão shows him opening his eyes, turning his head, and softly saying, "My land."

Back at Edite's house, a thirteen-year-old girl named Tina (Sandra do Canto Brandão) awakens Mariana from her sleep on the couch, telling her she needs help; Mariana rises from her position next to Edite's still sleeping, seminude son and goes off with Tina. On a rocky area near the volcano, they find Tano lying unconscious. "Dead man tried to kill Tano," Tina says. She is Tano's lover, and she wants Mariana's help not only in tending to Tano but also in persuading him not to go to Portugal. At the hospital, Mariana helps with the wound on Tano's arm, which was made by an animal's teeth. (We realize it was Tano who killed the dog on the beach.) She then gives Tina the letter she stole from Edite, asking her to translate the Creole. The girl reads: "My love, our meeting will give us at least thirty years of happiness. I'm growing younger and stronger. I'd like to give you 100,000 cigarettes, a dozen fashionable dresses, a car, and a house built of lava. . . . A bouquet of wildflowers. Most of all I want you to drink a bottle of wine and think of me." Cut to Edite, now awake and brushing her hair. Tina's voice reading the letter continues over this shot as though it is Edite's memory.

The letter, which Costa used again in later films, is loosely based on French surrealist poet Robert Desnos's 1944 letter to his lover Youki. Desnos was imprisoned in Auschwitz, Buchenwald, and the Nazi-occupied Czechoslovak prison at Terezin. He died of typhus in 1945. (Desnos's words are also used at the end of this film as the lyrics to Andrade's "Mornas de Sombras" [Mornas of shadows].) We see Edite searching frantically through a collection of letters among the keepsakes from her deceased husband, seeking a treasured memento about love's yearnings that Mariana has concealed in the pocket of her red dress.

But for all her curiosity about Edite's past, Mariana is no romantic. Edite's son pursues her, and she rebuffs him, saying, "I just like boys." In the evening, they have sex. "Did I hurt you?" he asks, apparently referring to their first experience. Costa keeps the effect on Mariana and her reactions ambiguous. Did Mariana lose her virginity? Is the youth simply a passing fancy, or is she determined to avoid erotic entanglements during her limited stay in Fogo?

After a few days, we see her back at the hospital, lifting the semiconscious Leão to his feet. He falls. Later, on regaining full consciousness, he sits unhappily in his hospital bed and angrily asks Mariana why she brought him back from Lisbon, to which she replies: "You were alone there." She adds that she was alone also. In Fogo, she has found a haven of sorts by treating patients, learning the culture, and being recognized as a familiar part of the island community. Leão sits with her on the hammock outside the hospital and allows her to shave him; he is angry and rebarbative, and they quarrel. Soon she begins pushing him around the village in a rickety wheelchair while he complains.

At a neighborhood party to celebrate Leão's dual return from both Lisbon and near death, Leão reveals his kinship with the violinist Bassoé, who now plans to leave Fogo with his sons.[26] Leão tries to play Bassoé's violin on stage, but the only sounds he manages to produce are out of tune and wildly off beat. He spots Mariana in the audience and dances with her to a lively piece, falling to the ground and laughing. Still suffering from concussion and loss of memory, he seems happy but off key, out of step with his island.

The film as a whole has a telluric quality that conveys the magnetic and erotic nature of the island. The day after the neighborhood celebration, Mariana walks up a hill toward the volcano. Leão follows her on crutches; he falls again and laughs, and so does she. They sit together on the volcanic rock. "I went to die in Portugal," he says, and embraces her as they slowly roll toward the ground off screen. It is suggested that they make love on the hillside.

That night, the bodies of Tina and Tano, the young couple, are discovered on the ground outside the hospital. Tano's tendency toward violence during the film is one of the few signs of a rage most islanders hold in check. Dispensing Xanax as a palliative for him along with what she does not realize is a suspicious vaccine, Mariana becomes the unsuspecting means for the two

Leão and Mariana

troubled lovers (and, we discover, recent parents) to use the medication to stay together, even if it means death.

Down to Earth does not disclose the fate of Leão, who denies writing the love letter Mariana took from Edite's house. Love, death, and guilt have marked Mariana, who looks for Leão after the party and sees him and Edite standing in a distant doorway in an intimate pose. This is one of the film's enigmatic, ambiguous elements, like the ones in *Blood*. Are Edite and Leão lovers? She is almost surely the woman who provided money for his return from Portugal. He probably did not write the love letter Mariana discovered, but he has affinities with the man who did.

After several days, we see Mariana caring for a child with hepatitis, then bathing and changing into a white blouse and dark-colored skirt—subdued attire suggesting her forthcoming return home. Bassoé and several of his sons are on their way to Lisbon, helped by Edite and funds from her widow's pension. As Edite walks with the departing men, a woman sitting on the street cries out, "When will my time come?" The supposedly fortunate men heading to Lisbon take mementos with them. The film does not tell us, but the history of the island confirms that some of them will send back remittances to support

Edite following men departing Fogo

their families, and the families left behind will send occasional missives from the archipelago to Portugal. In time, the remembered faces of loved ones will fade, with only letters as reminders of the past.

Notes

1. Pedro Costa, "I Have to Risk Each Shot," interview by Michael Guillén, April 5, 2008, http://pedrocosta-heroi.blogspot.com/2008/04/i-have-to-risk-each-shot.html.

2. Quoted in Michael Guillén, "Pedro Costa and Others on *Blood* (*The Blood,* 1989)," Cinematheque Ontario program notes, March 7, 2008, https://theeveningclass.blogspot.com/2008/03/pedro-costa-and-others-on-o-sangue.html.

3. See Nuno Barradas Jorge, *Refocus: The Films of Pedro Costa* (Edinburgh: University of Edinburgh Press, 2021), 14. As of this writing, Medeiros is mayor of Almada, a city across the Tagus River from Lisbon; she served in the Assembly of the Republic from 2009 to 2015.

4. From our conversations with the director in Lisbon in March 2024.

5. Adrian Martin, liner notes for *Blood,* Criterion Collection DVD, 2009.

6. Giovanni Marchini Camia, "Interview with Pedro Costa," in *Fireflies #4: Pedro Costa / Ben Rivers,* ed. Giovanni Marchini Camia and Anabel Brady-Brown (Berlin: Fireflies Press, 2016), 56. In an early review of *Blood,* critic Augusto M. Seabra compared it to *Os verdes anos* (*The Green Years,* 1963), Paulo

Rocha's first film about troubled teens in love, which Costa greatly admired and helped to restore. See Barradas Jorge, *Refocus*, 30.

7. Pedro Costa, "A Closed Door That Leaves Us Guessing," *Rouge*, 10, 2007, http://www.rouge.com.au/10/costa_seminar.html.

8. Quoted in Barradas Jorge, *Refocus*, 24. Dollar equivalencies for the Portuguese *escudo* and the euro, which replaced the *escudo* in 2002, are based on the value of Portuguese funds Costa received then and at different periods for his later films.

9. Quoted in Mark Peranson, "Pedro Costa: An Introduction," *Cinema Scope* 27 (Summer 2006): 9.

10. Quoted in Barradas Jorge, *Refocus*, 25.

11. For more on this subject, see Estela Vieira, "Pedro Costa's Cinematic Walls," *Journal of Lusophone Studies* 2, no. 1 (2017): 165–80.

12. Quoted in Guillén, "Pedro Costa and Others," https://theeveningclass.blogspot.com/2008/03/pedro-costa-and-others-on-o-sangue.html.

13. Guillén, "Pedro Costa and Others."

14. Guillén, "Pedro Costa and Others."

15. Luís Batalha, "Cape Verdeans in Portugal," in *Transnational Archipelago: Perspectives on Cape Verdean Migration and Diaspora*, ed. Luís Batalha and Jorgen Carling (Amsterdam: Amsterdam University Press, 2008), 62.

16. Batalha, "Cape Verdeans in Portugal," 66.

17. Patrick McGilligan, "Letters from Fontaínhas: Interview with Pedro Costa," *Film International* 8, no. 3 (2010): 82.

18. Pedro Costa, *Casa de lava – Caderno* (Lisbon: Pierre von Kleist Editions, 2013).

19. Barradas Jorge, *Refocus*, 42.

20. Peranson, "Pedro Costa: An Introduction," 11.

21. Peranson, "Pedro Costa," 11.

22. Barradas Jorge, *Refocus*, 40.

23. In some ways, the focus on Mariana's desire and sexual experience is a variation on the Portuguese (male) tradition of racial mixing with native inhabitants in the colonized tropics.

24. Tarrafal was known as the "slow death camp."

25. Amália's character is a reminder that locals employed at Tarrafal often supported prisoners. Perhaps the best-known case is Ana de Tchuntchum, a laundress at the prison who smuggled out Angolan writer Luandino Vieira's manuscripts and kept them until his release. See José Vicente Lopes, *Tarrafal-Chão Bom: Memórias e verdades*, vol. 1 (Praia: Instituto da Investigação e do Património Cultural, 2010), 148–50.

26. Bassoé's sons in the closing scenes of the film are the actor's actual sons.

PART II

The Fontaínhas Trilogy

Ossos (*Bones*, 1997)

Initially spurred by worker shortages in the 1960s, migration from the Cape Verdean archipelago to Portugal continued, driven by drought, famine, and the constant lure of better paying jobs. It was further stimulated by the 1974 revolution, the end of the colonial wars in Africa, and Portugal's recognition in 1975 of Cape Verde and other lusophone African territories as independent nations. Portugal's entry into the European Union in 1986 (of which Costa was deeply critical because of the nation's turn toward neocapitalism) and larger investments to modernize the country drew workers from Africa as well as Brazil, which was experiencing acute economic and political problems in the early 1990s.

Barely noticeable in Lisbon in the 1960s and early 1970s, the dark-skinned, largely male Cape Verdean population became increasingly visible, as did the arrival of some wives and mothers, who initially sold fish in the markets and later cleaned homes for the growing Portuguese middle and upper class. Creole-speaking children from the islands, most without knowledge of Portuguese, were sent to schools where they faced learning difficulties leading to significant dropout rates. By the early 1990s, plans were underway to raze shantytowns and relocate residents into "bairros sociais" (social neighborhoods), ostensibly to integrate communities into the larger Portuguese population. Lisbon's rapid development into suburbs demanded the removal of slums, which were all too visible in a city eager to promote its image as a modern capital.[1]

As Costa was preparing to leave Cape Verde after filming *Down to Earth*, locals he had befriended asked him to deliver packages and letters to relatives living in the Lisbon shantytowns, one of which was called Fontaínhas. Dating back to the early 1960s, Fontaínhas began as a group of wood and tin shacks built by migrant workers and poor white people with material from construction sites. Given the dearth of housing for Black workers in the city, company owners had little option but to supply them with lumber and aluminum to build homes. Erected side by side and often sharing walls, the dwellings grew in number as needs increased. Bricks and cement were used for newer housing and to fortify older structures.

In the early 1990s, Fontaínhas was home to a mix of Cape Verdeans, Africans from Portugal's other former colonies, and poor and working-class Portuguese. Those without jobs sold drugs to get by while others worked construction or low-paying jobs in the city. Drug use in the shantytowns was widespread. Fontaínhas had a reputation as a dangerous place, with armed guards posted to watch over comings and goings and profit from the drug trade.

As the bearer of packages and letters from home, Costa was warmly welcomed in Fontaínhas. Dissatisfied with his middle-class life in Lisbon, marked by his experience of filming in Cape Verde, and disturbed by conditions he found in the slums, he remained in Fontaínhas for periods between 1995 and 1996, growing close to a community whose Creole language he learned to speak.[2] During that time, his idea for a film about Fontaínhas took shape; he titled the work *Bones*, possibly referring to the bare-bones aspect of life in Fontaínhas, its skeleton of alleyways, or the bones beneath characters' faces that Costa tenderly registers. The title, like the work itself, tends toward the mysterious.

Paulo Branco, who produced Costa's earlier work, asked him for a script to secure backing for the new project. The script was a rudimentary document without dialogue, and Costa soon tore it up. The Portuguese Cinema Institute and RTP, which had supported *Down to Earth*, nevertheless approved financing, as did the Council of Europe's Eurimages. The film was a coproduction with Madragoa Filmes (Portugal), Gemini Films (France), and Zentropa (Denmark), a company started in 1992 by Danish director Lars von Trier. Cinematographer Emmanuel Machuel and sound technician Henri Maïkoff from *Down to Earth* returned to work with Costa on *Bones*, and he cast Inês de Medeiros in a supporting role in her third picture with him. The film was nominated for the Golden Lion prize at the Venice Film Festival, where it first appeared in 1997, and was popular with audiences back home—not always the case with Portuguese art cinema. In an interview, Costa commented somewhat wryly on its unexpected box-office success and the probable reasons why moviegoers flocked to see it:

> It played for months and months, and everybody wrote about that film, because it was the first time this reality was on the big screen. There was the smell of drugs, danger, lives that were not cheerful, and at the same time everyone could see that it was a real film, a story yet truthful. People knew about this place but it was hidden; nobody had showed it before. After *Ossos* it has been less and less because of course people don't want to see that again, and they saw it already, so they think they will be seeing the same thing all over again.[3]

In some ways, *Bones* is a film about Costa's Lisbon experience of crossing between two worlds: the noisy, labyrinthine Fontaínhas, with its cramped quarters, dark narrow passages, high outer walls, and Escher-like staircases seemingly leading nowhere, and the cosmopolitan city, with its shops, monuments, bustling streets, apartment buildings, and modern conveniences. Numerous shots feature a telephone pole near one of Fontaínhas's hidden entryways, a boundary marker of sorts where people mingle to talk or await loved ones returning from work in the city.

Capturing the disparities as well as the proximity between these two worlds, Costa employed a few professional actors from Lisbon, like Medeiros, to appear alongside nonprofessionals from Fontaínhas. We see no older people; Costa concentrated on his own generation, feeling an affinity with the impoverished community members and gaining confidence in their ability to become actors. The film altered the way Costa approached his subsequent work. His aim was simple: to represent the raw, quotidian lives of the poor accurately and respectfully. But like all his work, it is not a conventional social problem picture. As Costa later said, film as "a revolutionary gun does not exist. Or if it did exist, it failed completely, because the guys . . . who believed in it didn't succeed."[4]

Bones begins with a striking precredit close-up of a poor, attractive, nameless young woman (Zita Duarte—the sister of Vanda Duarte, who has a significant role in this film and the major role in Costa's next film). She is seated on a bed in a darkened room near a wall of peeling green paint. The close-up is a good illustration of a point made by critic Adrian Martin, who writes that Costa took a lesson from Jean-Marie Straub and Danièle Huillet: "Start

A young woman in Fontaínhas

the piece instantly, with a gaze, a gesture, a movement, some *displacement* of air and energy, something dropped like a heavy stone to shatter the calm of pre-fiction equilibrium. To set the motor of the intrigue going—even if that intrigue will be so shadowy, so shrouded in questions that go to the very heart of its status as a depiction of the real."[5] The close-up lasts almost a minute. The young woman, who is obviously poor, looks almost at us. She seems listless. She blinks and lowers her lovely eyes sadly, then wearily tilts her head to the side, resting it against the wall so that she looks out the edge of her eyes. Her expression changes. Is she resentful or suspicious? The change is small, ambiguous.

It is never clear who the young woman is, although she appears in other scenes—in another extended close-up later in the film, she again looks almost at us, her eyes shadowed with fatigue, smoking a cigarette. She becomes a watcher, perhaps a rebuke to cinema's voyeurism, peering out a restaurant's pass-through where she and another young woman (Clotilde Montron) are working or standing as if on watch at the door or in an alley in the shantytown. We never see the object of her interest in a subjective angle that would explain the focus of her gaze. Perhaps she is looking at nothing—here as almost everywhere else, Costa avoids the shot/reverse shot that is the basis of conventional film grammar. The young woman is simply an emblematic representative of her neighborhood, a character with no obvious significance for the narrative whom one would never find in the usual "well made" film.

It would be wrong to describe the opening shot as painterly, but Costa's films often work on a boundary between motion picture and portraiture or still photography (not surprisingly, his shorter work has often been shown in museum spaces), just as he increasingly works on a boundary between documentary and fiction. The opening close-up is pregnant with indeterminate meaning; the angle of light and the green of the wall are as fascinating as the young woman's face. It could almost be exhibited as art photography, but the tiny movements have an implicit narrative importance, as if the viewer is being invited to contemplate the smallest details and develop empathy.

Bones contains many lingering close-ups, and they become a motif. They are always silent, with the character lost in a somber attitude, making it difficult to sense exactly what the character is thinking. Costa has often been described as a director of "still life" because of his faces and occasional close-ups of inanimate objects, but as Ana Balona de Oliveira has pointed out the term has a double meaning in Costa's films: "Not only does it refer to the painterly, shadowy objects that accompany the quietly empty despair of Fontaínhas's inhabitants, but also to these characters' lives themselves."[6] In the close-ups of their faces, the actors never serve as "models," as Robert Bresson called his actors; for all their stillness, they convey an enigmatic inner expressiveness or a detached fatigue. The effect is mysterious and makes most movies seem artificial.

As a whole, *Bones* is a beautifully photographed 35mm color film that privileges long takes and extended close-ups of a community of Black and white people bound together by poverty and life in tight quarters. Like *Down to Earth*, it draws its slight plot from a newspaper account, in this case about a young woman's desperate attempt to sell her baby in a train station. The film's mother is Tina (Russian-born actor Mariya Lipkina), a teenager living alone in Fontaínhas who has recently given birth to a boy. During most of the film, she appears lifeless, her vacant look belying her desperation; she seems to have postpartum depression exacerbated by drugs. After she gives birth and returns home from the hospital, she shuts the windows in her house and prepares to kill herself and her newborn with gas from a propane tank placed near a sofa. Sitting motionless, as if in a trance, she completely ignores the baby, who looks at her while gurgling and waving his tiny hands and feet. (No one has noticed that Costa used two babies for the film; virtually indistinguishable, they are equally docile and charming.)

Portrait of a family

With the arrival of the nameless young father (Nuno Vaz), we discover that Tina's plan has been abandoned. Perhaps she expected him to arrive. He finds her and the baby asleep on the sofa and, exhausted or drugged, falls fully clothed into her bed. Awakened, Tina enters the bedroom and tugs at his inert body to get his attention, but he resists. She pulls him from the bed to the floor and drags him toward the sofa as if demanding he take responsibility for the baby, who continues to nap. Sitting on the floor with her back to the wall, she looks off in the distance as he lies sprawled in front of her. The shot holds for a time on a family portrait: two young people ill equipped and unprepared for parenthood and an unwanted child whose fate hangs in the balance.

Bones withholds more than it reveals, showing us often-nameless characters whose identities are slow to develop. Characters are sometimes shot in ways that conceal information. Our first glimpse of the young father, before he joins Tina, is from behind, sitting on a doorstep next to an unidentified woman who appeared in close-up in an earlier scene but whom we do not know at this point. Part of the film's obliqueness also has to do with the relative paucity of dialogue.

Throughout, we hear the sounds of life around mostly silent characters: Henri Maïkoff's soundtrack mixes sounds of children's voices, doors closing, and barking dogs into a discordant symphony of Fontaínhas white noise. As a result, the intermittent sound of a deep cough or a rattle of kitchen pans is palpable and startling against the continuum of background murmurings. When characters do talk, they sometimes surprise us by shouting and cursing each other. The sounds are fractured and incessant, contrasting the usually unmoving, carefully framed images.

Our first glimpse of Tina is a frame-within-the-frame close-up of her looking out a pane of glass set in a hospital door leading to the room where her baby has been delivered. The next shot, a close-up of another young woman looking through an identical pane, introduces her friend Clotilde (Vanda Duarte), who has come to the hospital to accompany Tina and the baby. Nothing is said between the two women as they ride a bus to Fontaínhas; comfort comes not in words but in gesture, as Clotilde places her hand over Tina's. Clotilde holds the baby and carries him off the bus as if she were the mother, handing him to Tina with instructions to show him to neighbors. (We have previously seen Clotilde trying to console the father, covering his hand with hers as they travel by bus to her workplace in the city.) As she walks through Fontaínhas, all too aware of the child's insecure situation, she angrily remarks to herself, "That baby should have been mine."

Costa struck gold with his discovery of Vanda Duarte, who lived in Fontaínhas and helped shape the character of the intrepid Clotilde. "I had seen her in the neighborhood two or three times," he told Mark Peranson. "I thought she should be in *Ossos*, but people on the crew were afraid of her, because she's a very direct person, and also this boy-girl mixture . . . when we were shooting, she always resisted hitting her mark or saying the lines, and she would say it's all bullshit. . . . [In one scene] I gave her the directions, 'Look here. You're not very happy, and you're making soup,' and she disagreed, 'No, no, I should be happy in this scene.' That was the end of all my fears."[7]

Vanda's androgenous quality pairs well with her role as Tina's protector, the father's judge, and, presumably, his eventual executioner. She has a remarkable presence, a sullen gaze that sometimes breaks unexpectedly into a tiny smile, and a distinctive walk (something all great movie stars have). She moves in a determined way, and her smallest gestures seem large. And has any actor ever deeply inhaled a cigarette and sonorously coughed as she does?

In many scenes, Costa uses a partly opened door to give little glimpses of Vanda's performance. A cracked door opening onto her home shows her in the role of wife and mother, serving dinner to her husband (Angolan-born actor Miguel Sermão). In the light from the kitchen, we see her daughter, Maura, nibbling a piece of bread on the front stoop and her nameless son

Vanda Duarte as Clotilde

walking silently past as he leaves the house. Later, through a narrow doorway concealing parts of a living room, Clotilde appears in cleaning clothes, vacuuming a bourgeois Lisbon apartment with spacious windows. At the center of the frame, sitting in a chair, is the young father, waiting to accompany her to the hospital to pick up Tina and the baby. Nonprofessional Nuno Vaz, whom Costa discovered on a Lisbon construction site, has a ponytail, almond-shaped eyes, and a thin, wispy mustache and beard. His thoughts and feelings, like everyone's, are difficult to read. A feckless, mostly silent character, he leaves work to women, simply lifting his feet so Clotilde can vacuum under them. He eventually slips out, causing Clotilde to call him a "bastard." The scene is memorable for its close-up of the slowly closing apartment door and the sound it makes as the father exits. A similar closed door will be important in a later scene and at the end of the film.

We cut to the walk-in closet where Clotilde is cleaning. A paean to middle-class consumerism, the clothing squeezed together on hangers sharply contrasts with Clotilde's work attire and the paucity of material goods in Fontaínhas. We never see the apartment's inhabitants, who have no contact with their cleaning lady. Later in the film, a weary Clotilde returns to the apartment and picks up dirty dishes and glassware; she has just arrived from her own home, where her daughter had a breakfast of bread. Still later, the same narrow living room doorway shows Clotilde sitting in the chair as Tina, now her coworker, vacuums. Clotilde smokes, smiles, and lifts her feet, hoping Tina's life might stabilize.

Hunger is a strong determining factor in the film. The father rummages for discarded food in a city market's trash bins. Sometime later, in one of the film's most astonishing shots, we see him walking briskly down a street outside Fontaínhas carrying a black plastic trash bag. The extended lateral traveling shot is formally reminiscent of one in *Down to Earth* in which Mariana walks briskly along a street in Fogo. Emmanuel Machuel, who photographed *Down to Earth,* does something similar here, but with important differences. In *Down to Earth,* the shot gives a sense of Mariana's vitality as she bounces along in her red dress; it shows us people and homes on side streets, providing a broader picture of the island community. In *Bones,* the shot is much longer, lasting over two minutes, and was photographed from the window of a slow-moving car. The father seems to be on a swift, determined march that covers a poor stretch just outside Fontaínhas, with cars rapidly passing in the foreground. The walk takes him past grim stone walls covered with graffiti and occasional closed doors that give the gray scene touches of color. There are only a few people on the street, among them a man with an umbrella and a small girl in a bright red dress. Suddenly lifting the bag from his side, where it has been partly out of our sight, he cradles it in his arms as he walks. It is a stunning moment. The baby is never visible in the shot, but we begin to realize that the father has absconded with his son, hiding him in the trash bag.[8]

Unlike the woman in the newspaper story on which *Bones* is partly based, the father does not try to sell his child. After the traveling shot, we see the baby in swaddling clothes, cradled in the father's arms outside a busy downtown metro station. This shot, too, is remarkable, in part because of the large crowd of people entering and exiting the station and walking in every direction: a businessman in a black suit, two elderly women who wrestle with a shopping bag, a woman who has difficulty opening or closing her blue and white umbrella, and innumerable working-class men who walk past the camera. Viewers might assume that several people in the shot are extras, but there is a very large crowd. The situation is so realistic that it resembles a film Costa discussed with his students at a seminar he taught in Tokyo:

> After *Workers Leaving the Lumière Factory* (1895, *La sortie des usines Lumière*), there is a second film, again workers leaving a factory. It is here that things . . . become complicated, because the Lumières were not very happy

Father with baby in a bag

> with the appearance of the workers coming out of their factory . . . they said to the workers, "Try and be a bit more natural. . . . You, go left, don't go to the right . . . you, you can smile a bit, and you, too. . . . You, go with your wife over there." And so there was *mise en scène*. Thus, fiction was born.[9]

When we asked Costa how his shot was done, he explained that there were no extras; the only person he directed was Nuno Vaz in the role of the father. The large 35mm camera was placed in the middle of the street, with a normal lens rather than a telephoto, which would have enabled it to move back and be less visible to the crowd. Only one of the many passersby seems to glance at the camera, but the look is barely noticeable. Before the scene was shot, Costa told Vaz that he could keep any money he got for begging with the baby. Vaz thought he would have a profitable day, but nobody gave him anything.[10] "Some food for the baby?" he asks the businessman, who ignores him, as do several women. His few words and the baby's mewling are lost in the sounds of a city at rush hour.

Weary, the father eventually sits on the low stoop of a small grocery shop with the baby and tells a nurse in a white uniform who is entering the shop

Begging outside a Lisbon metro

(Isabel Ruth) that he has not eaten in three days. When she exits, she hands him a sandwich and milk for the baby. He follows her down the street. We cut to a public restroom, where we see him sitting on the floor with the child in his arms, trying to feed the baby with bits of chewed bread and drops of liquid he spits from a half empty bottle of beer.

We cut to a hospital entryway, where the baby is rushed to emergency as the drunken father is pushed by an aide and sent sprawling on the floor. Still more information is withheld. In Fontaínhas, Clotilde asks Tina where the baby is, and Tina responds by pounding her fists on her friend out of fear and despair. At the hospital, a nurse (Berta Susana Teixeira) asks the father what is wrong with the baby, and he replies, "Ask nurse Eduarda Gomes," the nurse who earlier bought him food. When Eduarda appears, she apologizes for having had the baby taken to the hospital. It was a false alarm, but the child must remain overnight. The father simply bums a cigarette from her and goes out to a balcony for a smoke. Whether out of guilt, pity, or some other motive (sex is later implied), Eduarda takes him to her apartment and feeds him. "I do eat," he says as he downs a plate of scrambled eggs, "but not meals." She tells him he must go because her husband will soon arrive—apparently a lie, because we never see evidence of a husband. The next day, the father brings the baby back to the apartment, and when Eduarda asks about the mother, he replies, "She doesn't care." He adds, "It's your fault, you could have helped her," giving no explanation for the accusation.

Partly because he was using heavy equipment in Fontaínhas's tight spaces, Costa often filmed characters at windows and behind half-closed doors, revealing only a slice of life. Speaking to his students in Tokyo, he said that the technique enabled him to conceal the sight of people taking drugs, all too common in Fontaínhas.[11] Drug taking is regularly implied in the lassitude and dead stares of characters like Tina and the errant young father. (In one scene of people walking through Fontaínhas, we see in the background a quick drug handoff between two youths.)

In interviews, Costa has often talked about the onerousness of large cameras, lights, and crew; he tended to work around them in small spaces. One of the best examples of his strategy shows Tina stopping in an alleyway and looking into a window, where Clotilde and her husband are in bed, the husband pleading for sex. In the next shot, the camera has moved inside, looking through the couple's bedroom doorway opposite the window to show Tina looking in. In a later party sequence, the space is so small that couples mostly dance in place to music from a boom box. To capture a broader image of the action, the camera moves outside the room just beyond the doorway, which frames Clotilde dancing alone, her arms swaying at her sides. We also see Clotilde and Tina dancing close to one another, the latter a pale figure with glazed, half-closed eyes and an unsteady stance. Suddenly, Clotilde's husband appears, shouting that she has not fed her children, and drags her off. Without Clotilde's support, Tina falls to the floor. A nameless young woman kneels beside her, saying that Tina has "evil eye" and must pass it to her.

Costa also decided to minimize lighting equipment, opting for available light and often showing characters emerging from complete shadow. In a dark alleyway in Fontaínhas, for example, the young father, temporarily back from the city, hides behind a staircase, barely visible as Tina and her friend walk by. There is a ghostly, noir quality to the slum's barely lit passageways, where Clotilde becomes a sort of sleuth, tracking the father's location to Eduarda's apartment. Caught, he shoves Clotilde against a wall, hurting her arm, but she remains adamant, confronting him with the pain he has caused Tina, who is obsessing over the missing child. He tells her the baby is dead. Clotilde warns him that if anything happens to Tina, she will kill him. Following their angry exchange, the father takes the baby to the apartment/workplace of a prostitute (Inês de Medeiros); when he sees a customer going through her door, he leaves the baby lying on a tattered couch in the hallway and returns to Eduarda's apartment. Back from work, Eduarda asks him where the baby is, telling him she has found someone to take the child. Without explanation, the father simply replies, "I've found someone."

Next, we see Clotilde and her daughter, Maura, riding a bus. Viewed from behind, Clotilde keeps repeating a sort of mantra, identifying herself as a cleaning woman who needs work. She is rehearsing a speech she will make to Eduarda for a cleaning job that Clotilde gets and passes on to Tina so that she can confront the father. But no one is there when Tina enters the apartment to clean. She walks into the kitchen, opens the oven, turns on the gas jets, and waits for death. Her suicide plan is foiled by Eduarda, who finds and saves her, helping her return home.

In the meantime, the father goes back to the prostitute, where he finds the baby is no longer on the couch. Realizing that the prostitute has a customer, he leans against the wall just outside her door and waits. A long, sinister close-up shows him casually turning his head away from the door, looking to the side and concealing his face from the departing customer. When he enters, he has no money to pay for sex, but he and the prostitute go to bed anyway. (Costa mostly depicts sex off-screen or in darkness and never eroticizes it.) Afterward, talking while half naked in bed, he offers to sell her the baby. She agrees to keep the child without money and says he must leave. Suddenly we cut to a view of the narrow space beneath the bed, where the prostitute has stashed the baby, awake on the floor. As if to punctuate the infant's plight, the screen fades to black. It is the last time we see him.

Up to this point, the only people we have seen crossing from Fontaínhas to the city are workers like Clotilde and Tina, plus the father, who seems to live off the street and women. The pattern is broken when nurse Eduarda seeks out Tina in Fontaínhas. A crane shot looks down as she makes her way through a winding maze of alleys, stopping to ask a guard for directions to Tina's place. The high-angle shot gives us an idea of the size and complexity of Fontaínhas, with its outer walls and broad flat rooftops dotted here and there with objects and debris. Through a window, we see Eduarda meeting Tina in a small room, where the sound of the British punk band Wire's 1977 song "Lowdown" blares from a tape or radio. (When asked about the scene's deafening music, Costa recalled times as a young man when he would go stoned or on acid to retrospectives of John Ford movies and come home to play music loudly.)[12] The

Clotilde observing Eduarda and Tina

nurse's offer of help is rebuffed by Clotilde, who arrives and stakes her claim by kissing Tina.

But Eduarda does not leave Fontaínhas, and her behavior cannot be explained by a desire to do good. She is sexually attracted to Tina's errant lover and perhaps, as a white liberal, wants to experience slumming. We next see her in a small, dark café, where she is joined by Clotilde's Black husband. Sitting close beside her, he says she looks like Tina, whom he propositioned earlier in the film. Rejected by his wife, he presses his attention and a couple of glasses of beer on Eduarda, who ends up in bed with him. When Clotilde and her daughter arrive back at their home, the son, standing guard outside the door, stops them. The scene echoes an earlier one in which the boy prevents Tina from entering the home while his father is trying to have sex with Clotilde.

Sometime later, Clotilde arrives to clean Eduarda's apartment, where she finds the father of the missing baby alone, sleeping in the bedroom. Without hesitating, she walks to the kitchen, opens the oven, and turns on the gas jets. She leaves, triple locking the door from the outside and making good her promise of revenge.

This is one of the most dramatic moments in the film, and it leaves the audience unsure of how to react. The father is by no means likeable, but does he deserve death, and does he in fact die? He has treated the baby as a commodity to be sold or used on the street for begging, but he has also kept the child alive when the mother almost killed it. Although the loosely woven plot focuses on a desperate mother and an unwanted child, the action is driven mostly by the peripatetic father and the resolute Clotilde. Critics have been of two minds about the sullen, baby-faced father. For many, he is simply a deadbeat who takes the baby for personal gain. Others regard him as the story's ironic hero, who saves the baby from its suicidal mother and tries to find it a home. Tina's emotional crisis, which jeopardizes the baby's well-being, seems to spare her negative critique, but one of *Bones*'s praiseworthy qualities is that it never allows us to make easy judgments. It simply observes several lives—the father who goes from woman to woman with his baby, the drugged mother who swings from suicidal despair to maternal anguish, the nurse whose charitable actions have questionable motives, the working woman who protects her family and friends but is willing to kill—all while preserving their ambiguity and mystery.

As in *Blood*, a new family forms from a broken one, in this case consisting of Tina, Clotilde, and Maura, who is now sick and in bed. Viewed from outside their bedroom window, a scene of quiet domesticity unfolds as Clotilde tends to her daughter. In a sign of youthful rebellion, Maura dumps a glass of cold medicine out the window as her mother's back is turned. Another spill occurs in Tina's small kitchen, this time unintended, as Tina and Clotilde collide and a pot and its contents spill to the floor. They burst out laughing. Unlike the early scene of Clotilde silently serving her husband, this one creates a sense of domestic comradery and a kind of joy.

But while Clotilde's survival instincts and strength as a mother and friend are her greatest assets, they can also be disturbing. Her emotion when she turns on the gas and triple locks the door to kill the father seems no different from the way she performs routine tasks like drying dishes or vacuuming a rug. There are no apparent consequences for her vengeful act, nor do we learn what happens to Eduarda or others. As the film approaches its end, we merely see two nameless young women coming and going on the street, one of them carrying a travel bag.

Bones reveals a community that is sometimes warm but constantly at risk. We are left to speculate on the significance of the film's final close-up of Tina slowly closing the door behind Clotilde, who is likely going to work. Like the lowering of a theatrical curtain, the door's closing ends the drama, but without resolution. As Emma Fajgenbaum has put it, "*Ossos* is always withholding, repeatedly demarcating the limits of what viewers can see, not only with its multiple framings and elliptical editing that veil the ubiquity of heroin, but at the level of the image, with the symbol of the closed door."[13] It is the film of Costa's that best exemplifies the title he gave his lectures in Tokyo: "A Closed Door That Leaves Us Guessing." It also marks his passage from 35mm production to a radically different kind of cinema.

No quarto da Vanda (*In Vanda's Room*, 2000)

In addition to a successful box office run, *Bones* was nominated for prizes at several international festivals, garnering top awards in 1997 at the Entrevues Film Festival in France (best foreign film) and the Venice Film Festival (best cinematography). While *Bones* did not end Costa's relationship with Fontaínhas, it did change the way he made movies. Forgoing a cumbersome 35mm camera, heavy lighting equipment, and large crew for his next projects, he adopted a Panasonic DX 100 digital video camera, a virtually amateur instrument, and worked with a much smaller professional crew.

In some ways, that radical change was already on the horizon when he made *Bones*. Costa expressed frustration at losing desirable shots in the film because of the time and cost of rearranging equipment and crew.[14] As we saw, the space required for positioning a large camera, lights, reflectors, and personnel made filming in the narrow corridors and tight interiors of Fontaínhas especially difficult, often impossible. More difficult for residents was the everyday presence of technicians and large equipment, with lighting setups shining directly into people's homes at night. Costa consulted the community about the shooting schedule, filming only during times that would not conflict with drug operations, but, as in his two previous films, he was frustrated by the size of the crew, some of whom cared nothing for the film, and by quarrels with his producer and actors.

In various interviews, Costa credits Vanda Duarte, the woman who was so effective in *Bones*, for urging him to find another way to approach life in Fontaínhas, to create a film that would give an intimate view of life without professional actors. This encouragement helped determine his choice of technical process. The digital camera allowed greater intimacy between himself, his principal players, and community members (all of whom played themselves), as did his use of light from windows, small lamps, candles, and unobtrusive reflectors made with mirrors or polystyrene sheets, used to create shots of astonishing beauty. Two of his previous films had shown Costa's impressive skill with landscapes, but henceforth he would work mostly in small interiors.

Ironically, during his long period of meticulous work on *In Vanda's Room*, Fontaínhas was being destroyed by the city of Lisbon, its residents gradually moving to a distant public housing project. The destruction of the community is intermittently documented and heard on the soundtrack, providing a kind of understated plot. Vanda's family home was nevertheless an ideal location. As Costa explained to Mark Peranson, "Vanda's house was the first in the Fontaínhas neighborhood to be built . . . and probably she will be the last to leave. The government wants the African population to leave first because it's nice for the papers and public attention."[15]

Costa spent two years, 1998 and 1999, traveling between his own home and Fontaínhas, living for periods in Vanda's place or rooming with young men in the neighborhood, becoming a trusted member of the community. According to critic João Bénard da Costa, Vanda suggested that Costa center the film completely in her room.[16] In an interview with filmmaker Jean-Pierre Gorin, Costa said he initially planned to follow her suggestion, making the film a conversation piece between himself, Vanda, and anyone who might visit her.[17] That plan changed when Zita, Vanda's sister (who had a minor role in *Bones*), moved into Vanda's bedroom to accommodate their sister Nela, who was being released after serving three years for shoplifting Knorr bouillon cubes, widely used to cut dope. As a result, Costa decided to remain behind the camera while Vanda and Zita took center stage.

Challenges were posed by the sound recording, which is as important to this film as the images. Even with an external mic, the sound of conversation was a problem, and specialists Philippe Morel, Mathieu Imbert, and Stephan Konkan were contracted during postproduction to improve the quality of voices and other sounds. Vanda and Zita also rerecorded some of their conversations for postproduction. Costa tells an amusing story about the many sounds of the government's demolition of Fontaínhas, which was going on at the time. Some of the racket in the movie is actually from an archive of sound editor and designer Xavier Waldir, who recorded the demolition of a building in Cairo for a film he made there.[18]

The resulting film, *In Vanda's Room*, required nearly a year to edit, including work to enhance the digital image and transfer the material to a 35mm exhibition format for festival competition.[19] Accustoming himself to the new technology, Costa shot 180 hours of video, much of it in Vanda's compact bedroom, where he positioned his camera between a wall and the door and sat on a crate, filming over a period of six months. The space was so tight that there was no room for a tripod for an external mic, necessary given the insufficiency of the camera's mic, so a setup was improvised.[20]

Although the original idea was to film exclusively in Vanda's room, Costa shot other spaces inside her home and outside, where empty houses were being bulldozed into ruins. The result is a 170-minute film—a coproduction between Portugal (Contracosta Productions), Germany (Pandora), and Switzerland (Ventura Films) with funding from ZDF, RTP, ICAM, RTSI (Radio and Television for Italian-speaking Switzerland), and Filmförderung Hamburg Schleswig-Holstein. Premiered at the 2000 Locarno Film Festival, it had limited distribution and did not do well at the box office, but it won the International Federation of Film Critics prize at the 2001 Yamagata International Documentary Film Festival (despite the fact that its status as a documentary can be questioned). The following year, Costa took home the Cannes Festival's France Culture Award for Best Foreign Director.

Despite the realist power of the completed film and the fact that many regarded it as a documentary, Costa's decision to use a digital camera for *In Vanda's Room* placed him in an emergent field of artists who, for theorists in the 1990s, seemed to threaten cinema's relation to reality. Because digital reproduction is different from celluloid reproduction, and because it can be manipulated in postproduction or embellished with computer-generated imagery, a few theoretically inclined viewers in the years leading up to Costa's film argued that the digital was guilty of a death of the human.[21] To them, the digital undermined André Bazin's famous argument about realism in "The Ontology of the Photographic Image," which describes photographic emulsion as a surface on which objects from the real world are imprinted, like an old book page that preserves the imprint of a leaf or sand that preserves a footprint. The semioticians call such imprints "indexical" signs, a language closest to the real.

Viewers of *In Vanda's Room* will recognize the fallacy of such arguments. Volker Pantenburg has been of great help in clarifying debates about realism by enumerating four ways in which the impression of reality is created in cinema, nearly all of them relevant to Costa's film. First is the means of production: "The fewer people involved in making a movie, and the fewer props and technology you need, the greater the chance to capture something 'real' without suffocating it in technology." Second is the indexical imprint, which has less to do with celluloid film strip than with "lenses and physical transmission of light onto whatever support these are then transcribed onto." Third is what Roland Barthes calls the "reality effect" of narrative fiction, which in film can be created by various means, including "excessively long takes that do not use time for narrative necessities" or "dialogue that does not aim at getting somewhere." Fourth has to do with the subjective impressions of the viewer, as when computer-generated imagery (not used in *In Vanda's Room*) reached a new level in the 1990s and made viewers unsure of whether what they were seeing was real.[22]

By now, we should recognize that the digital is fully capable of recording the real world. There can be no doubt that Vanda Duarte and the other occupants of Fontaínhas are really there, and the sense of reality is heightened by the small digital camera and minimal equipment, which are less distracting to the performers. The digital camera enables Costa to shoot extremely long takes that create a sense of real duration, often involving aimless or inconsequential conversations that give the impression of the real. More than that, the actors are not professionals, as they often are in Italian or Hollywood neorealism, and they are playing themselves, speaking dialogue of which they are the primary authors.

If the film is in one sense a documentary, in another it is a theatrical and at least half-fictional representation. The images Costa captures with his unmoving camera are far more thoughtfully and artfully composed than most documentaries, which sometimes foreground a reality effect by employing grainy or handheld shots. Furthermore, the performances were subject to many retakes under Costa's direction. No matter what interventions he made, however, he has said that he placed emphasis on the real:

> I'm always within a kind of realism. Everything feeds into this realism: the way I work, the decision what to spend the money on, which camera you use, which microphone. All that is what I call "realism." And I know very well that every transgression—of a threshold or border that I vaguely call realism—makes me risk losing myself and the film. . . . I think we have established a kind of balance between the technical means, the people, and the money, all these things. We have established an equilibrium that runs into the film . . . something runs from us into the neighborhood, and from the neighborhood a lot runs into the camera and to us.[23]

All this being true, Costa has never fetishized the digital camera or claimed it to be flawless. In a 2012 interview with David Jenkins, he remarked that he would like "more than ever" to work in 35mm because of its true-to-life qualities: "If it stays the same price, I could do another film in 35mm. Something that annoys me: the fake stillness of digital. The depth and distance of things with DCP is very fake. We filmmakers and technicians feel that the black is not black."[24]

It is impossible, however, to think that *In Vanda's Room* could have been done in any other way, and no one has ever complained about the force of its imagery. It is a revolutionary film because of its production methods, and it points to what Jonathan Rosenbaum calls "Films of the Future."[25] As Pantenburg indicates, it also raises fundamental questions about the ontology of the image and the distinction between documentary and fiction. Part of the film's greatness is that it gives a new answer to Bazin's question, "What is cinema?" At the same time, it makes the viewer ask, "What is documentary and what is fiction?" Even if we had no knowledge of its means of production, we would feel uncompromising reality mediated by art.

In this regard, the film raises still another question: "What is acting?" Erving Goffman has accurately defined theatrical performance as an arrangement that transforms an individual into someone who can be "looked to for engaging behavior by persons in an audience role."[26] The individual could be on stage, in a film, or on a street corner, as long as a conceptual frame of some kind separates performer from audience. Anyone who steps into this frame, even an ordinary passerby, becomes a performer. In *In Vanda's Room*, for example, the camera looks through an open doorway onto a street where a small bicycle is standing, and a cute toddler waddles up to the door, looks inside, turns, and waddles off. After a while, the child comes back, pushes at the handle of the cycle, and toddles off again. This child is a performer, perhaps inadvertent but charming.

Performers are more likely to be called actors when they become agents in a narrative of some kind. Even if the actor is playing herself and performing her typical daily activities, she remains an actor. Vanda had already become an actor in *Bones*, where she played a fictional character, but here, the sense of fictional narrative is almost nonexistent—the film has no plot other than the systematic, ultimately total destruction of Fontaínhas by bulldozers and the residents' drug usage and mounting fear for their survival. Vanda is living the experience she enacts. Is she acting when she sits on her bed, spreads heroin on a piece of tinfoil, lights the foil with a Bic, uses a tube of foil to inhale the drug, and follows it up with a strong drag on a cigarette, all while raucous noise goes on outside? The answer is yes because actors both pretend and do. When they kiss in a film, they are really kissing, even if they feign passion. Vanda is really taking the drug, and her emotions are real. Costa has said that this is the film "where I directed least and there was really very little imposing of anything. What's there are the feelings—the emotions, the sadness or joy . . . comes from the people themselves."[27]

Vanda nevertheless has the fascinating personality of a movie star. If she is occupying her room with others, it is to her sculpted face we are drawn. Her dark eyes and prominent nose give her a raven-like intensity, even in repose. She and her sister Zita, with whom she shares heroin and many conversations, have long legs and are thin as fashion models. Both are magnetic presences despite being unkempt and ravaged by drugs. Zita looks a bit like someone from a hard-rock band. In one scene, we can see the bones on her thin chest; in another, we watch her eating a banana, chewing the pulpy fruit with an abstracted, dreamy, perhaps drugged expression. In yet another, we see her playing with a toy gun like one she saw on TV in *Police Academy*. In many scenes, Vanda has fits of asthmatic coughing and sneezing. Even so, she is assertive and dominates every conversation, determining the emotional substance and course of dialogue with everyone she encounters.

In interviews, Costa has recalled his uncertainty about how to start the film and, more pressingly, deal with the hours of footage and decide what to select. In a 2019 interview, he referred to regularly shooting thirty to forty retakes of scenes. He has also spoken about what he was trying to achieve with the retakes, giving as an example a conversation between Vanda and her friend Pedro, a flower seller, about their friend Geny's fatal overdose. Geny had great appeal as a personality, and Costa's early plan was to feature her prominently; because of her death, however, her one appearance is an extended mid-range outdoor shot of an unidentified Black woman wearing a colorful cloak and gracefully smoking a cigarette while a passerby says to her, "Geny, they pulled your house down." Costa filmed Vanda and Pedro's conversation about her death in Vanda's bedroom. Dissatisfied with the results, he asked them to reenact it a couple of days later. During the reenactment, Vanda and Pedro began crying as they talked about Geny, which Costa said made the scene too sentimental. Six months later, he asked Vanda and Pedro to do the scene again, which involved another four takes. The second of those four appears in the film.[28] Costa's patience won out for an important scene, and his actors displayed an ability to recreate from memory the words they had spoken some six months earlier.

To help work through the hours of footage, Costa hired French editor Dominique Auvray with ZDF funds, which also paid for sound mixing. Their intense work schedule involved watching rushes from ten a.m. until seven p.m. each day for a three-week period.[29] But the problem of how to begin the film was still unresolved, so Costa took a hiatus. On learning that Jean-Marie Straub and Danièle Huillet were reediting a version of their 1998 film *Sicilia!*, he took the opportunity to make a documentary about their work in the editing room, using his digital camera. By then, he had plenty of experience using the camera in a contained space. (More will be said about the film he made, *Où gît votre sourire enfoui?* [*Where Does Your Hidden Smile Lie?*, 2001], in part IV of our book.) According to Costa, it was during the two-month shoot that he came up with the idea of turning *In Vanda's Room* into a story about two "gangs" in Fontaínhas: "the girls and the boys and their separate worlds with parallel stories." He also decided he wanted to begin the film with a scene that would be like "girls on a beach."[30] (The film begins with two girls on a bed.)

Unlike his earlier works, no professional actors were hired for the film. The girls are the Duarte sisters Vanda and Zita, with occasional appearances by their Cape Verdean–born mother, Lena, and grandmother, and a few unidentified women, one of whom, Clotilde Montron from *Down to Earth*, came to Lisbon for the shoot. As in his earlier works, Costa starts the film in media res with a remarkable scene. A five-minute precredit shot is preceded by the briefest sound of breathing over a black screen, which segues into the explosion of Vanda's stertorous coughing. The opening shot features the sisters, who face one another on Vanda's rumpled bed in a lighted corner of her room. As in many interior scenes, the room is only partially lit, with areas that are dim or dark. Probably thanks to postproduction, Costa achieves true blackness and a splash of color—in this case, a green wall behind Vanda bearing the markings of longtime occupancy. She and Zita are taking turns smoking heroin, which they share along with a cigarette. Desperate for the drug, Zita tells Vanda to hurry up with preparation, complaining about her sister's greasy hands. Equally fixated on Zita's hands as she prepares a hit, Vanda urges her also to hurry up and licks her lips. The camera here and throughout the film is completely still. From somewhere off-screen, a recording of a woman singing soulfully is heard, followed by the sound of neighbor children's distant voices.

Despite the rawness of what we are witnessing, the sequence has artistic power. With her back to one wall, Vanda's ravaged face is aglow, not unlike a woman in a Vermeer painting, although in conversation with sculptor Rui Chafes and others, Costa has argued against such comparison: "To name drop Vermeer when talking about a shot, a composition, or specific ambient setting of a film constitutes a refusal to see and think about the film itself and is an insult to cinema's intrinsic capabilities."[31] One could argue, however,

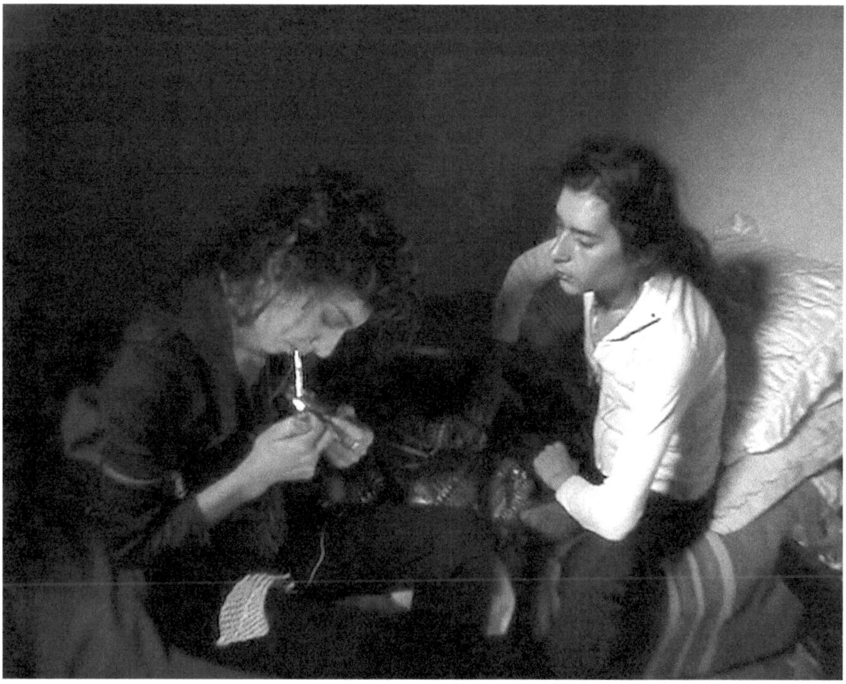

Costa's "two girls on a beach"

that by placing mirrors to reflect light into the darkened room and illuminate a relatively still face, the film elicits the comparison. (Costa himself has said that he admires the Dutch realist school of painting.) The composition of the shot also neatly contrasts Vanda's countenance with Zita, who, turned from the light, disappears into the shadows as she stretches out on the bed. The long take and stillness and lighting of the scene evoke paintings of women seated or reclining by classical as well as modern artists like Edward Hopper, whose *Morning Sun* portrays a girl sitting on a bed, gazing out of a window. And there is a strangely luxuriant aspect to Vanda as she leans back against a shiny pink satin pillow, one arm tucked almost seductively behind her head. It is a momentary image, quickly dispelled as she bends forward, gives a wracking cough, and wipes her nose and mouth on her sleeve.

The conversation in the scene is limited, the sisters' attention focused on firing, chasing, and inhaling dark liquid heroin over a narrow foil strip with a thin tube. They rhythmically pass the paraphernalia back and forth, first inhaling the dope and then drawing deeply on a cigarette to push the dope

Excavating the yellow pages

deeper into their lungs and lessen what Vanda calls the "agony" of the intake. There is meticulousness in the way Vanda studies the yellow pages in an old telephone book in her lap, evaluating and scraping up powdery residue left from a hidden stash. Toward the end of the scene, a sense of greed and urgency develops. Zita chides her sister for taking a double hit. After the screen goes black and the film's title appears, we hear Vanda again yelling at Zita to "hurry up!"

Similar scenes of Vanda using heroin recur in the film, one of them especially ghastly. She loses control, her thin arms falling to her sides as if she were dying, unable to stop her violent coughing and asthmatic spasms. Even in the midst of this fit, she manages to take a hit of the drug and a drag on a cigarette. In an interview, Mark Peranson asked Costa if he ever thought of intervening in such scenes, and Costa replied: "Yes, there was a moral dilemma. In the end, though, how could I not show that? What I feel about it is what they feel, which is what the boy says in the film: 'We're unemployed, but that's work.' After the Portuguese 'discovered' India in the 16th century, we became unemployed forever: unemployment, poverty, and sadness. It's something to do with that—they're unemployed, the worst capitalist exploitation.... Drugs are just another punishment imposed on them. And it became clear to me that they are working, and not in terms of dealing."[32]

Costa leaves both himself and the audience complicit in the grim scenes of Vanda and heroin. His approach is somewhat Brechtian in the sense that unlike the typical social problem filmmaker, he never pushes the audience's buttons or manipulates desire for catharsis. He wants viewers to *think*, not become emotionally absorbed. He therefore avoids the sex or violence of commercial cinema, and his treatment of drug taking is coolly objective.

The boys in the film include Pango (António "Pango" Semedo), Paulo (Paulo Nuno), Pedro (Pedro Lanban), and others who are nameless. Unlike the girls, they shoot up with syringes carried at the ready like a pack of cigarettes in a shirt pocket; sometimes, they leave syringe needles dangling from their arms as they go about occupying homes abandoned by people who have relocated or died. Zita tells Vanda that Pango (also known as Nhurro) has moved into a place where a woman killed her baby. Later in the film, Pango tells a slightly different version of the story to a friend, saying the girl tried to sell her baby for 1500 *escudos* (approximately $10.00). The friend asks, "The blond who put her baby in the trash?" Pango replies, "Whether she put it in the trash or killed it, I don't know." Their conversation evokes the desperate mother and unwanted baby in *Bones*. We are often reminded that death is omnipresent, haunting the world of the film. Pango refers to living in "ghost houses," places where a "witch wouldn't live." Crews of workers paint bright yellow *X*'s on buildings to signal their imminent demise, but there is also a general feeling that leaving Fontaínhas is like death. When Vanda's mother is asked, "Where we will end up?" referring to their forced displacement, she replies, "In the cemetery."

With some exceptions, the young men in the film lack the individuality of the women. Most of the time, they are anonymous, nearly invisible figures inhabiting dark rooms lit by a single candle or a shaft of light seeping from a boarded-up window. In the audio interview for the Criterion DVD, Costa says the youths regularly kept indoor lighting to a minimum to avoid police raids, presumably for illegal trespassing and drugs. (In his next film, *Juventude em marcha* [*Colossal Youth*], men also live in dark Fontaínhas rooms to avoid detection, but the times and reasons are different.)

Most of the scenes inside the vacant spaces are artfully composed, with inky blackness and minimal light. In one segment, two young men stand inside a softly lit doorway as the noise of demolition roars on the soundtrack. One of them is Pango, shown naked and in silhouette as he washes himself. Drying off, he reaches to the side and tumbles over, light from a nearby shuttered window illuminating steam slowly rising from his wet back. Costa cuts to another spot, and we see a still life of the injured Paulo's crutches; posed against a bare wall, the metal supports gleam in the dark like a silvery objet d'art. Then we see Paulo sitting in semidarkness, eating a sandwich and sipping a drink. A somber young man with little or no prospects, he looks at the floor as he eats and softly utters, "May the Lord help me."

Pango, Paulo, and Pedro spend most of their time together in rooms of an abandoned house where they find a couch, a mattress, some folding chairs, and a small, round table. Costa keeps returning to this space. In the daytime, there is plenty of light, and we watch Pango arrange things while the other two chat and shoot up. An anal personality with something of an artistic bent who seems uninterested in drugs, Pango finds a wooden box and converts it into a piece of furniture with an added shelf; he also finds a soccer ball, which he carefully balances atop the box like a decoration. He is constantly sweeping, dusting, and trying to get the others to take out the garbage. "I'm cleaning up so we can feel at home," he says. During one of his labors, he complains, "There's nothing but assholes here. All I hear is 'in a minute.'" Then he studies the walls, adding, "What would look good here is some nice, flowered wallpaper." When he begins using a hammer and nails to hang photos from advertisements on the wall, Paulo and Pedro completely ignore him, jabbing needles into their arms and getting into a bragging contest about who has suffered most from hematomas caused by needles. "Talk about hematomas, man," Paulo says, "I'm a fuckin' martyr, a walkin' blood clot." He goes into a lengthy history, describing ones on his feet, chest, and neck and recalling visits to the hospital and attempts to sleep under a blanket in an open field. "What about me?" Pedro asks, "One in each foot." Paulo does not want to hear about it. "So, who won the championship?" Paulo finally says, "The hematoma championship."

Pedro seems to get a little money from capturing and selling finches. We see him holding one of these tiny birds and giving it a kiss, and we hear one of them chirping as Pango, silhouetted in the dark room, speaks a grim soliloquy: "My hair's filthy. I look like a tramp. And the dirt makes your hair grow even quicker. Soap and water—we'll see if that will wash away all this grime. I've really gotta wash it. . . . I've washed cars. I've been a thief. A street paver. I've helped out in construction. I don't know what else I could do in this world." Paulo, meanwhile, tries begging, and one evening, he gives his

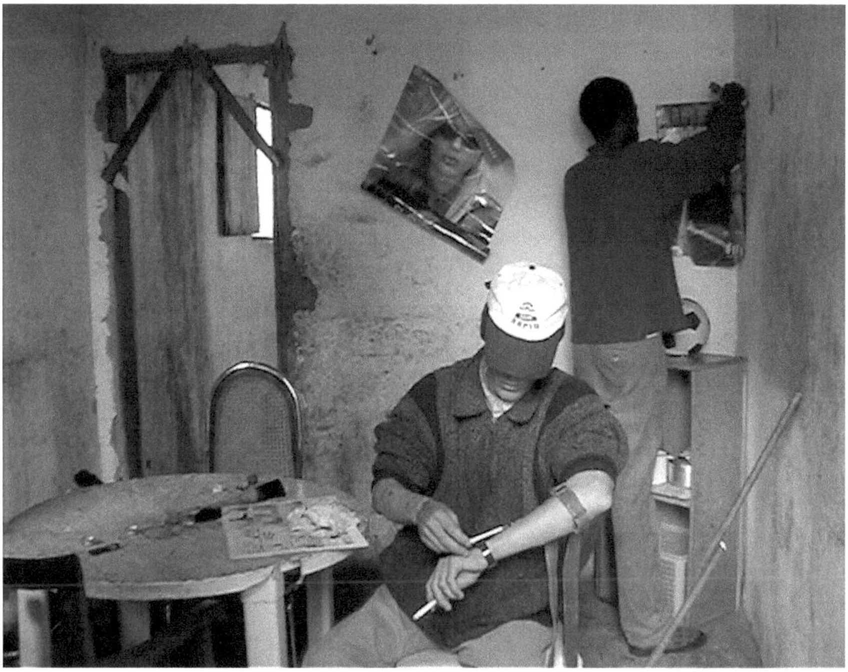

Pango decorates while Paulo shoots up

roommates a darkly comic account of a recent experience. He went to an apartment house where the elevator was broken: "Imagine walking up six flights on crutches. I finally get there. I ring the bell. 'Dona Rosa, how are you and your husband? Could you help me out a bit?' She comes back and hands me two yogurts. Two fuckin' yogurts. I was fuming. I was expecting money. Anyway, I put the yogurts in my bag and prayed all the way down that they'd be strawberry. . . . I hope they're the ones with fruit chunks."

It is impossible to say how Costa elicited such remarkable speeches, memorable and believable as the dialogue of trained writers, and how much coaching he did. With nonprofessional actors from Fontaínhas, he said, "the basic fundamentals of doing a film are changed. You either open up to it or not. It's difficult, but I choose to work this way and sometimes it doesn't work, of course, and you have to say so. But sometimes, and most of the times, what comes out, or what I hear, is a germ to build on in the story."[33]

Occasionally, in pillow shots, brief cutaways from scenes during conversations, Costa shows the once tidy Fontaínhas passageways of *Bones* now strewn with rocks, empty bottles, and other debris. In shots of longer duration, we see that the outer walls of homes are either heavily damaged or completely torn away. The place looks increasingly like a war zone, but there are also moments of liveliness. In the morning, a crowd of residents gathers around a fire where water is being boiled, and a man kisses his wife on the cheek as he heads off to work. Warmth comes from small outdoor barbeque grills heaped with wood and set ablaze. Uneven pathways with puddles of water here and there have little human foot traffic, but a dog meanders down a narrow, empty alleyway. The sounds of voices, some raised, others of children, seem at odds with the emptiness and rubble. At one point, several schoolchildren in colorful clothes enter the frame from below; following one another down a corridor as they move away from the camera, they bring a modicum of joy and color to a desolate setting. Later, a large woman wanders into an open area and tugs at a door to a home. She seems disoriented, possibly on drugs. A white plastic bag lands on her from above, but she fails to notice. Thwarted by the closed door, she turns and walks away with an unsteady step.

Although much of the film takes place in Vanda's bedroom, we also see other spaces in her home, including a large room stacked with crates of fruits and vegetables the family sells. A washing machine sits among the crates, and a small living area with a red sofa and chairs occupies the back corner. Across the room, perched on a high shelf, is a tiny television that seems constantly on. One of the most interesting scenes occurs in this crowded storeroom/living room area, when Vanda carries in a crate of vegetables and stacks it on top of others. Seated on the sofa are her mother (Lena) and Lena's husband, Miranda, holding the child Diogo, who is Vanda and Zita's much younger brother. The intermittent sound of a violin being tuned is heard in the background.

Vanda leaves the room but soon returns with a large replica of an old sailing vessel she found among the cast-off items of destroyed houses. Lena is scornful about the find: "What is it? What do you want that for?" Proud of her discovery, Vanda treats the ship like an art object, calling it an "antique" and placing it atop a nearby crate. She sits back on the sofa to admire it and consider its sale value, which might be high despite a broken wire on the sailing rig. Picking it up and looking closer, she wonders about a shiny substance on the ship's deck, which she touches and smells, believing it to be wax or oil. Sitting beside Vanda, Lena does the same and agrees. Asked where she got the ship, Vanda says she found it outside, behind some streetcars. She starts to place it higher up on top of some fruit, and Lena immediately reacts, telling her the ship is dirty and should be kept off the food. Suddenly, a nameless

Displaying a prized find

woman enters the room, declaring the ship to be hers and claiming that she left it near the trash to later retrieve and clean. A muted discussion ensues between the women to the sound of the violin played off-screen.

The scene has ironic implications. The ship model resembles the swift-moving caravels the Portuguese built in the late fifteenth century and sailed in search of trade routes and luxury items such as spices from India. Ships of this kind became symbols of Portugal's maritime skill and vast empire. The historical and symbolic significance of Vanda's ship goes unnoticed in her household, but her wandering and discovery of it evoke the long Portuguese history of going out and coming back with goods to sell. Like a merchant, Vanda gathers and stockpiles fruits and vegetables she hawks to residents in Fontaínhas. (How the family affords them is never explained.) The produce is far more valuable than the dirty and damaged ship, but from Vanda's perspective, its "antique" status makes it salable—possibly, she says, worth up to 5,000 *escudos* ($20–$25 in 1998). Her mother's scoffing is reminiscent of the grumblings of the Old Man of Restelo in Luís Vaz de Camões's epic

Os lusíadas (1572, *The Lusiads*), who calls Vasco da Gama's idea of finding a route to India and its spices pure folly. The trouble comes when the unnamed woman appears, proclaiming ownership and creating a miniature conflict not unlike the ones between colonial powers over property. We never learn who wins the argument, but the model ship remains a kind of symbol or allegory of Portugal's former empire.

The film continues moving back and forth between the women and men. One remarkable scene shows Vanda doping and coughing as usual in her room when suddenly, a long string of phlegm runs from her mouth, hangs in the air, and lands on the bed clothes. She seems to feel blithe about the viscous mess, covering it with a blanket and whistling as she turns the yellow pages for traces of dope. A few seconds later, she is chewing gum and singing as she excavates the telephone book. In a later scene, we see her struggling to get a flame from a disposable lighter to fire the heroin; undaunted, she reaches for a green plastic bag at her side, bulging with used Bics she keeps testing and tossing toward the floor until she finds one that works. We cut to a still life: a large red bucket on the floor, overflowing with colorful lighters. The image is powerful evidence of her addiction, but the jumble of colors also has striking beauty.

Vanda occasionally has visitors, like Carla, who drops by to share Vanda's heroin. The shot has a disorienting, almost cubist effect. Vanda is seated on her bed, intent on finding bits of the drug in the yellow pages, while Carla sits across the room opposite her. Costa avoids the shot/reverse shot this arrangement might require for an ordinary filmmaker. (After his first films, he abandoned the shot/reverse shot.) Instead, he shows Carla's face reflected in a mirror placed near Vanda's bed; as a result, she appears to be sitting next to Vanda on the right while Vanda occasionally looks left to speak to her. The dialogue has to do with Vanda's visit to Nela after her arrest and imprisonment. "It's real degrading," Vanda says, "They treat you like a convict. At 5:00 am they took me straight to a cell at the prison. Shit. . . . I don't know what they call it, that 'you're under arrest' thing. A piece of paper to take me to the women's prison . . . you can't wear jeans or anything." Carla seems to understand these precautions: "But [Nela] had a long career stealing," she says. Vanda strongly disagrees: "But Jesus Christ, doing time for a few Knorr cubes? Only here in Lisbon. Three fucking years . . . Our country is the poorest, most pathetic of them all."

Costa has said that the chief difference between the young women and men in the film is that because the males used needles, "the boys were dying, the girls were not dying."[34] (In one scene, Paulo says to Pango, "I'm dying," and Pango replies, "Go to sleep, Paulo. Bad guys like us never die.") The boys do not have protective families like Vanda, Zita, Nela, and Diogo, who have a strong and caring mother. According to Vanda, her mother is a survivor of domestic abuse by her first husband, Vanda and Zita's father. Despite their addiction, the sisters have a home and food and carry out tasks for the family. Vanda sells vegetables door to door, calling out to customers who respond from inside their homes. The family's house has bedrooms, a kitchen, a storeroom, and a dining room where Vanda and Zita stand and fold clothes. At one point, we even see what appears to be a small family party in the house, with a couple dancing to Cape Verdean music. The mother's room has comfortable furnishings, including a canopy-style bed and a large trunk filled with clothing. We see Vanda pulling different items from the trunk and coming across a rat; frightened and angry, she steps back, picks up a broom handle and warily returns to the trunk as if ready for battle. In another scene, she holds a skein of pink yarn between her outstretched hands as Zita rolls the yarn into a ball. (A similar shot occurs with Cape Verdean women in *Down to Earth*.)

This is not to say that all is at peace. Lena, who grew up in Cape Verde, skins a rabbit outside the house and shouts to both Vanda and Zita: "That's what's wrong with Portugal. . . . In Cape Verde you'd be locked in your room. . . . On my island you'd get up at 3:00 or 4:00 in the morning to work in the fields." Sitting on her bed and hearing her mother's voice, Vanda lights up her fix and coughs. "You're gonna have to shape up," her mother shouts. But nothing deters the sisters. In a nostalgic moment, they sit together on the bed, pleasantly high, and happily recall their childhood, when their mother would send them out to purchase something. Zita says, "When we were kids, we'd repeat to ourselves, 'Salt, salt, salt.'" Vanda smiles and chimes in, "And when we got there, we couldn't remember! 'Ma'am, my mother said she wants . . . I forgot.' That was back then . . . I loved playing ball. You know, we had a good childhood in this neighborhood."

Despite Pango's efforts at homemaking, the boys live in much more depressed circumstances, and as wrecking crews near, they are forced to leave the abandoned house. Pango keeps cleaning as the other two exit with their belongings. He is especially concerned about the round table in the front room, which normally holds a bottle of water, candles, and drug implements. Night has fallen, and moonlight from a window illuminates the tabletop, giving it a lovely surface. Costa holds this shot for over three minutes, observing the table's pale blue color as Pango obsessively, methodically scrapes it down, smoothing it with a table knife and treating it as an art object. "You're

The aesthetics of poverty

a stubborn fuck, man," one of his off-screen roommates says, "They're tearing this place down." Pango replies, "Let me finish this. I like things tidy." (A brief variation on this scene, involving different characters, occurs in Costa's *Colossal Youth*.)

French theorist Jacques Rancière has commented on the importance of the scene to Costa's aesthetics and politics:

> Perhaps complicity between the aesthetic sense of the filmmaker, who does not hesitate to exploit all the "beauty" available in the shantytown, and the aesthetic sense of the poor addict gets closer to the heart of the matter. . . . By setting aside "explanations" of the social and economic reasons for the existence of the shantytown and its destruction, the film sets forth the specifically political dimension: the confrontation between the power and the impotence of a body, the confrontation between a life and its possibilities. There is no aestheticizing formalism or populist deference in the attention Pedro Costa pays to every beautiful form offered by the homes, and the patience with which he listens to the often trivial and repetitive words uttered in Vanda's room.[35]

Pedro and Vanda

Vanda is generous, even a bit maternal with males who come to her room, as when she and the flower seller Pedro are shown together in a 50–50 composition, seated at either side of her bed, talking about the death of Geny. Pedro is a gentle soul, and Vanda remarks that since getting off drugs, he has gained weight and looks better. He worries about his shortness of breath and what that might portend—it seems everyone has asthma. Vanda takes on the role of caregiver, warning him about needles, handing him some of her asthma pills (avoid the inhaler, she advises), and giving him strict instructions on how to take them. He asks if she would like to buy the two bouquets of flowers he has yet to sell. She declines, and he decides to leave them as a gift, reminding her (mistakenly) that the cemetery only accepts plastic flowers. After he leaves, she picks up the bouquets from her bed and looks at them without any sign of pleasure, as if they are a specimen from another world.

Perhaps the distinction Costa makes between the young women and men in Fontaínhas is best captured in a scene toward the end of the film, when Pango, now on his own, pays a visit to Vanda's room to ask if he might stay with her for a while. Vanda chides him for coming into her bedroom, where she has been sleeping. Because they are childhood friends, she agrees to let him stay. Sitting on the floor with his face toward the camera, he looks clean and neat, but his despair is evident. (Earlier, we saw him going door to door like a beggar, passing the shells of destroyed houses, trying to sell a small silver spoon that belonged to Paulo.) His back to Vanda, who reclines on her bed, he talks about his mother, her loving support, her alcoholism, and his decision to stay away from her to avoid becoming a problem. Vanda talks about the strength of her own mother, knowing that her family will be broken by the destruction of Fontaínhas. "This is the life we are forced to live," Pango says. Rejecting defeatism, Vanda tells him twice: "This is the life we have chosen." But talk of mothers affects Vanda in a way not previously seen. The idea of her mother caring for a large family and of what lies ahead after Fontaínhas seems to overwhelm her. She cuts short the conversation, leaving the bed and moving out of the frame. Pango sits alone, a young man who has nothing except a few clothes and a comic book he holds in his hand.

As destruction proceeds, there are scenes of daily life beyond the younger generation. As a bulldozer chips away at Fontaínhas, we watch a man in a café clean the tile floor. On the wall behind him is a large mural depicting the Fontaínhas of an earlier time, a fortress city with a modern, high-rise apartment building behind it on the horizon—the same building we saw in an earlier shot of Fontaínhas being reduced to rubble. Another shot contrasts the new and the old in the form of a man wearing fashionable shoes and black-and-white slacks, casually leaning against a scarred slum wall. His head is out of the frame, and we see only his slim body dressed in stylish clothes. Given the other people in the film, who are ruined, addicted, or working odd jobs, the man in fashionable clothes looks wildly out of place; perhaps he is a drug dealer waiting for customers, many of whom come from outside Fontaínhas to score.

A powerful shot, typical of Costa's style of portraiture, shows a stocky old woman wearing a simple dress that might be one of her best, sitting alone in her room. Costa holds on a close-up for a long time, inviting viewers to contemplate her face in the absence of narrative information. She seems to be waiting patiently for something. Her face is worn and wrinkled; she has a bit of a mustache, and her right eye is missing. We eventually see tears running down her cheek.

One of the final shots is about family. Zita sits on the bed holding Diogo, who is wielding a jagged piece of plastic, possibly a damaged ruler. She tends

A remnant of Fontaínhas

to him like a mother, telling him not to hurt himself as she reaches for the object, which splinters and falls apart in the boy's hand. Her concern for her brother's safety echoes the figure of the protective mother from Vanda and Pango's conversation. Despite his family's care, Diogo's future as a visually impaired boy growing up in a tough world is grim. In Costa's next film, we discover that even Zita, who seems quietly resilient but drugged throughout *In Vanda's Room*, does not survive.

We cut from the boy's shattered toy to a large, lonely chunk of rubble, possibly from a wall, standing at the edge of a passageway like a memorial sculpture or ruined marker of the kind the Portuguese used to make claim to foreign land. Costa holds the shot for almost a minute. An older man lingers near the stone and walks away. Another middle-aged man walks by without taking notice. They are the last of a generation making its way out of Fontaínhas. Others have disappeared from the life they chose. On the soundtrack, an elegiac score by Hungarian composer György Kurtág adds to the atmosphere of departure and loss. The film ends as it began, with the sound of a breath.

Juventude em marcha (*Colossal Youth*, 2006)

While filming in Fontaínhas, Costa was aware of an older Cape Verdean man standing quietly like a sentry, sometimes disappearing like a ghost into the darkness of eroding corridors and abandoned homes. Called Ventura, he was the link between the diaspora of islanders who saw Lisbon as a land of economic opportunity and another kind of diaspora, a forced migration from Fontaínhas to a place without any connection to the community's language, customs, or past. In Costa's next film, Ventura becomes the guide to understanding what that past signifies for those living in Fontaínhas and what is at stake now and in the future.

Colossal Youth was produced by Francisco Villa Lobos's Contracosta company, the French Unlimited and Les Films de l'Étranger, the Swiss Ventura Film SA, and Franco-German Arte television. Additional support came from ICAM and RTP in Portugal. Like *In Vanda's Room*, it was shot with minimal equipment. "We had no lighting, no cables, no makeup, no generators," Costa said. "We often filmed in locations without electricity. We used only eight or nine mirrors, some reflectors, polystyrene sheets, everything that could increase available light." The basic equipment, he explained, was a digital camera, a couple of microphones, and some tripods. "I shot 320 one-hour DVCam cassettes. The shoot lasted 15 months, six days per week, practically all day long, shooting sometimes twenty or thirty takes per scene."[36]

In an interview with Jean-Pierre Gorin for the Criterion DVD and Blu-ray edition, Costa says that the nearly three-year production cost approximately 500,000 euros ($800,000). It used a crew of four, with all performers present for every day of shooting. After appearing at festivals in Turin, Toronto, London, and Cannes in 2006, where a portion of the audience walked out, it won the Los Angeles Film Critics' Association Award for Best Independent Film in 2007. The 150-minute picture was theatrically released in 2008 and became one of Costa's most admired works.

The film's Portuguese title is from a leftist marching song of the Portuguese revolution recorded on a 1980 album by the punk band Young Marble Giants (a recording Costa no doubt heard). The English title, *Colossal Youth*, fails to capture the important historical reference to revolution but has an equally ironic effect because the film is about old age, memory, and the failures of the revolution. The action takes place at the moment Fontaínhas has been almost completely demolished and most residents have been relocated to Casal da Boba, a large social housing project in Amadora that is a one-hour bus ride to downtown Lisbon. Between 2001 and 2005, over 90 percent of the Fontaínhas population was moved there, losing daily contact with one another because of the separate blocks of multifloor housing.

Like Costa's previous work, *Colossal Youth* has a strong documentary element but is quite different from gritty neorealism. There are no bumpy, handheld shots, and most of the film is composed of lengthy takes with painterly compositions and little or no camera movement. As in *In Vanda's Room*, the light from windows, in which Costa often situates his actors, sometimes resembles the lighting effect in a Vermeer painting. (Little wonder that brilliant art photographer Jeff Wall, who specializes in staged documentary, is a great admirer of the film.) Compared to *In Vanda's Room*, however, this is an unusually quiet, often silent film interspersed with important dialogue, much of it suggested or improvised by the performers. There are only a few sounds of a buzzsaw and hammer, but the precredit sequence begins with a startling crash.

We see metal boxes and furnishings being shoved out the upstairs window of an almost destroyed two-story house in Fontaínhas and landing in pieces on the ground. We cut to a close-up of the person responsible—an embittered Black woman surrounded by darkness, brandishing a small knife. She (Isabel Cardoso) identifies herself as Clotilde and seems to make a speech to a person we never see, recalling her youth in São Filipe, a town on the island of Fogo in Cape Verde. She was a wonderfully strong swimmer, she says; she would go to the sea with her son while boys on the rocks above sang, "Come back, my love, back to my arms." She gradually retreats into the darkness, only her knife visible.

Costa told Jean-Pierre Gorin that he wanted this moment to be a "theatrical" expression of anger addressed to both an unseen auditor and the film's audience. He said that a theme of the scene and the film as a whole can be described with the untranslatable Creole word *mórti*, which means death, but not in the conventional sense. A liminal state of the kind we have already described, *mórti* is a kind of living death. *Colossal Youth* is about the dying of Fontaínhas but also the dying of individuals who lived there and their memories and culture. As Vanda says at one point in the film, "I feel I am mourning myself."

The star of the film and the most important of Costa's growing company of performers and collaborators is José Tavares Borges, known to the cinema simply as Ventura—a tall, slender Black man from Cape Verde with a quiet demeanor and a haunting presence. According to Costa, Ventura was a "diabetic, an ex-alcoholic, a diagnosed schizophrenic, and anemic." Costa nevertheless regarded him as an actor with the power of old Hollywood stars: "I think he's the last in a great line of studio actors. . . . I need him to stand tall. . . . He's my oracle, and he has a double face. He's the pioneer, the immigrant who survived the violence of this sick society. At the same time, he's the fool, the broken hero."[37]

Costa intended the film to be mostly about older characters and was surprised to learn that Ventura, who has gray hair, was not as old as he seemed. "I wanted him to look good," he told Gorin, so most of the time, Ventura wears a white shirt and slightly rumpled black suit; despite his poverty and homelessness, he looks distinguished and a bit funereal or priestly. Costa agreed with Thom Andersen that Ventura gives off a heroic air reminiscent of Black actor Woody Strode, who starred in John Ford's *Sergeant Rutledge* (1960).[38] Probably as a result, Costa often photographs him Ford's style, with the camera at a low angle looking up at him.

The film's plot has mostly to do with Ventura's wandering between the remains of Fontaínhas and the new construction at Casal da Boba in search of his "children," some of whom may be his actual children but most of whom are his lost community. The woman in the opening turns out to be his wife; he explains to several people that she left him, destroying all his furnishings and stabbing his hand with a knife. His daughter, Bete (Cila Cardoso), still lives in what is left of Fontaínhas. Outside her home is one of the most evocative objects in the film—a once plushily upholstered, rose-colored chair of indeterminate vintage, where Ventura often sits. Like the shell that was once Fontaínhas, in one scene, it is missing its two front legs and slumps to the ground. There is something venerable, even majestic about the chair's ruined yet brightly colorful presence, a vestige that stands as a lame sentinel to the shantytown and a reminder of the place a community built and called home for decades. Now Ventura is on the list for a place in Casal da Boba, where perhaps the chair can be moved and his children can live with him again.

The film never provides the audience with signposts to indicate locations and has an initially bewildering flashback structure, without explanatory intertitles such as "X years earlier." We occasionally shift to scenes that take place around the time of the 1974 revolution, when a younger Ventura, a construction worker whose wife is in Cape Verde and whose head is bandaged from a fall, shares a tiny shack with his friend Lento (Alberto Barros). These unannounced flashbacks result in one of several moments that constitute what Dominic Lash calls a "cinema of disorientation"—for example, when Ventura wakes up from sleeping on the floor in an empty room in Casal da Boba, leaving us wondering if the preceding scene with Lento was in a dream. There are also scenes in which we are unsure about the relationship between Ventura and the people he meets, such as the tall, silent, older white man he encounters twice in a Fontaínhas passageway. As Lash puts it, these bewildering moments are "thematic, or, we could say, mimetic of Ventura's experience, which is one of profound disorientation."[39]

Colossal Youth is mainly a series of skillfully lit, carefully composed long takes or sequence shots in which Ventura meets his children and either talks about his life or listens to others talk about theirs. The film uses a short, slightly wide-angle lens that opens space around the characters and presents them in depth. It also has longer speeches than usual because it is about people who reminisce or talk about their troubles. Early on, for instance, Ventura meets André (Gustavo Sumpta), a construction worker in red overalls who may or may not be his son and is Vanda's husband. The worker goes to a small concrete building with "Cantina" scrawled in fading red paint above the open doorway and gives Ventura a meal, which Ventura does not touch. "Your mother left me," Ventura says. "Stabbed me, wrecked the house, took the new black suitcase, smashed up all my furniture. She had Clotilde's face, but it wasn't her."

Next, Ventura visits Casal da Boba, standing outside the vast complex and shouting "Vanda!" Ventura's face first appears in the lower left corner of the screen with the apartment buildings looming over him. As he moves from one building to another, his shouts echo as if in a canyon or cave. Unlike Fontaínhas before it was demolished, this place has no narrow alleyways or crowded spaces—it looks blankly futuristic, deserted.

Vanda finally calls out to him in reply. When he goes to her new rooms, we find them in radical contrast with those in *In Vanda's Room*. Her bedroom walls are unadorned, stark white, with light from a partly shaded window. Ventura sits beside her on her bed while she watches over her little daughter, Bia, and occasionally looks toward a TV. She is almost unrecognizable—aged, toothless, heavier, on methadone rather than heroin, but as assertive as always. When Ventura mentions his troubles, she goes into a monologue, confessing her worries about keeping her daughter and getting unemployment money. She also talks about the loss of her mother, who was buried in Amadora. At one point—a rare instance of humor in the film—she rubs her eyes and asks herself, "Why'd I wipe my eyes with those Dodots?" Ventura asks,

Ventura at Casal da Boba

Ventura, Vanda, and her daughter

"Dodots?" Vanda looks off toward the television, which is showing a nature program about reptiles. Ventura keeps asking, "What are Dodots?" She finally shows him a package of tissues used for "wiping a baby's ass."

Ventura decides to leave, saying, "See you, daughter." When he exits, we cut to one of the film's "empty shots," filmed in the manner of Yasujirō Ozu, who is among Costa's influences. Ozu made quiet films about small domestic interiors and often cut to close shots of household objects with no direct narrative purpose. In this case, Costa shows the wall outside Vanda's bedroom door, where a beam of light falls across a vase of artificial flowers, the red blossoms providing a touch of vivid beauty in contrast to the stark white interior. Like the molten lava beneath volcanic rock in *Down to Earth,* Costa uses brief touches of red, pink, and rose to suggest warmth and passion beneath a cold setting. (The flowers are also reminiscent of Pedro's gift to Vanda in *In Vanda's Room.*)

At this point, we have the first unannounced flashback, signaled by an opaque glass window on the doorway of a shack. Ventura and Lento, bearing what appear to be lunch pails or thermoses, arrive from a day's work and play cards (a game similar to the child's game called "Battle") at a small table. Ventura always wins these games, throwing a card down hard and shouting to claim points. Lento says, "I need you to write a letter for me for my wife . . . to tell her I miss her, a sort of love letter." There is nothing to write with, so Ventura recites a letter, telling Lento to "listen good." He launches into a recitation of the missive by Robert Desnos heard in *Casa de lava.* This letter becomes a motif, an expression of Ventura's own sorrows. After Lento retrieves a couple ballpoint pens, Ventura leaves him to scratch the surface of the card table with them. Lento cannot read or write, and Ventura keeps insisting that he memorize the letter, learning it by heart as he has apparently done. The fullest of his recitations, based loosely on Desnos, runs as follows:

> Nha crecheu, my love. Being together again will brighten our lives for at least thirty years. I'll come back to you strong and loving. I wish I could offer you one hundred thousand cigarettes, a dozen fancy dresses, a car, that little lava house you always dreamed of, a three-penny bouquet. But most of all, drink a bottle of good wine and think of me. Here, it's nothing but work. There are over a hundred of us now. Did my letter arrive safely? Still nothing from you. Some other time. Every day, every minute I learn beautiful new words for you and me alone, made to fit us both like fine silk pajamas, wouldn't you like that? I can only send you one letter a month. Still nothing from you. Some other time. I get scared building these walls.

> Me with a pick and cement, you with your silence. A pit so deep it swallows you up. It hurts to see these horrors that I don't want to see. Your lovely hair slips through my fingers like dry grass. Often, I feel weak and think I'm going to forget you.

How did the apparently semiliterate Ventura come to know this letter? Was he in Cape Verde when Mariana, the Lisbon nurse in *Down to Earth*, found it in Edite's home? The film never explains, leaving a poetic mystery.

Without notice, there follows the most stunning, even shocking image in the film: an "empty" shot of Peter Paul Rubens's baroque painting *The Flight into Egypt*, beautifully framed and hanging on a dark wall, its colors ablaze. This shot is held for almost five seconds, allowing the audience to feel baffled and amazed. Next, we see a wider shot of a wall in the Calouste Gulbenkian Museum, with Ventura casually standing near Anthony van Dyck's seventeenth-century *Portrait of a Man*. The aristocratic figure in the painting is dressed in black and white, and so is Ventura, who looks casually elegant and uninterested. We soon realize that he is visiting the temporarily closed museum with the help of a young Cape Verdean guard, who pulls him away from the wall and wipes the floor where he has been standing. Cut to a beautiful, deep-pink, tapestry-covered Gobelins sofa on a low platform—a kind of doppelgänger of the rose-colored chair outside Bete's door back in Fontaínhas. Ventura sits in a relaxed pose on the sofa, one arm stretched across its back, his long legs extended with the casual grace of Henry Fonda in Ford's *My Darling Clementine* (1946).[40]

The guard takes Ventura out of the museum via a back door, and an equally stunning scene follows. Of the few moving camera shots in *Colossal Youth* (critics have counted five), this is the most elaborate. We are outside the Gulbenkian on a sunny day, looking up at green, leafy treetops, and off-screen we hear Ventura's voice delivering his longest speech in the film. His quietly spoken words deserve quoting in full. Note that when Ventura mentions a statue of a penguin outside the museum, he is speaking of a stylized sculpture of a falcon that stands beside a sculpture of the wealthy Armenian Calouste Gulbenkian:

> On August 19, 1972, I was on a big jet with four hundred immigrants plus serving girls. It was me and my cousin Augusto. In the air, he started to cry. They served us horse steak and wine from Castelo Branco. He didn't eat. I ate his entire portion. At the airport, we met his cousin. [At this point, the camera starts panning from the treetops, angling slowly downward.]

Ventura in the Gulbenkian Museum

> He took us to Salitre Street. The next day, we started work with Technical Construction on the Borges Brothers bank downtown. I earned 1,800 escudos every two weeks. At the barracks, a parrot would sing, "Nigger, nigger, stinky face!" I left to work for Gaudêncio Construction. They sent me to the Gulbenkian Museum. [The camera reaches the ground, and we see Ventura's feet. He steps forward, and the camera pans to show him sitting down on a row of concrete steps, looking off in the distance.] I earned 7,500 escudos, plus overtime, or 16,000, plus the Christmas bonus. This was all brushwood here. Me and Correia, the mason, cleared out the brushwood and eucalyptus and laid down sewer pipes. It was a carpet of frogs here, thousands of them. One day we set up the statues of Mr. Gulbenkian and the penguin. We planted grass to make it prettier. We watered it. They say Mr. Gulbenkian has lots of heirs.

An on-line cut to a wider angle reveals that Ventura is talking to the young museum guard, who sits on the step below him, also looking into the distance. Ventura raises his arm and points to the spot where he fell many years ago. In quiet, ghostly counterpoint to Ventura, the guard makes his own speech:

"Here is another world, an ancient world. . . . No one shouts or spits on the floor. It's nice and easy. I can even take a little nap, so afternoons here in Egyptian art are sacred to me. It's trouble when someone like you turns up. But you don't see people like you or me here often."

Another flashback takes us to Ventura and Lento in their dim but warmly lit shack, playing cards. The banging of a loose piece of tin housing in the wind can be heard in the background. "Get this into your head," Ventura says, again reciting the Desnos letter. Lento replies, "You were lucky you had your hard hat when you fell." Saying nothing, Ventura steps off-screen and comes back with a small record player. He puts on a recording by Cape Verdean rock group Os Tubarões of the song "*Labanta braço*" (Raise your arm) about the revolution and independence: "Shout, o liberated people! July 5, the road to happiness!" There is obviously nothing liberating about Ventura and Lento's place in the new order, and as the song continues, Lento uses a pen to gouge deep marks into the table where the phonograph sits. He seems indifferent to the lyrics, and his movements cause the needle to skip. The distorted music suggests an unharmonious aspect of liberation and portends the struggles that beset Cape Verde in the years following independence, including the 1980 coup in Guinea-Bissau that strained relations between the two former colonies and ended Amílcar Cabral's dream for their political union. His patience tested, Ventura taps Lento's hand to stop his relentless gouging.

Back at Casal da Boba, Ventura visits Vanda and drinks a beer with her in her bedroom. The light is stronger than before and the whiteness more oppressive. She gives a ten-minute monologue about the agony of childbirth, when her tiny baby seemed pushed inside her almost to her chest and she was desperate to get out of the hospital. "Without my husband and daughter," she says, "I'd still be on drugs." Coughing loudly, Vanda tells her daughter, "Momma's sick, baby," and gets a small inhaler. Half reclining on the bed with a bottle of beer, Ventura waves a hand absently. "I went to visit my daughter, Bete," he says, a remark Vanda ignores. The drug-ridden Vanda of *In Vanda's Room* seems to reappear for a moment when she experiences a wracking, open-mouth cough. Her toddler daughter watches her from next to the bed. In a tender moment, Vanda urges Bia to dance to the music of a small toy. "Dance, baby, dance!" she laughs as Bia smiles, moves her arms following her mother's example, and sways her tiny bottom.

Ventura repeatedly tries to visit Bete. He brings her a roast chicken in a plastic bag and hums a song about love at her front door, where the rose-colored chair sits. At one point, she throws a pail of water outside and asks

Ventura playing a record for Lento

Outside Bete's home in Fontaínhas

him, "You know you have a dead son?" He sits brooding in the rose-colored chair; when he sniffs snuff from a white container, she joins him for a moment. He then goes to a used furniture outlet and meets his old friend Nhurro (António Semedo), who chats with him. "You like this living room set?" Nhurro asks, and adds, "I'm not the same Nhurro you knew back then" (a reference to *In Vanda's Room*). When Ventura asks if he is completely clean, Nhurro says, "Nobody can claim that. Clean means three meals a day, knowing all the tricks. . . . I'm here with you but my mind's back there with my mother. She stopped drinking three weeks ago. She's going through withdrawal. . . . I know you've always hoped to go back to Cape Verde to die."

The film now shifts back to the construction shed where Ventura and Lento live, which is mostly in darkness. The camera focuses on a ledge where empty bottles of different colors, lit from behind by a lantern, resemble a still life. On the soundtrack, footsteps are heard. We cut back to the present, with Ventura standing on an interior ramp in Casal da Boba, his legs crossed at the ankles, looking casually elegant as he awaits a real estate agent, who arrives in a suit and tie and shows him a two-room apartment where he might live. The agent introduces himself as André Semedo, a former locksmith born in Tarrafal, Cape Verde. He escorts Ventura to a bare room on the fourth floor, which gets lots of sun. "My head's spinning," Ventura says, "I ache all over." The agent prattles about rules and regulations and the home as a temple for a household god, a place where we can "open our house to God." Ventura looks around at the white walls, more alien to him than anywhere he has lived, and complains that there will not be enough room for his children.

Unhappy, Ventura returns to Fontaínhas and the wreckage of his old dwelling. He rifles through broken furniture, finds some old letters and mementos, and sits on a cushion on the floor for a long time, his back against the discolored wall, weary, depressed, perhaps thinking of the move to Casal da Boba. He visits Vanda again, sitting with her at her small dining table and drinking a beer. She has a wracking cough and says she wants to take her baby to the religious shrine at Fátima while she still can. "Here comes the lord and master," she suddenly announces, and André arrives. She brings him food, and the three sit around the table, not looking at one another, silently meditating. Vanda says she wants to get rid of two old sofas, which remind her of ghosts. After a long silence, Ventura turns to André and asks, "Are you married to Vanda?"

Costa then cuts to a bewildering scene in which Ventura is sleeping on the floor of the apartment in Casal da Boba. Is he now a resident? Whose place is this? The doorbell rings and Ventura answers, admitting Paulo (Paulo Nunes), a young man with a crutch who first appeared in *In Vanda's Room*. Paulo is still impoverished and struggling with a leg wound caused by a bullet. A surprised Ventura tells him, "A guy came by asking five thousand escudos for your funeral." Paulo hobbles across the bare, empty room and sits pathetically on the floor with his back to the wall. Ventura stands over him, silhouetted by pale, ghostly light from a window. Looking like a ghost himself, Paulo explains that he had been begging door to door in the apartment complex. A fellow he knows "picked up on the racket" and lied to residents, telling them Paulo committed suicide and using the ruse to collect donations for a supposed funeral. It seems, however, that the con man ran into trouble and was sent to jail because he did not realize that one of Paulo's good Samaritans at the complex, Dona Júlia, is married to a policeman. "Your mother left me, Paulo," Ventura says, adding, "This place is for all of us." The weakened Paulo replies, "No use begging around here. Everybody is poor."

Another flashback shows Ventura and Lento in their shack at the moment of the 1974 revolution, when many Cape Verdeans were not celebrating in the streets but hiding in fear of soldiers. Lento says that he and Ventura need to stock up on cooking gas and cigarettes: "Just when things were working for us, this coup d'état breaks out! Soldiers all over in their cars, asking for IDs. Don't go out for anything. Yesterday they came by in a Jeep. They took Yagan up in the hills and beat him up." Ventura asks Lento to learn the letter. Lento tells him it is too late: "There's no mail." He has a machete in his hand.

Back in the present, Ventura returns to Casal da Boba, where the real estate agent shows him a larger apartment. The agent expands on the advantages of living there: a kindergarten for kids, social services, a health-care center, a library, an ice-skating rink, and police services. "Five rooms is the best we can do," he explains and adds that unpaid rent means eviction. "This move is important for our future," the agent says, spouting the official line. Ventura points in a graceful gesture toward the ceiling and says, "It's full of spiders." The scene has many ironies: locks fail to work, and doors close on their own as if pushed by a ghost.

Things begin to spiral downward. Ventura again visits Bete, who at last admits him to her shadowy dwelling, where the conversation is brief and somber. Stretched out on Bete's bed with his head on her lap, Ventura announces that Zita, a resident of Fontaínhas and one of Ventura's children, has died, apparently from "poison," meaning drugs. The reference is to Zita Duarte, Vanda's sister. (In one of their conversations in Casal da Boba, a confused Ventura calls Vanda by her sister's name.) Bete looks at the marks on her wall

"Spiders on the ceiling"

and says, "I see two turtles, see 'em in the corner?" Then she quietly asks if Ventura is a good man or a bad man. "I'm a good man," Ventura replies. Still looking at the wall, Bete makes a prophetic, poetic comment on the haunted environment of Fontaínhas: "In the houses of the departed there are lots of figures to see. When they give us those white rooms there'll be nothing to see. It'll be all over."

We cut to an unmoving sequence shot of over two and one-half minutes, showing Ventura with Vanda again, seated between her and her husband at their table. Everyone is silent, lost in thought, until Ventura gets up and says, "It's hot." He leaves, casting a shadow against the white wall as Vanda says, "Papa, Zita was your daughter, but she was my sister first." Another brief flashback takes us to Ventura and Lento. Ventura again recites the letter, and when he comes to the phrase "pushing you ever deeper into a pit of forgetting," Lento says, "That's an awful letter."

In the most haunting sequence of the film, Ventura visits Paulo, who is now in a hospital bed with a young woman seated beside him. The light is gray and ethereal, the figures shadowy; Ventura, standing with his back to us and looking down at the suffering Paulo, seems a revenant, returned from death to witness the dying. Paulo's leg has become worse, and he is subject to an experimental treatment doctors have been wanting to try. "The doctors are running around like crazy," he says. "They filmed [the operation] and sent it to the United States to study the method. It's costing me a lot. I'm paying twelve and a half euros for a room." Paulo turns toward the wall, looking like a corpse, and speaks in a monotone voice. It has been seven or eight years since he has seen his mother, and he wishes Ventura could take him to her: "Remember this boy? Does this face mean anything to you? This dirty hair, these hands blue with the cold.... I've brought you your son, just as he is." Paulo wants his mother to tell him his daughter's address: "I haven't seen her in fifteen years. I found out a few days ago that I'm a grandfather."

In another flashback, we return to Ventura and Lento, removing their door from its hinges and replacing it with a metal barrier to conceal where they live from nearby soldiers. Lento says, "Is it that rat again? Are you barefoot? Tonight, we'll sleep warm and cozy." Ventura complains that Lento does not want to hear the letter again, and Lento replies, "I can't learn it. I can't write and you won't write it out." He goes outside and climbs a utility pole to try to fix the electricity; in the next shot, his body appears at the bottom of the pole. He has been electrocuted and lies dead on the ground. We cut to a close-up of Ventura unwrapping the bandage on his head and dropping it on the floor.

Back in the present, Ventura goes to Vanda's apartment and lies face down on her bed, shoeless, while she watches TV. She wants him to babysit for her: "Tomorrow I have to go to Social Security. I have to go to the cemetery to clean mother and Zita's graves.... It's like I'm mourning myself." She turns, looks at Ventura's feet, and says, "Poppa, your socks don't match." She picks up his shoes from the floor and begins polishing them. When we last see her, we realize she has a job as a cleaning woman. She steps outside her apartment and with a vigorous flourish dons a cleaning robe like the one her character wore in *Bones*. Looking as determined as a soldier going off to war, she exits the film.

Unlike the other Fontaínhas films, *Colossal Youth* ends on what might be described as a qualified happy ending, although one that does not alleviate the aging and suffering in the film as a whole. In his interview with Jean-Pierre Gorin, Costa explained that one of the closing scenes came about by accident. A fire at Casal da Boba, probably caused by a drunken male resident who wanted to kill his family, had destroyed one of the apartments. Costa stages a scene in which Ventura and the ghost of Lento reunite, holding hands and surveying the charred ruins of the place. Lento, looking youthful and well

Ventura and the ghost of Lento

dressed, describes how his family escaped the building fire by leaping through a window, and shows Ventura the burn marks on his hand. As they stand side by side, Lento says he has finally memorized the letter. We have already seen Lento's death in one of the flashbacks. This is the first of several scenes we find in later films in which the schizophrenic Ventura has conversations with the dead, who look as alive as he does.

A more touching and poignant scene, though it contains bitter historical ironies, shows a reconciliation between Ventura and Bete. We see them seated together at a dinner table in her darkened Fontaínhas room, eating grilled chicken. For the first time in the film, characters smile at one another. Ventura recalls, "I took some grilled chicken to your mother in the hospital the day you were born. I was working construction on a bank in the Rossio." Bete asks, "How did you win my mother's heart?" In a closer shot, Ventura tells her the story:

> It was at the Águas Podres river in Assomada. She was scooping up water in a pan. I was riding my donkey, Fogo-Serra. It took three years to win her over. At first, she wouldn't even look at me. On July 5, the Independence

Bete and Ventura

> Day holiday, she was there among the violins, flags, accordions, and drums, and she started to sing: "Fifth of July! Raise your arms and shout, Freedom! Shout 'Cabral!' people of liberated Guinea and Cape Verde!" But she didn't know how to sing. I started to tease her: "You sorry looking little country hick!" She whacked me with a flagpole, but she took a liking to me.

We cut to a closer shot of Bete, who asks, "Was she pretty?" Ventura says, "Yes, she was." Then Bete asks, "Am I pretty or ugly?" Ventura says, "Pretty." She replies, "It's a wonderful story to tell your children and grandchildren. Good thing you told me."

As Bete's remark suggests, the history of the peoples of Fontaínhas and Cape Verde is essentially oral, dependent on memory, always in danger of dying as inhabitants age and disperse, scattered by the shortcomings of the revolution. In one of the last shots of *Colossal Youth,* we see Ventura with a bandaged head. Is this a flashback or another appearance of a ghost? He and Lento are out of their shed and in a small boat traveling down a stream in a park. The film shifts to the present with Ventura babysitting for Vanda, lying on his back on Vanda's bed. He is a relaxed man, one leg crossed over the other at the knee, waving a shoeless foot in the air. Perhaps he is dreaming of the past or thinking about the future. Bia makes baby talk, and a piece by György Kurtág plays nondiegetically on the soundtrack. Ventura's trials are not over, as Costa reveals in his next feature, but he has family and, for better or worse, a place to call home where marks on the walls are beginning to appear.

Notes

1. For a discussion of the razing and relocation plans, see Rita Ávila Cachado, "O plano especial de realojamento: Ambiente histórico, político e social," *Análise social* 206, no. 48, 1 (2013): 134–52.

2. See Costa's commentary in Aurélien Gerbault, "All Blossoms Again" (2006) in *Supplements: Letters from Fontaínhas,* DVD (New York: Criterion Collection, 2010).

3. See Patrick McGilligan, "Letters from Fontaínhas: Interview with Pedro Costa," *Film International* 8, no. 3 (2010): 86.

4. Quoted in Nuno Barradas Jorge, *Refocus: The Films of Pedro Costa* (Edinburgh: University of Edinburgh Press, 2021), 47.

5. Adrian Martin, "Reviews: *Blood:* The Inner Life of a Film," *Film Critic: Adrian Martin* (blog), accessed December 15, 2022, https://www.adrianmartin filmcritic.com/reviews/b/blood.html. The essay also appears in Portuguese in *Cem mil cigarros: Os filmes de Pedro Costa,* ed. Ricardo Matos Cabo (Lisbon: Orfeu Negro), 91–97. The quote is on 92.

6. Ana Balona de Oliveira, "Rooms of Colossal Bones: Pedro Costa's Trilogy," *Mute,* June 26, 2008, https://www.metamute.org/editorial/articles/rooms-colossal-bones-pedro-costas-trilogy.

7. Quoted in Mark Peranson, "Pedro Costa: An Introduction," *Cinema Scope* 27 (Summer 2006): 12.

8. For further discussion of the traveling shots in *Down to Earth* and *Bones,* consult Shiguéhiko Hasumi, "Aventura: Um ensaio sobre Pedro Costa," in Matos Cabo, *Cem mil cigarros: Os filmes de Pedro Costa,* 133–8.

9. Pedro Costa, "A Closed Door That Leaves Us Guessing," Tokyo Film School lecture, *Rouge,* 2004, http://www.rouge.com.au/10/costa_seminar.html.

10. From conversations with Pedro Costa in Lisbon (March 1–10, 2024).

11. Costa, "A Closed Door."

12. Peranson, "Pedro Costa," 10.

13. Emma Fajgenbaum, "Cinema as Disquiet: The Ghostly Realism of Pedro Costa," *New Left Review* 116–7 (March/June 2019): 148.

14. Pedro Costa and Jean-Pierre Gorin, audio commentary for *No quarto da Vanda* (New York: Criterion Collection, 2010). See also Pedro Costa, Cyril

Neyrat, and Andy Rector, *Um melro dourado, um ramo de flores, uma colher de prata: No quarto da Vanda, Conversa com Pedro Costa* (Lisbon: Midas Filmes and Orfeu Negro, 2012), 39.

15. Peranson, "Pedro Costa," 13.

16. João Bénard da Costa, "O negro é uma cor ou o cinema de Pedro Costa," in Matos Cabo, *Cem mil cigarros*, 24.

17. Costa and Gorin, audio commentary, *No quarto da Vanda.*

18. Costa and Gorin, audio commentary, *No quarto da Vanda.*

19. Barradas Jorge, *Refocus*, 66.

20. Costa and Gorin, audio commentary, *No quarto da Vanda.*

21. See, for example, Paul Virillo, *The Vision Machine*, trans. Julie Rose (London: BFI, 1994).

22. Volker Pantenburg, "Realism, Not Reality: Pedro Costa's Digital Testimonies," *Afterall* 24 (2010): 59.

23. Quoted in Pantenburg, "Realism, Not Reality," 60.

24. David Jenkins, "Some Violence Is Required: A Conversation with Pedro Costa," *Notebook*, March 11, 2013, https://mubi.com/notebook/posts/some-violence-is-required-a-conversation-with-pedro-costa.

25. Jonathan Rosenbaum, "Films of the Future (on Pedro Costa)," June 19, 2021, https://jonathanrosenbaum.net/2024/02/cinema-of-the-future.

26. Erving Goffman, *Frame Analysis* (New York: Harper, 1974), 124.

27. Patrick McGilligan, "Letters from Fontaínhas: Interview with Pedro Costa," *Film International* 8, no. 3 (2010): 84.

28. Costa and Gorin, audio commentary, *No quarto da Vanda.*

29. *Um melro dourado*, 101.

30. Costa and Gorin, audio commentary, *No quarto da Vanda.*

31. Pedro Costa and Rui Chafes, *Fora! / Out!* (Oporto: Fundação Serralves, 2007), 64.

32. Peranson, "Pedro Costa," 14.

33. McGilligan, "Letters from Fontaínhas," 84.

34. Costa and Gorin, audio commentary, *No quarto da Vanda.*

35. Jacques Rancière, *The Emancipated Spectator*, trans. Gregory Elliott (London: Verso, 2009), 80.

36. Costa, 2006 promotional leaflet, quoted in Barradas Jorge, *Refocus*, 87.

37. Aaron Cutler, "*Horse Money*: An Interview with Pedro Costa," *Cineaste* XL, no. 3 (Summer 2015), https://www.cineaste.com/summer2015/horse-money-pedro-costa-aaron-cutler.

38. Thom Andersen, "A Band of Outsiders," in *Letters from Fontaínhas: Three Films by Pedro Costa*, supplement (New York: Criterion Collection DVD, 2010), 29.

39. Dominic Lash, *The Cinema of Disorientation: Inviting Confusions* (Edinburgh: Edinburgh University Press, 2020), 119.

40. Jacques Rancière writes at length on the relation between the museum art in this sequence and the still life of glass bottles in Ventura and Lento's shack. See his "Política de Pedro Costa," in Matos Cabo, *Cem mil cigarros*, 54–58, and his *Pedro Costa: Os quartos do cineasta* (Lisbon: Relógio d'Água, 2003), 18–20, 40–1.

PART III

After Fontaínhas

Cavalo dinheiro (*Horse Money*, 2014)

Although it stars Ventura and deals with themes that had preoccupied Costa since *Down to Earth*, *Horse Money* is a stunning departure—hallucinatory, surreal, and filled with what Jonathan Romney has termed "poetic authority."[1] More praised by critics than carefully described and analyzed, it largely abandons the long sequence shots in Costa's previous films and leaves us searching for a coherent narrative in what is essentially a nightmarish cinematic poem.

A relatively good analogy, although in a different medium and with little otherwise in common with Costa, would be T. S. Eliot's *The Waste Land* (1922), which has discernable themes—the devastation brought by World War I, mourning for a poetic tradition, sex, death, spirituality, mental breakdown, etc.—but resists the many critical attempts to interpret it logically. C. K. Stead has offered an insightful way to account for *The Waste Land*: "It is composed of a series of projections of states of feeling, having no fixed centre but their common origin in the depths of one man's mind. [It] traces in its rhythms, in its music, and in the sequence of its images, the events of that mind at a particular time and in relation to a particular set of circumstances . . . it is the feeling, not the experience, which is the poem's 'subject.'"[2] Compare to Jonathan Rosenbaum on *Horse Money*: "Discontinuity of time, space, and even identity is superseded by an underlying continuity of mood and feeling that belongs to . . . a private and personal consciousness."[3]

In the period between *Colossal Youth* (2006) and this picture, Costa made several short films and the feature-length musical documentary *Ne change rien*

(2009, *Change Nothing*), which we discuss later. When asked in an interview why it took years to make *Horse Money*, he described the film's "erratic" history, which began with a plan to work with US musician and poet Gil Scott-Heron, whom he hoped would compose music, contribute to the script, and act:

> When I thought about Scott-Heron, I was in New York with *Ne Change Rien*, around the festival or something. That was the moment when I started talking to people about the music from the New York scene. And then I remembered that, especially with the African-American poets, the lost poets, there were a lot of very, very strong political rappers working in the Sixties and Seventies in New York and Chicago. I like that very much. Between poetry and rap and music. Rock, funk, books. Scott-Heron was a writer too: he wrote a great novel called *Vulture*. I thought of something like that—that the film could be a long rap, and Scott-Heron could do that. I thought we could get him, and Ventura would sing and Scott-Heron would say poems. Because Ventura likes to sing, and in *Colossal Youth* there's not really that chance.[4]

Costa met Scott-Heron in May 2010 while the musician was performing in Lisbon. Regarded as the father of rap for his 1970 song "The Revolution Will Not Be Televised," Scott-Heron liked Costa's idea for the movie and agreed to collaborate. (Costa once remarked that Ventura and Scott-Heron resembled one another: slim Black men of a similar age with health problems.) But the plan never materialized; a drug addict, Scott-Heron had tested positive for HIV several years earlier and died from the disease in 2011.

Music was much on Costa's mind in this period, and *Horse Money* uses it in interesting ways, including a bit of singing by Ventura. Prompted by a story Ventura told him about a traumatic encounter with a soldier during the Carnation Revolution, Costa moved forward with the project. He began by filming a lengthy sequence on a set designed as an elevator car's interior; trapped inside with a revolutionary soldier who is carrying a rifle and painted to look like a dark silver statue, Ventura, wearing pajamas, relives and gives voice to personal traumas, most of them connected with the 1974 revolution. This sequence, one of the most powerful in the film, required working six to eight hours every day for three months. The trembling Ventura was older, frailer, and dealing with physical and mental issues that obviously made performing and remembering lines more difficult. In addition, the actor playing the soldier (António Santos) could work only three hours per day because of the paint's toxicity.

Asked to contribute to an anthology film called *Centro histórico* (2012) for the celebration of Guimarães as the 2012 European Capital of Culture, Costa offered the elevator sequence, a modified version of which appears in *Horse Money*. Initially called *Lamento da vida jovem* (*Lament of Young Life*), the title was changed to *Sweet Exorcism*, a choice better attuned to Ventura's confrontation with the past and his emotional struggle and release in the elevator. It appeared in *Centro histórico* alongside short films by Aki Kaurismäki, Manoel de Oliveira, and Victor Erice. The Guimarães commission also financed the short's intricate sound mix of voices and music.

Supported entirely by Portuguese sources, the 104-minute feature film was shot in color by cinematographer Leonardo Simões with a Panasonic AG-DVX100 digital camcorder. João Dias is credited as editor, and there was an eight-person crew plus a significant number of postproduction workers. The cost was estimated at 120,000 euros ($158,000), although producer Abel Chaves has said that it was actually "a lot more."[5] Whatever the cost, it was a low-budget film, and in artistic terms, every euro was well spent. The completed film premiered in August 2014 at the Locarno International Film Festival, where it won the award for best director. The following year, it received the prize for best film (international competition) at the Munich Film Festival and the Critics' Award for best film at the Recife Cinema Festival. It also won the Robert and Frances Flaherty Prize at the 2015 Yamagata International Documentary Film Festival (though it is by no means a documentary—Ventura plays a character who experiences a confused, mostly imaginary reality).

After making three features in Fontaínhas and Casal da Boba, Costa changed course in *Horse Money*, the locations of which include a hospital, the catacombs beneath historic Lisbon, an abandoned construction company building, and a wooded area outside the city. Asked in an interview about the specific sites, Costa explained that his actors did not want to make another film in housing projects such as Casal da Boba because they were "damp and violent places" with "cold white walls."[6] Although he mentioned the catacombs, he demurred from specifying the location of the hospital (actually, there are two hospitals). Except for a shot of a statue of physician António Egas Moniz outside Lisbon's Santa Maria Hospital, we could be in any medical facility; the film's focus is always on generic common areas such as hallways, a cafeteria, and a patient's room. This approach may have been Costa's way of representing Ventura's myriad experiences in the larger hospital system where he received various treatments over the years. The wooded area, Costa said, was a no-man's-land across a highway not far from the projects where he had previously shot two or three short films.[7] It and some other exteriors were shot night-for-night and required large floodlamps.

Although it appears late in the film, the elevator segment set the course for *Horse Money* and its fragmented, hallucinatory journey into the labyrinth of Ventura's thoughts and anxieties about his past. His history is quite different from Costa's. "While I was [in school] studying the Middle Ages," Costa has said, "Ventura was building the Banco de Portugal. . . . Ventura and all his brothers and sisters are caught in intervals of time and space in which nothing belongs to them. . . . It's a sort of prison, or an asylum. . . . They have been cheated, exploited, beaten, and murdered by ruthless governments for over five hundred years."[8]

As we have pointed out, for most Portuguese, the revolution was an unexpected and joyous event, bringing an end to a nearly fifty-year-old fascist dictatorship and its colonial wars in Africa. Celebrants like the young Costa rejoiced in the streets, placing red carnations in the gun barrels of revolutionary soldiers. But Ventura's experience, like that of most Cape Verdean immigrants, was at another extreme; he and others were terrified of what the soldiers might do to them.[9] *Colossal Youth* makes this point, showing Ventura and his coworker Lento hiding in near darkness in their boarded-up worker's shack. The fear of that moment never completely went away. In interviews about *Horse Money*, Costa has said that for Ventura's entire life after the revolution, he had recurring nightmares featuring a helmeted soldier.[10] History was a nightmare from which he could not awake.

Horse Money opens in unusual fashion, with ten mesmerizing Jacob Riis photographs of immigrants and tenement life in late nineteenth-century New York City. A Dane who moved to New York in 1870, Riis is best known for his book *How the Other Half Lives* (1890), which lays bare a destitute immigrant population largely invisible to the middle and upper classes. Displayed in Costa's film on a virtually silent screen, the black-and-white Riis images document men, women, and children in crowded indoor spaces, sitting idly and resting their heads on tables, or walking through alleyways strung with laundry where young and old lean out of tenement windows for conversation and a breath of fresh air. In one photograph, a policeman carries the front of a stretcher bearing a dead man with his hands folded over his chest and a hat covering his face. "I have always thought that I belonged to Riis's world," Costa has said. "Even if his pictures portray scenes of great social distress, they never surrender to demagogy. They are not 'candid' shots. They give us the freedom to choose what we see." He has also said that both *How the Other*

Ventura enters a nightmare

Half Lives and the partly photographic James Agee/Walker Evans book *Let Us Now Praise Famous Men* (1941) "have been as important to me as the greatest of films."[11]

From the still photographic images of immigrants and poverty, Costa cuts to a motion-picture image. His slightly canted camera pauses on a portrait, partly in shadow, of a handsome African male, possibly a slave, by nineteenth-century French painter Théodore Géricault, housed in Lisbon's Palácio Nacional da Ajuda. The painting, *Portrait of a Negro,* shows a young, slim man with somewhat downcast eyes wearing a white shirt and dark jacket—not unlike Ventura's attire in *Colossal Youth*. Connecting the last Riis photographs with the painting is the barely perceptible sound of footsteps and voices.

The camera slowly pans across the painting as the sound of footsteps grows. As if by magic, the wall to the right of the portrait becomes a dark, sloping passageway leading down to a locked door with iron bars. The footsteps belong to Ventura, who walks into the frame, moving away from us, wearing his cap but shoulders bared. As he slowly makes his way down the dark passage, a man in a doctor's white coat opens a door for him to pass through. The scene is extravagantly mysterious, resonant of urban Gothic. Where is this place? Why is Ventura there, and what is behind the door? Adding to the mystery is the aging Ventura's unusual appearance. As he approaches the doorway, a patch of soft light momentarily illuminates his body, which is naked except for the cap, red briefs, and shoes.

Descent into hell

Ventura then slowly walks in a tunnel toward Costa's slightly tilted camera. His bare chest, stiff stride, and wide, staring eyes resemble Carrefour (Darby Jones), the bare-chested zombie in Jacques Tourneur's *I Walked with a Zombie*. Suddenly, we cut to Ventura in a pajama top, his long fingers trembling violently as the man in the white lab coat helps him with a robe; they descend an ancient stone staircase. At the bottom, barely visible in the darkness, is a naked Black man sitting in a hunched position.

Commentors have described this place as a dungeon, but residents of Lisbon would recognize it as the Roman catacombs deep beneath the city. The catacombs date from the first century BC and were originally marked by a chiseled stone dedicating the crypt to Aesculapius, god of medicine. (At certain seasons, tourists can still visit them.) In symbolic terms, the scene is evocative of Dante's *Inferno,* in which the ghost of Virgil leads Dante through a gate famously inscribed, "Abandon hope, all ye who enter here." The naked man near Ventura's feet has the tortured look of the sinners Dante passes on his journey. Costa's deep focus allows us to see past the staircase to a concatenation of open entryways in a long, dark corridor of the catacombs through which Ventura and his guide proceed, its mise en abyme of doorways conjuring circles of hell. We cut inexplicably to a canted, deep focus shot of Ventura and the doctor, walking toward the camera but in a different corridor—a hospital with a near infinity of doorways. Costa emphasizes the hallway's eeriness by using a single light that keeps the edges of the frame in blackness.

The juxtaposition of the two corridors, one ancient and the other modern, is emblematic of the film's treatment of history and Ventura's shattered memory. The catacombs are deep below such urban landmarks as the Banco de Portugal, the depository of money Ventura helped build. They represent the buried consciousness of both Ventura and Lisbon but also merge with the hospital corridor, indicating the persistence of the past in the present. One thinks of William Faulkner's remark, "The past isn't dead. It isn't even past."

Faulkner may have been on Costa's mind when he started *Horse Money*. Around the time Costa made the film, he wrote a short essay on Howard Hawks's historical epic *Land of the Pharaohs* (1955), which has a screenplay by Faulkner and deals with the building of the pyramids. Commissioned for a Hawks retrospective at the Cinemateca Portuguesa, the essay quotes Faulkner and shows what a fine writer and critic Costa might have been had he wanted. It also has themes and images that strongly resonate with *Horse Money*, as in an excerpt from the English translation:

> The presence of Time and Death . . . is like an open wound that was already there from the start. . . . Time and space become saturated, full of emptiness. [Hawks] filmed the most ancient and most modern, immobility and movement, time standing still. . . . Hawks is a hard worker: he builds his shots brick over brick like a mausoleum, like a huge graveyard. . . . It is a science of nightmares . . . he guides his fragile and nervous Pharaoh by the hand through the secret chamber corridors. . . . The builders of the Great Tomb are building their own grave.[12]

Unlike *Colossal Youth*, in which scenes from Ventura's past interrupt the present day, *Horse Money* collapses past and present to convey Ventura's often hallucinatory experience. Like the builders of the ancient pyramids in the Hawks film, Ventura was building his own grave when he helped build the Banco de Portugal. A fusion of past and present is suggested by his transversal of something akin to memory, which shapes his "fragile and nervous" feelings (similar to Hawks's pharaoh) as he is led through the corridors of the strangely empty hospital. The hospital elevator also has a duality: in its brief initial appearance, it is simply a detail of the setting from which Ventura and the doctor emerge and walk to his hospital room. In the much longer scene near the end of the film, it becomes a time machine, carrying Ventura into the past to confront the soldier of his nightmares.

As Costa says in the essay on *Land of the Pharaohs*, "time and space become saturated," resulting in a "science of nightmares." Throughout *Horse Money*, Ventura is confused about past and present. Taken to an examination room in the hospital, he sits atop a padded table and is asked his age. (Doctors in the film seldom appear and are never depicted as full characters—they merely lead Ventura from place to place, give him pills and injections, and ask formulaic questions.) He tells his physician that he is "nineteen years and three months old," mixing up this hospital visit with one in 1975. When asked if he has a family history of nerve problems, he responds only, "I know my sickness." The doctor asks, "Has this happened to you before?" Ventura replies, "It will happen again, yes, it will."

From the confluence of past and present, other figures appear to Ventura. As he lies in a hospital bed with a blank stare and trembling hands, five former Cape Verdean coworkers file into his room, bringing a potted plant for his window. They appear thoroughly real but are ghosts from his past. Dressed in red pajamas, the unidentified spokesman for the group describes various injuries and losses from falls, drugs, beatings, and acts of madness he calls "our sickness." He explains the group's uncanny presence in a soft voice, telling Ventura: "We're together through life and death." We later learn that this spokesman, who reappears in several scenes, sometimes dressed in a red ruffled shirt, is Joaquim (Tito Furtado). He is dead, having left behind a widow, Vitalina Varela, in Cape Verde and afflicting Ventura with persistent guilt.

At one point, as Ventura is sitting on the floor in the hall near the entrance of the hospital and taking snuff, a silhouetted figure emerges from the shadows of a nearby doorway; the figure is revealed to be Vitalina. Costa discovered her for this film and made her the eponymous character for his next feature. An imposing figure, she is often viewed from a low angle that emphasizes her power and regal attitude. In this scene, she slowly approaches Ventura, dressed in black, becoming gradually visible and pulling behind her a wheeled suitcase.

Costuming is important throughout *Horse Money*. Except for doctors in the hospital, male characters wear a strange mix of solid and striped pajamas (the latter resembling prisoner uniforms), street clothes, and, in two cases, ruffle-front shirts like those popular in the 1960s and 1970s. Vitalina's attire is consistent with her widow status but also evokes the black clothing adopted by rural women in northern Portugal whose husbands emigrated to other parts of Europe, the US, and Brazil for better paying jobs. Called "widows of the living," these women might spend years or the rest of their lives awaiting their husbands' return—not unlike Vitalina, who long waited in Cape Verde and has recently arrived in Lisbon to attend her husband's funeral, only to discover she is three days too late.

In Ventura's mind, perhaps to assuage his feelings of guilt, Joaquim is still alive. He leads the ghostly group that visits Ventura in the hospital, and we later see another vision of him from the past, wearing a red ruffled shirt, holding a straight razor, and slinking down an open stairway in Fontaínhas. After the revolution, he and Ventura were apparently both injured in a knife fight with one another in the woods. As Ventura reclines on an examining table, Joaquim again appears, his red shirt slashed, revealing a long scar on his arm. Ventura says he had ninety-three stitches from the fight. Joaquim accuses him of having sent him into retirement with no way to support his family.

Soon after Vitalina arrives, she and Ventura are seen outside the hospital, where she tells him of her traumatic flight to Lisbon. Costa photographs her striking face in a low angle close-up against the darkness of the city sky. She gazes upward, her eyes deliquescent and her voice slow and soft. During her soliloquy, the longest speech in the film, Costa occasionally cuts to the back of her head, but he always returns to her face. She talks as if to herself:

> It happened on June 23rd, 2013. My sister Isabel showed up with heart-stopping news. I rushed to Assomada to get my visa and passport. I was so confused, so lost. I couldn't recognize anybody. I couldn't recognize myself. My face was all disfigured. I couldn't even take my photo for the passport. I was blind, I was numb. In Praia I bought an airplane ticket. On the night of the flight, I nearly died. A policeman took me to the stairs of the plane. The plane girls took me by the arms and showed me to my seat. I was burning up. They sat me down and gave me two big pills. They undressed me. I was left in my nightie. Miss Filomena, sitting next to me, helped me to the toilet. I couldn't pee. We went back to my seat. Had to pee again. The pee kept coming. She had to ask for nappies from the girls. I arrived in Portugal burning in fever, soaked. Freezing. This was June 30th, 2013. My husband's death was three days earlier.

Still gazing upward, she responds to Ventura's questions about his own island home and possessions. Nothing survived, she says, including his horse,

Dinheiro (Money), who was eaten by vultures—possibly Costa's nod to Scott-Heron's novel.

In a film where dialogue is often minimal and Ventura's actions are mostly limited to lying in bed, sitting in a chair, or meandering in empty spaces, objects take on special importance—especially a set of beaded necklaces. The first thing Ventura sees on one of his entrances to his darkened hospital room is a black beaded necklace dramatically displayed in close-up on a gleaming white bed pillow. Nothing explains its mysterious presence, but it is next seen worn by Vitalina in a hospital office, now in a white lab coat and without her headscarf. This is another of Ventura's hallucinations. Seated at a white table in front of a white lightbox projection screen, Vitalina opens and closes a drawer, which contains a straight razor. She reads details from her own official documents piled on the table, then stands to remove the lab coat and put on her headscarf as Ventura enters the room. Wearing his cap and a white ruffled shirt, he picks up Vitalina's passport from the table and takes a seat against a wall. She plays with three long black necklaces taken from her pocket, arranging them into elaborate patterns on the desk.

The scene enhances Vitalina's oracle-like persona. She speaks in whispers, contributing to the otherworldly atmosphere, and the necklaces seem to have a mystical significance. She studies them, rearranging them on the table like a fortune teller reading tarot cards or tea leaves. She begins to speak with Ventura, as if channeling his conscious:

VITALINA: How are you doing, Ventura?
VENTURA: Feeling a bit better. You're a kind of doctor or what?
VITALINA: Look at you, all dressed up, fancy.
VENTURA: Should have seen me in my teens.
VITALINA: Showing off your ruffle shirt . . . razor in your back pocket.
VENTURA: I left the barracks of the construction site. I caught the subway train. Got off downtown. I walked to Estrela Garden. It was a warm Sunday. Me and my brothers bought five bottles of wine. We all got drunk. I was thirsty.
VITALINA: [As if reading Ventura's thoughts and speaking for him] I drank from the fountain. I saw him coming with a smiling face. He wore bell bottoms, passport in his pocket, the red shirt I gave him on his birthday. It was his day off from his boss, J. Builder.
VENTURA: I've worked at J. Builder too.
VITALINA: You know the deal, Ventura. The life of Cape Verdean folk is always hard.

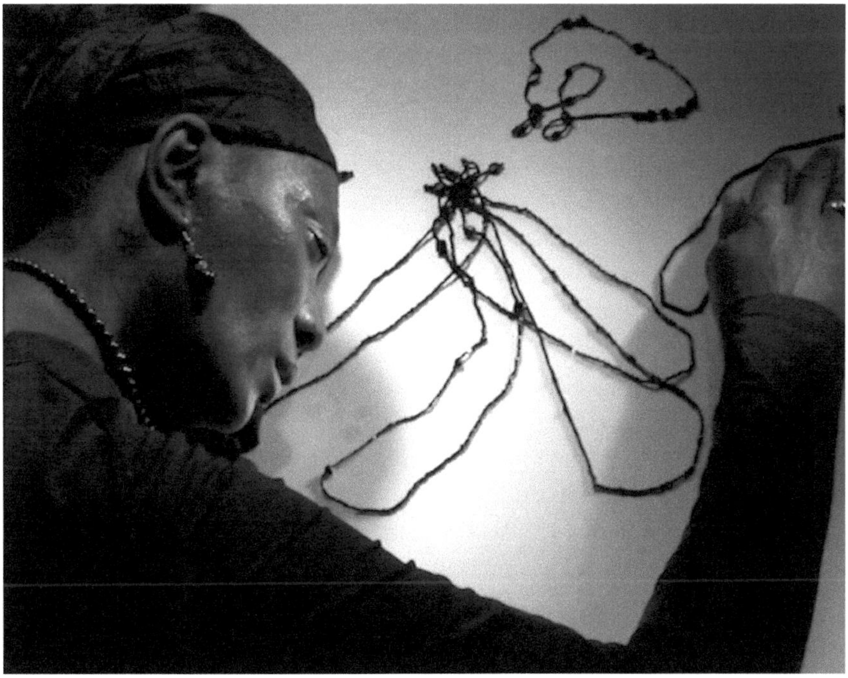

Vitalina and her necklaces

VENTURA: True. Whites cracked their whips on our back.

VITALINA: [Again channeling Ventura's thoughts] Then I lowered my face. He attacked me with his razor blade, slashed my forehead, so I cut his arm with my knife. Paralyzed him right there. I wanted to kill him with an axe. My brothers stopped me. The soldiers picked me up, put me in a jeep and took me to the hospital.

Watching Vitalina's hands still moving the necklaces, Ventura says: "You see a lot, Vitalina." She replies as if still in a trance, "You're still breathing . . . blood drips to the ground but nobody sees the razor. You've wrecked your life. Mine, too." Ventura removes his hat, hair askew and head bowed in shame. The camera tilts up as he stands. Cut to a large close-up of Vitalina, her head lying flat on the table atop the necklaces, her eyes open, staring in grief and despair. Ventura says, "He is not dead."

The next scene shows Ventura's partly hallucinated memory of the fight with Joaquim. We see helmeted soldiers armed with clubs moving through a wooded area, where one of them finds Joaquim seated on the ground and holds a baton against his neck. Another bends over Ventura, who is prone on the ground with a head wound, holding a knife in his trembling hand. (The trembling hand suggests that all this is a memory of the hospitalized Ventura.) The soldier takes the knife and a wedding ring from Ventura's finger, loads him in a jeep, and drives to the hospital. In the hospital, the aged, white-haired Ventura is strapped to an examination gurney, and Joaquim appears in the darkened room, wearing his red shirt and accusing Ventura of putting him into retirement with no way to provide for his wife.

Another important object, as usual with Costa, is a letter, the contents of which we never see. Ventura enters a vacant hospital office, sits in a chair, and begins writing on a sheet of paper with a pen from a doctor's pocket. We vaguely see the words on the paper but have no clue what or why he is writing. The scene has a mysterious effect because of an African mask hanging on an otherwise blank wall near him. Seated opposite the mask's inscrutable face, Ventura contemplates it with a sad expression. The paper on which he writes is seen at later junctures but remains a mystery until he gives it to Vitalina, saying it is a letter to her from Joaquim.

This letter evokes other missives in Costa's films, all from the long absent or recently dead, about family, love, and loss. Vitalina reads it to herself in a hallway with Ventura sitting nearby as she waits to collect her widow's pension. The letter's contents are never disclosed, only movingly suggested by a small smile she gives Ventura after finishing it—her only smile in the film. The effect is ambiguous. Perhaps the letter was for Zulmira, Ventura's wife in Cape Verde, to whom he has said he intends to write. Costa once described the letter writing in *Horse Money* as a metaphor for his relationship with the Cape Verdeans: "You don't know what is there," not unlike the letters he brought back years earlier from the island.[13]

Whatever its contents, the letter differs from the official documents Vitalina carries with her and reads aloud in her whispery voice. Her slow recitation of dry facts provides information about important events: her birth and parentage, her civil marriage to Joaquim, and his birth and death. His death certificate leaves "Cause of Death" blank, suppressing the fact that either his construction job, known to be dangerous, or the knife fight with Ventura contributed to his demise. Reading her own birth certificate with dates and places in Cape Verde, she becomes tearful, as if mourning herself, her parents, and everything Cape Verdean she has left behind. Unlike these documents, Ventura's letter, ostensibly from Joaquim, offers a measure of comfort and solace. Costa shows the emotional connection between Ventura and Vitalina in a Bressonian close-up of her hand over his, tenderly stroking his trembling fingers.

Old-fashioned rotary telephones also play a role in Ventura's reckoning with the past. We see him on what seems to be a summer day, inexplicably lying on the ground outside an abandoned construction building. Has he fallen or is he napping? He rises and dusts himself off. Dressed in his white ruffled shirt, pants, jacket, and cap, he enters the abandoned Gaudêncio construction firm, passing through the empty carpentry, mechanics, and woodwork areas to a locker, where he hangs his jacket as if readying for work. In a close-up, a white rotary phone with a detached cord sits atop faded and dusty blueprints. In the carpentry room, Ventura picks up a similarly disconnected black phone and asks if anyone is there. He mentions Miss Singela, identifies himself as José Tavares Borges, and says he wishes to speak to Mr. Ernesto. A stopped clock hangs on the wall. From there, he walks in a kind of daze along a factory tunnel, carrying the black receiver with the base connected to its cord scraping along the floor behind him. (As Jonathan Rosenbaum has noted, the grating sound of the phone "rhymes plaintively" with the sound of Vitalina's roller suitcase we saw earlier.)[14]

In an office with an old photograph of the building on the wall, Ventura spies a green phone, picks it up, and asks for the management. Pulled loose from the receiver, the speaker part of the phone dangles from a wire as he talks. Carrying the telephone into Mr. Ernesto's vacant office, he uses it to call his boss, with whom he talks about cuts to his wages. He also places an order for bricks and bags of cement to use to build himself a house.

These scenes, which show an aged and trembling Ventura in one-way conversation with ghosts, occupy over ten minutes in the film. Like the phones, Ventura's mind has frayed wiring, and in this altered state, he mysteriously encounters his godson and former coworker Benvindo (Benvindo Tavares) seated in a hallway in the abandoned construction building. (This scene may have been one that Costa imagined earlier with Ventura and Scott-Heron.) Benvindo says he has been waiting twenty years to collect his salary from the owner, who fled with the money and machines after the revolution. Responding to Ventura's questions about coworkers, he describes poverty, injuries, displacement, and death. Ventura sits next to him, cradles the broken telephone in his lap, and casually dials a few numbers. During the warm, beautifully lit scene, the two men begin singing a song in Creole about a Cape Verdean migrant's suffering and the memory of a comrade called Pépé Lopi. A small argument breaks out, with Ventura insisting the word "comrade" must be used to describe Pépé. In

Calling no one

the song, the migrant asks, "Doctor, what is wrong with me?"—a line Ventura sings alone as he struggles with his own maladies. The song finished, Ventura leaves, holding the telephone in front of him with both hands. It seems to offer a measure of comfort, connecting him to his younger self.

"Pépé Lopi," the song Ventura and Benvindo sing, is the title of a 1976 album by the popular Cape Verdean group Os Tubarões, whose song "Alto Cutelo," a traditional morna, plays off-screen over an impressive montage of portrait shots, most of them of older Cape Verdeans living in depressed conditions. The lyrics speak of the drought that drove a husband to Lisbon, leaving a wife and son behind. The husband works as cheap labor, exploited "even more than his white brother," living in a shack without electricity. He dreams of a day when the water returns and he can go back to Cape Verde to work as the boss of his own land.

Appearing halfway through the film, the song and montage of faces serve as a hinge leading to the remainder of the action and a companion to the Riis photographs of immigrants from the beginning. Here, the immigrants are shown as color, motion-picture images backed by music. They occasionally move expressively, acknowledging that they are being photographed. A couple of them smile at the camera. Like the figures in the Riis pictures, they are poor and working-class men, women, and children. Many of the shots seem fashioned to replicate still photographs; in one, a man does nothing but rest his head on a table—an apparent homage to Riis's images of men and women with their heads on tables. Except for Vitalina, who appears in two shots (one a low-angle view of her that ends the sequence), the subjects have no other role in the film. As a group, they function as a synecdoche for Lisbon's large Cape Verdean community.

Like the montage of faces, several shots in the film pause on significant outdoor statuary. As we have seen, a large statue António Egas Moniz graces the front entry of the Santa Maria Hospital, where Ventura is undergoing treatment. Moniz won the Nobel Prize in Medicine in 1949 for his groundbreaking work in psychiatry and psychosurgery, having performed the first lobotomy for mental illness in the mid-1930s. Built in 1974, the figure of Moniz, shot from the back, looms in a full-length academic cape. Costa also includes nocturnal shots of a female statue standing and holding what appears to be a torch or sword and another of the god Poseidon riding the waters on a majestic rearing horse in the Luminous Fountain of Alameda Park. Both sculptures are rendered in a classical style, but Costa gives them ironic implication; on the soundtrack, we hear Vitalina reading in her whispery voice a letter sent to Cape Verde confirming her husband's demise and requesting embassy support of a visa to allow her to travel to Lisbon for the funeral. The female statue suggests strength, care, and resilience—characteristics of Vitalina, who has braved illness and a traumatic flight to reach Portugal. But as the camera pulls back to a broader view of the soaring, exuberant sea god and horse, a weary Vitalina slowly treads past, pulling her roller bag. The powerful steed reminds us of the film's title, although Ventura's horse is now dead. (A reference to the horse occurs in another form in the song sung by Ventura and Benvindo about migrant hardships, which begins with the harrowing line, "I scream like a horse.")

One of the most astonishing, surreal instances of Ventura hallucinating is a sequence of him walking at night in his red underwear down an empty Lisbon street; suddenly, he is confronted by two helmeted soldiers with rifles, and when he raises his trembling hands, a tank rolls up behind him, its cannon pointed directly at his back. Costa used toy rifles for the soldiers, but the tank is real, an expensive addition to the film. Portuguese viewers would recognize it as an iconic Chaimite armored vehicle, associated with the colonial wars in Africa and the revolution.

Ventura surrenders to soldiers and a tank

The most disturbing of these visions, however, is the lengthy hospital elevator sequence, where Ventura confronts his recurring nightmare in the figure of a helmeted and armed soldier-statue. We see Ventura walk alone down a corridor in his striped pajamas, hands trembling at his sides, and arrive at the elevator door. The door slides open, and several people exit, leaving one barely visible, shadowy person on the right side. Ventura enters, the door closes, and the nightmare begins.

A tour de force, the sequence is a good example of what Alfred Hitchcock called "pure cinema." Hitchcock often pointed out that movies do not require vast landscapes, armies in battle, or men in tights fighting with swords; they can be confined to tight spaces because, in his opinion, the essence of cinema is editing. Costa stages the claustrophobic elevator scene in even more restricted fashion than in Hitchcock's films, without point-of-view shots, shooting at several angles but keeping his camera aimed toward the rear of the elevator car. The sequence lasts roughly twenty-three minutes and has thirty-eight shots—rare for Costa, who avoided montage and relied on long takes in his previous films. Each cut involves changes of angle and

Ventura trapped by his fears

character position, and almost every new shot lands with surprise and the force of a blow.

Although the scene chiefly involves Ventura's experience during the revolution, it becomes a crucible of his confused memories and emotions—a mix of terror, anger, sadness, nostalgia, anguish, and guilt. The statuary soldier's eyes and lips are always closed; we only hear his voice, sometimes mingled with other voices that may be Ventura's memory or hallucination. Ventura often moves, but the soldier moves in only one shot. Between shots, he changes position from one frozen pose to another, sometimes standing, sometimes kneeling, once sitting with his hands covering his ears.

A great deal is required of Ventura. Films, much more than stage productions, depend on an actor's eyes, and the many close-ups of him, together with expressive changes of posture, result in the most impressive of his performances. The dialogue is also important. Costa based it on Ventura's experience, subtly weaving in different styles of speech until it becomes a kind of oratorio or surreal poem. Below is a description of each shot, together with abbreviated excerpts of dialogue.

ONE: Seen from a slightly low angle, Ventura stands alongside the statuary, discomforted, staring ahead, hands trembling. The soldier stands at attention with his rifle at shoulder arms. Soldier: "*You're in the shade, boy, stay calm.*" Ventura raises his hands and clenches them. Soldier: "*Don't cry. Are you with the people? United we stand!*" Ventura bows his head in desperation and says, "*Always with the people.*" Soldier: "*It's been thirty years since I've seen you, maybe thirty-seven.*" Ventura straightens and moves to a handrail at the back of the elevator, grasping it and looking sidelong at the soldier. Soldier: "*I heard you've been ill. You're with better doctors now.*" Ventura crosses his arms nervously. Soldier: "*Your time has come.*" Ventura: "*A lame nurse sticks me with a needle every night. I'm shitting black.*" Soldier: "*Remember when you came in.*" Ventura turns his back on the soldier.

TWO: Low angle close-up of the soldier's face. Ventura: "*When I heard you were coming my guts slashed open.*" Soldier: "*You're in good hands. The fight has just begun.*" Ventura: "*I'm not healthy. I can't move no more cement sacks.*"

THREE: Close-up of Ventura's profile, turned away. Soldier: "*Where does it hurt?*" Ventura: "*My whole body. In matters of the flesh, I'm no help.*" Soldier: "*Know your prayers?*" Ventura turns his head and shouts: "*Our Lord of Nazareth, son of the Holy Mary, taste the mother's milk. The Beast's gun is not yours.*" Soldier laughs: "*You're worshipping Satan, boy!*"

FOUR: Close-up of soldier, head turned toward Ventura. Soldier: "*This is no joke, Ventura. This is a revolution. Do you think I like being locked in here with you for thirty-eight years? I'd rather be harvesting the grapes. I'd rather be helping Father with mass. We weren't made for this.*"

FIVE: Close-up of Ventura, now in semidarkness, a light above his head. Soldier: "*Remember, Ventura? We left the barracks at a snail's pace . . . Marched all night, our eyes closed.*"

SIX: Low-angle close-up of soldier, chin held high. Soldier: "*There was nothing else to do. Overthrow the regime. Didn't you see the people cheering in the streets?*"

SEVEN: Close-up of Ventura. Ventura: "*Am I in jail?*" Soldier: "*Lisbon is sealed off, didn't you hear the reports?*" Ventura: "*Are you going to kill me?*" Soldier: "*You've died a thousand deaths. What's one death more?*" Ventura: "*I've built a good life . . . family.*" Soldier: "*You call this living with your miserable pension?*" Ventura: "*I've built lots of buildings, banks, schools.*" Soldier: "*You've broke your body, messed up your head.*" Ventura: "*You know nothing about my life!*"

EIGHT: Low angle close-up of soldier, chin up proudly, turned toward Ventura. Soldier: "*Your boss stopped the work because of the coup, remember? We took up arms against the fascists.*"

NINE: Wide profile of soldier, rifle now at his side. Soldier: "*You were up at the scaffolding. I was ambushed in a corner. I wore my steel hood, you your yellow hard hat. . . . A sparrow flew past and I looked up. You were up there singing a song.*" Ventura: "*I wasn't the only one singing, we all sang—masons, bricklayers, pavers. . . . It wasn't springtime. It wasn't a sparrow.*"

TEN: Close-up of Ventura, head turned away, lips not moving during his speech. Ventura: "*It came to me one night, a big black bird flew over my shack on great black wings.*" Ventura's voice cries out in song: "*Monster's mommy!*"

ELEVEN: Close-up of soldier, rifle held high, looking toward Ventura. Soldier: "*You screamed. You cried. It wasn't the fascists, it was you. Dirty briefs, lost in the streets.*"

TWELVE: Low-level close-up of Ventura. Ventura, quiet, determined: "*Open the door in the name of General Spínola, the Cyclops.*"[15] Soldier: "*You ingrate! Can't you remember nigger against nigger with knives? You weren't dancing in Estrela Garden.*" Ventura, slowly bowing his head: "*Did you wash the blood off my face?*" Soldier: "*Who picked you up when you were half dead?*" Ventura: "*Did you hide the killing knife?*" Soldier: "*Who took you to the hospital?*" Ventura: "*Did you put ninety-three stitches in my head?*"

THIRTEEN: Close-up of soldier's hands. The only time we see the statuary soldier moving, loading his rifle.

FOURTEEN: Low-angle close-up of Ventura. Ventura: "*You're a son of the people.*"

FIFTEEN: Wide shot. Soldier is now on one knee, aiming his rifle toward the door of the elevator. Ventura eases behind him fearfully. Ventura: "*Did you shoot those fascist policemen?*" Ventura bends forward, looking with soldier. Ventura: "*If you killed a nigger you'd already be a general. Can you see them so far away? Hidden in those shacks. Fontaínhas, Damia, Black Cat.*" Ventura looks down at the soldier. Ventura: "*My children, my grandchildren. My brothers.*" Ventura stands, hands trembling, and moves to the side of the elevator.

SIXTEEN: Medium shot of Ventura. Soldier: "*Stand up, Ventura! The fight has just begun.*" Ventura: "*I'm dying.*"

SEVENTEEN: Close-up of soldier, head bowed. Soldier: "*Relax, Ventura. I'll never die.*" Ventura: "*I don't know you.*"

EIGHTEEN: Close-up of Ventura. Soldier: "*Don't you? But your night does, and the tiles of your shack, and the step of your door. What are you afraid of?*" Ventura: "*Losing my work contract.*" Soldier: "*You have to get to build your shack.*"

NINETEEN: Larger close-up of Ventura. Ventura: "*I can't fight no more. Can't work no more.*" Soldier: "*You still have to get Zulmira from Cape Verde.*" Ventura's eyes raise, and he smiles with a memory. Ventura: "*Bought a wedding dress with a veil and shoes. You've met Zulmira? . . . Bought a watch*

The soldier takes aim

for seven grand. I lived a hell of a life, working ill, raising my children. Now I'm retired." Soldier: *"Shut up, Ventura."* Ventura: *"They're all grown. It's time for them to help daddy."* Soldier: *"Shut up. All your children are yet to be born."*

TWENTY: Close-up of soldier looking at Ventura.

TWENTY-ONE: Close-up of Ventura, looking down solemnly. Ventura: *"I'm retired now."* He folds his arms. Soldier: *"Where are you now?"* Ventura: *"I'm at work. . . . Boss tells us there's no work today, there's a revolution going on. . . . I'm scared."* He smiles. *"In Estrela Garden . . . lots of Cape Verdeans, lots of whores."*

TWENTY-TWO: High-angle close-up of the soldier, arms folded. Suddenly, there is a frighteningly loud blast of organ music, "The Apparition of the Holy Church" by French composer Olivier Messiaen.

TWENTY-THREE: Close-up of Ventura, arms and hands crossed over his face, as if fearful of the organ music.

TWENTY-FOUR: Close-up looking down at soldier, hands over his ears.

TWENTY-FIVE: Close-up of Ventura looking down at soldier. The organ music stops, and Ventura sings quietly in his reedy voice some verses from the migrant's song "Alto Cutelo," heard earlier in the montage of Cape Verdeans.

Warding off terror

TWENTY-SIX: Low-angle close-up of the soldier looking toward Ventura. Ventura singing: "*Cheap labor, shack in the dark . . . my conscience and me.*" Soldier: "*Spare me the singing.*"

TWENTY-SEVEN: Close-up of Ventura.

TWENTY-EIGHT: Low-angle wide shot of Ventura and soldier, soldier on his knees, both looking toward the door. Ventura turns to look around, hears an unidentified call: "*Ventura!*" He backs away toward the corner fearfully.

TWENTY-NINE: Ventura: "*Zulmira!*" Soldier: "*Fight it. Stay with me.*" Ventura: "*This freedom trooper wants to kill us.*" Ventura looks at his hand. "*He stole our wedding ring. Stole our life. Says I'm not married to you. Says we haven't got any children. . . . I hear you sing but I don't hear you happy.*"

THIRTY: Low-angle close-up of soldier looking toward Ventura. Ventura: "*I hold you in my sleep but I don't feel you at peace. If you go now what will become of me?*"

THIRTY-ONE: Close-up of Ventura sitting on the floor of the elevator, hands on his head. Ventura: "*I feel your belly bloated but I don't see you eat.*"

> THIRTY-TWO: Close-up of soldier, also seated, propping his head on a hand. Ventura: "*You like this and with me unemployed we won't pay the rent.*"
>
> THIRTY-THREE: Close-up of Ventura, head turned away. He looks up. An unidentifiable voice speaks: "*This is the story of the young life . . .*"
>
> THIRTY-FOUR: Wide shot of Ventura looking up at the standing soldier. The voice continues: "*and of the life yet to come and of all things that will follow. Stay close to me, the time will fly. The day will come when we'll accept our sufferings.*"
>
> THIRTY-FIVE: Close-up of the seated Ventura. He looks up sadly, eyes tearing. Voice: "*They'll forget our faces. You shall sing no more.*"
>
> THIRTY-SIX: Soldier looking down at Ventura. Soldier: "*This story is not over yet. Our sufferings will be joys for future men. They will say nice things about us. It won't be long before we know why we live and why we suffer. We'll know everything.*"
>
> THIRTY-SEVEN: Close-up of Ventura. Soldier: "*We lay with the dead locked in silence.*" Ventura looks up at soldier with quiet anger. Ventura: "*See how I tremble.*"
>
> THIRTY-EIGHT: Wide shot of Ventura and standing soldier. Soldier: "*This is what I had to tell you, boy.*" Ventura seems very weak. Soldier: "*On your guard, pay attention!*" Ventura scratches his leg slowly. Ventura: "*I'm paying attention, Master.*"

One of the many remarkable aspects of this conversation is the way the soldier's voice seems to represent not only Ventura's horrified memories of the revolution but also a mixture of a doctor's psychological prompting and a quasireligious prophet's proclamations. The elevator sequence ends suddenly with a cut to Joaquim, dressed in his red pajamas, sitting in an empty hospital cafeteria with his crutches leaned against the wall. Joaquim tells Ventura, who sits beside him, that he cannot feel his arm because of the knife fight that led to him losing his job. There has not been a clear explanation of what caused this fight, which also resulted in Ventura's head injury and one of his many hospitalizations.

The cafeteria encounter shows the two older men in a moment of reconciliation, with Ventura, his hands no longer trembling, spoon-feeding soup to his former foe. Ventura's compassionate act might be imaginary contrition for inflicting the injury that left Joaquim unemployed and his family without support. In any case, Ventura seems liberated from his demons. As he feeds the soup, he returns Joaquim's gaze with a small smile. He then says that the doctor has discharged him.

Unlike when he entered the hospital, Ventura is fully dressed when he leaves, walking more firmly with the doctor and shaking his hand farewell. The doctor lights a cigarette and watches him go. Again like Dante led by Virgil, Ventura has escaped from private circles of hell with the doctor's help. The skyline with its soft orange glow announces a new day, but there are hidden ironies. Costa shot the hospital exit at the entrance to a Lisbon morgue.

We suddenly cut to a shop window displaying a row of Opinel knives, sharp and deadly. A cobblestone sidewalk is reflected in the glass along with the shadow of Ventura's legs stopping in front of the display. This unexplained and unsettling image closes the film, harking back to the knife fight between Joaquim and Ventura and the statuary soldier's forewarning: "*The fight has just begun. Pay attention, be on your guard.*"

In an interview with Costa, Michael Guarneri asked what the knives in *Horse Money* signify. Costa initially demurred but then spoke at length about how the ending came about:

> As I watched and re-watched Ventura's walk, I realized there was something missing. The film couldn't simply end with Ventura leaving the hospital. Not with that kind of walk. So I delayed the closing of the film, and let it rest a little.
>
> One day I opened the "Ventura's Sunday" folder [Costa's photos of Ventura walking around Lisbon], and I saw the knives in the shop window. There it was. Ventura found his purpose. Somehow the three steps he takes toward the knives reassured me. He would be safe. He would be protected. I don't know what the knife means, though.[16]

The knife may just be a knife, but, like the soldier, it is linked to a harrowing experience that marked Ventura both physically and mentally for decades. His approach toward the knife display may be less about his safety than about conquering something unsettling from his past, this time not as a hallucinating patient in a hospital elevator but as a man somewhat restored, walking along a city street in daylight.

Vitalina Varela (2019)

One of Pedro Costa's most critically acclaimed films, *Vitalina Varela* was the recipient of several awards, among them the 2019 Locarno Film Festival's

Golden Leopard Prize for Best Film and Leopard for Best Actress for the star, Vitalina Varela. Cinematographer Leonardo Simões, who also worked on *Colossal Youth* and *Horse Money*, garnered top prizes at the Dublin, Mar del Plata, Coimbra, and Gijon festivals. Shot over a nine-month period, six days a week, with an Arri Alexa camera and a four-person crew, the two-hour-four-minute color film cost 600,000 euros ($720,000). In a 2020 interview, Costa discussed its funding sources and costs: "The film was funded in its totality with Portuguese money, mainly with the support of the Portuguese Film Institute, an aid from the Lisbon City Council, a participation of Portuguese Public Television, and a small grant from the Gulbenkian Foundation. That would make a total of around 600,000 Euros. But I must stress that we managed to get part of the funding for *Vitalina Varela* while we were still working on *Horse Money*, a film for which we had only 90,000 Euros. This means that we did the two films for around 700,000 Euros! 350,000 Euros each."[17]

The premiere was projected on a large wall in the Cova da Moura neighborhood, where filming had taken place; located about ten kilometers from metropolitan Lisbon, Cova da Moura's population includes a Cape Verdean enclave, some parts of which have a reputation for poor housing. Vitalina herself lived there, and Costa said that he made the movie for its Creole-speaking community. Roughly 80 percent of the dialogue is in Cape Verdean Creole, requiring subtitles even for Portuguese-speaking audiences: "They gain something, recognize themselves, what they lost, [and are] trying to find." He described the audience response at the premiere in three words: "They loved it."[18]

About Vitalina's role, Costa remarked, "She was the co-author, the co-director. . . . She is the history of that place [and] is so exposed . . . seventy percent is her."[19] In another interview, he added: "We wrote the screenplay together. Actually, she wrote more of the screenplay than I did; she didn't write it by hand, but she memorized it. You see ten or five or one minute of dialogue or monologue, in the beginning it was ten or twenty minutes. My work was to contain, to compress."[20] Probably no Costa film better represents his lengthy, painstaking collaboration with performers, which always results in a dialectic of the harshness of lived reality and the beauty of art.

There are many obvious connections between *Vitalina Varela* and Costa's other films about the Cape Verdean diaspora, but the closest is with *Horse Money*, in which Vitalina is introduced and meets Ventura, recounting her traumatic journey to Lisbon and belated arrival for the funeral of her estranged husband, Joaquim, who had left Cape Verde decades earlier. She is

Ventura's link to his island past as well as a voice for the many Cape Verdean women who remained in Cape Verde, sending letters abroad to loved ones, working, raising families, and suffering abandonment by their husbands in Portugal. *Vitalina Varela* continues her story, mostly in her own words, about her young married life in Cape Verde, her grievances and fears after waiting forty years to join Joaquim, and her new life in Cova da Moura.

Vividly featured in *Horse Money,* where he wears a red ruffled shirt and carries a razor knife, Joaquim in this film is a structuring absence. On the death certificate Vitalina reads in *Horse Money,* his cause of death is left blank; it remains a mystery in the tight-lipped, patriarchal Cova da Moura community, where Vitalina moves into the dead Joaquim's dark, ramshackle house. About the real-life Joaquim, Costa said, "This guy was a nasty guy. The guy who plays his friend [in *Vitalina*] told me that in the last months Joaquim was probably one of the biggest dealers in the neighborhood, and then he got diabetes or heart disease or whatever. There was blood in the house, diarrhea on the floor, he was kaput."[21]

Vitalina Varela also features Ventura, who plays a fictional character—a disgraced island priest sent to serve in a humble, mostly empty Cova da Moura church. Vitalina and Ventura are alone and adrift in a foreign land, their tender words and consoling gestures growing out of Vitalina's sorrow and the priest's battle with his demons. Costa has emphasized a special bond between the two films and characters, describing *Vitalina Varela* as the "companion piece" to *Horse Money.*[22] Like most of his digitally photographed pictures (except *Horse Money*), *Vitalina* has long takes, an unmoving camera, striking depth-of-field compositions, eloquent portraiture, and a fascinating play of deep blackness with areas of beautiful color. But the primary difference with *Horse Money,* and what makes it a counterpoint as well as a companion piece, is that the earlier film is about a man while *Vitalina Varela* is about a woman. This has important consequences for its narrative and style.

Where narrative is concerned, *Vitalina Varela* resembles most of Costa's work in that it devalues plot in favor of themes and characters. For *Down to Earth,* Costa threw away the script he had written, turning the film into a young Lisbon woman's exploration of landscape, culture, and people in Cape Verde. *Bones* has a feuilleton-style plot about the fate of a baby, but that plot is subordinated to the portrayal of various characters and their relationships. *In Vanda's Room* oscillates between the rooms of "girls" and "boys," but its only plot is the gradual destruction of Fontaínhas, mostly heard in the background. *Colossal Youth* involves Ventura's wanderings in search of family and friends and is loosely held together by an understated picaresque structure, a series of vignettes that circle around Lisbon and environs. *Horse Money*, for all its hallucinatory action and incidents, is basically a film about a traumatized, psychologically broken man who goes to the hospital at the beginning and leaves better than when he entered. As for *Vitalina Varela*, it is shaped by nothing more than a traumatized woman dealing with grief and anger, coping with her late husband's leaking roof, and trying to adapt to a strange new community.

Costa's films have a great many virtues, but audiences do not go to them for the pleasures of classical narrative. On this level, his work has something in common with literary high modernism's treatment of plot. Virginia Woolf's *To the Lighthouse* (1927), for example, is shaped by a series of almost unrelated and undramatic events: the preparation of a family dinner, a short rowboat trip to a nearby lighthouse, and the completion of a painting. The real subject is time, death, and the interrelated consciousness of several characters, and important moments often come when nothing is happening—as when Mrs. Ramsay is merely sitting by a window contemplating the flowers outside.

Virginia Woolf may seem a wildly inappropriate example in this context because Costa's films are largely about an extremely poor, Portuguese-speaking African world, while Woolf's novels belong to a privileged, even snobbish Bloomsbury culture. But comparison to Woolf is appropriate to a degree because her fiction has a great deal to do with the experience of women. Without arguing that there is an essential difference between female and male narratives, we can at least say that women have more experiences of a certain kind than men do—not only of childbearing, which is essentially female, but also of domestic or care-giving duties common in conservative, patriarchal societies.

Vitalina Varela is just such a traditional woman, and as a result, Costa's film about her has different qualities than his other pictures. The action is centered on the subjectivity of a lonely character who often does nothing more than clean her house and garden, or boil water. Like *Horse Money*, *Vitalina Varela* is about memory, but Ventura's memories are hallucinatory, and events of his past life are reenacted in violent dreams or visions. Even when he feels trapped in an elevator alongside the frightening statue of a soldier, the soldier goes into dynamic poses with a rifle. If *Horse Money* is full of movement, *Vitalina Varela* is full of stillness. It has a different kind of statuary quality, with long silences in which minor characters stand in unmoving, almost Brechtian poses, making the viewer aware of time passing when nothing happens. Apart from her conversations with a priest, Vitalina is nearly always alone, and most of her memories are shown not as dreams or flashbacks but as soliloquies addressed to the spirit of her dead husband. One of the longest of these occurs when she is doing nothing more than sitting on the bathroom toilet, lost in thought.

Vitalina Varela is also unique in Costa's career because it is his only film in which an older woman plays the lead. Several of his films feature young Cape Verdean or Portuguese women, but middle-aged and older females in those films play supporting or minor roles: the reclusive widow Edite (*Down to Earth*), the nurse Eduarda (*Bones*), and Vanda's mother Lena (*In Vanda's Room*). Vitalina has a prominent role in *Horse Money*, but that film remains Ventura's story. She appears in it as an invited guest, sharing in his suffering and consoling him while coping with her own misery and ghosts. *Vitalina Varela* is completely her story. She is a mature woman alone with memories encapsulated in the time span of a few days.

As critics have noted, *Vitalina Varela* has gendered and formal connections with *In Vanda's Room*. Both are films titled after strong, resilient female leads, and *Vitalina* could have been called *Na casa de Vitalina*, "In Vitalina's House," since much of the film takes place inside her Cova da Moura home. In her surrounding neighborhood, there are small affinities with Fontaínhas: dark, narrow passageways, occasional painted metal doors, and an outdoor stairway that seems to lead nowhere. A man selling cans of tuna door to door, whom Vitalina ignores, recalls Vanda's outings to sell cabbages to mostly uninterested neighbors. The soundtracks of the two films are also similar, with their subtle mix of distant adult and children's voices, an occasional barking dog, and ambient murmurings. Costa once remarked that *Vitalina Varela* "has a lot to do with *Vanda*, not only because it's a woman's story but a story of confinement."[23]

As in *In Vanda's Room*, the small bedroom in *Vitalina Varela* is an important space, first appearing during a precredit sequence. The film begins at night, with a strange, vividly mysterious wide-angle shot of a line of men, two of them supporting a priest by holding his arms over their shoulders. (Costa was especially pleased with the inky blacks Leonardo Simões achieved in this film.) They walk toward us in a procession down a long road bordered by the stone wall of a hillside cemetery, crosses visible in the black sky above the wall. (Crosses will become one of the film's motifs, always with funereal connotations.) Here and elsewhere, Costa does not explain what is happening, but we eventually realize that the men are leaving Joaquim's burial ceremony. The priest falls to the ground, and while some of the mourners bend over him, two men exit, going to the dead man's house. When they enter, the first thing we see is a bed with a heavily bloodstained pillow and coverlet, attesting to the wretchedness of Joaquim's last days. Over the course of the film, Vitalina will spend a good deal of time in that bedroom.

In the opening scenes, one man goes outside to burn Joaquim's bedding and photographs of a young woman; another vigorously mops the floors, muttering, "Fine son of a bitch you were. Took it all to the grave." When Vitalina initially enters the house, bumping her head against the top of a low doorway, it has been cleaned a bit, but the bedroom, where she goes first, is scary, the site of Joaquim's most intimate life in Portugal. Her eyes moist, she peeks in through a part in a curtain hanging across the doorway. (Female pinups are tacked to the door of another room.) She sits on the bed, holding a paper bag, removes her earrings and dark headscarf, and gazes out a window; her face is a study in contemplation, artfully lit and reflected in a bureau mirror. She eventually looks for traces of herself in Joaquim's satchels hung along the walls but fails to find any of her letters to him.

In *Vitalina Varela*, as in *Colossal Youth*, the theme of domestic displacement is given strong emphasis. Ventura roams the last vestiges of Fontaínhas and locates his "children," who have been forced to depart for Casal da Boba; for her part, Vitalina seeks solace in a wooded area near a makeshift church, where she tills a vegetable patch as if back in her homeland. But she has no community. Ventura is just as unhappy moving to Casal da Boba's sterile housing as Vitalina is when she occupies Joaquim's dark house with its small, barred windows and leaking roof. (She tells a group of Joaquim's mourners who comment on the state of the roof that she will "get some guys" to fix it.) Ventura amusingly expresses dissatisfaction to his housing agent by pointing out spiderwebs and improperly installed doors, while Vitalina, looking around the house she now owns, complains aloud to her dead husband about his shoddy workmanship.

An early scene in *Vitalina Varela* creates a surreal, dramatic sense of displacement and disorientation. We see a wide nighttime shot of a giant passenger jet on a noisy airport tarmac, its engines shut down and rear door open. The passengers have left, and in the lighted exit doorway Vitalina appears as a silhouette—a tiny, solitary figure dwarfed by the aircraft. We cut to a close-up of a portable stairway pushed against the exit door; a barefoot Vitalina steps tentatively into a new world, showing legs and toes marked by the incontinence she describes in *Horse Money*. She is greeted on the tarmac by five Cape Verdean cleaners waiting in still poses, one of whom embraces her and whispers, "Vitalina, condolences. You arrived too late. Your husband was

Vitalina arrives in Lisbon

buried three days ago. There is nothing for you here in Portugal." The group of women stands like figures in a tableau, immobile, their eyes mournfully downcast. (Costa once told an interviewer that this scene was inspired by his and Ventura's arrival for the Cannes Film Festival, where Ventura recognized a nephew from Cape Verde on the airport's cleaning crew.)[24]

Vitalina's excellent performance is supported by Ventura, who plays a frail, nameless priest, insecure in his faith and slightly deranged. Costa based the character on an actual priest known to both Vitalina and Ventura who was sent from Cape Verde to Lisbon after refusing to baptize a group of compatriots, all of whom died in an accident after he sent them to another parish.[25] Vitalina reminds Ventura's priest of this episode when she helps him recover from a fall as they walk from his church. She also reminds him that he knows her: "Don't you remember me, Father? You buried my husband seven days ago. It's me, Vitalina Varela." Despite his disgrace, she asks him to offer a mass for Joaquim and herself.

Rituals, symbols, and other signs of faith appear throughout the film, beginning with the eerie nighttime view of hillside cemetery crosses and recurring during the extended, traditional mourning after Joaquim's death. As part of the cleaning process in Joaquim's house, a man carries a plate of burning herbs, moving the smoke around the bedroom as if to purify a defiled space. Still-life close-ups show Vitalina's makeshift altar on a small table, with candles, flowers, two photographs, and a crucifix; the candles will eventually burn down, indicating the passage of a period of mourning and a slight change in Vitalina's life. Other extended shots picture rough-hewn telephone poles with metal crossbars that evoke crucifixes. In one close-up, the priest's trembling hand rests on one of these poles, which has been painted with a small purple cross. "Get thee behind me," the priest murmurs, as if speaking to Satan. As he slowly makes his way from the town to his church, he touches other poles, like a man walking the stations of the cross.

The priest's humble dirt-floor church has a prominent metal cross affixed to its corrugated tin facade. Inside, a collection of miscellaneous colored desk chairs from a schoolhouse faces a pulpit set before a bright red wall with a large crucifix. (The church's interior is a set that was assembled in an abandoned cinema. Some critics have found deep meaning in this, as if Costa were commenting on film substituting religion or the sanctification of a commercial space, but we would never know the place was a former cinema had he not mentioned it in interviews.) Walking on the dirt path to the church, the priest falls, losing a silver cross that, in close-up, gleams against dark earth. He is trembling and infirm, his various tumbles suggestive of his fall from grace. A close-up of the meager offerings on his collection plate in the church shows two coins alongside a small crucifix and a prayer card with a cross. Without a flock, he pays penance by helping a few needy compatriots and officiating at burials, often donning a purple prayer stole embroidered with symbols of the cross. When Vitalina confers with him about Joaquim, he tells her, "He left with a clean soul. I sang him a nice sermon. I hear a man crying all night. There is nothing sadder than a priest here." Vitalina becomes angry: "Men favor men! When you see a woman's face in the coffin, you can't imagine her suffering."

If the priest has floundered, Vitalina stands firm. Despite fear, loneliness, and suspicious neighbors who visit her house to offer condolences, she is determined to stay. In one scene, a group of mourners plays cards in her living room, and one of them talks about Joaquim's last days: "I bathed him, I changed him. . . . We found him covered in vomit . . . gave him a glass of water, he threw up." Vitalina only replies, "I've been waiting for my plane trip to Portugal for forty years. I'm not going to leave." She overhears one of the

Vitalina and a guilt-ridden priest

mourners asking about her: "Is this the same woman who was at the funeral?" Suppressing the gossip about the woman in question, who may have been Joaquim's lover, Vitalina shouts, "Leave, go out!"

Vitalina Varela was largely filmed in Vitalina's actual Cova da Moura home. As Costa told an interviewer, "It's very small: it's me, her, camera, and that's it, nobody else. . . . It's difficult. But it's her house . . . and in a way she needs that, too. When she's looking, she's looking at her mirror, her wall, her window. . . . We left everything there, lights, tripods, so she lived in a kind of studio for months and months, poor woman."[26] Vitalina's familiarity with the setting no doubt contributed to her performance, which is deserving of the award she received at Locarno. A tall woman, she has a stately presence and an aura Costa recognized when he first saw her. He emphasizes her physical strength by centering the film on her erect, almost statuary poses and ability to sit or move in expressive fashion.

Her power on the screen derives not only from strength but also from eloquent silence, whether gazing out a window, tending a vegetable patch, or searching for her letters to Joaquim. Costa regularly films her in portrait-style

Vitalina undeterred

close-ups, emphasizing her high cheekbones and thoughtful face. Her large, dark eyes are like windows to a soul—intensely expressive in wide shots and particularly in close-ups. More than any of Costa's actors, she has an ability to be what Lesley Stern has described as "simultaneously quotidian and histrionic."[27] Notice, for example, the close shot of her seated on her bed, eyes beginning to weep as she talks softly to the dead Joaquim: "You're surprised, aren't you? You didn't expect my visit. You don't want me close to you in your dying hours. I don't hurt you in life or death." Or see the moment when she is discussing Joaquim's death with the priest; in a wide shot, seated in a chair, she turns and looks behind her, wide-eyed, as if aware of some ghost or haunting event from her past.

Two scenes give an especially clear sense of Vitalina's abilities as a performer, both involving intimate moments in which she appears without her trademark black headscarf. In the first, she is sitting on the toilet in Joaquim's dingy bathroom, secluding herself from the mourners who have come to the house, her face toward the camera but gazing down and slightly to one side. With her short hair exposed, she seems vulnerable. Her only movements in

Pondering the roof

the first minute of this six-minute shot are the pulse in her throat as she slowly raises her head and widens her eyes, which roll up to glare at the roof as if it were about to collapse.

Her eyes upturned, she begins speaking to her dead husband about the house, their place in Cape Verde, and his betrayal. Her story of hard work and abandonment is movingly delivered in a soft, whispery monologue, without recourse to theatrical expressions or gestures—just a slight tilt of her head and gradual lowering of her eyes, fixed on what only she can see:

> This house of yours is a poorly done job. Windows like gutters. I keep hitting my head on these shitty doors. The house we built together in Cape Verde is incomparable. Ten rooms, a kitchen, a good bathroom, a big water tank. Close to the chapel of Figueira das Naus. I sold a small calf for 100 *contos*. I bought a truckload of iron, a truck of sand, cement and water. I built all the blocks with my own hands. You laid down the bricks, towed the walls, tiled the floor. People passing by couldn't believe it. We had done all that work all by ourselves in forty-five days. You came to Cape Verde forty-five days. We worked day and night. Sometimes we didn't even go to bed.

> "Lay down for a little bit."
>
> "No, I have to work. The cement paste is ready to make the blocks in the morning."
>
> One day you ran off to Portugal, you didn't even say goodbye. I went back home, made dinner, waited with the food in the pan . . . then I threw everything away. You ran all the alleys of the neighborhood, the other side of the river, France, chasing those street women, like a lamb that just escaped the barn. When I wrote asking for money you didn't reply, you kept silent. You thought it was a joke.
>
> "If I had known it would be so tiring, I wouldn't have come to Cape Verde on holidays, for forty-five days."
>
> After you left, I worked very hard. I took care of all the doors, all the windows. I built the water tank. I sold another calf and bought more doors and windows. I was working pregnant with a little girl that didn't even have a name. I carried fifty-kilogram cement bags on my head every day. One of my feet got bigger than the other. You never saw it. You never entered our house after it was finished, all painted. You said you would come, you would come. . . . And you died and never came.

Costa holds the camera on Vitalina for several more seconds, like the pause after a beautifully performed aria. The next shot is of a closed door Vitalina slowly opens from inside, giving us a partial view of the bathroom behind her. Now wearing her protective headscarf, she steps tentatively out as if steeling herself for something unpleasant. Walking past a group of visiting mourners posed like leaning statuary, she stands with her back to a wall in a low-angle shot, hiding from their view. This is the point at which she hears their low voices gossiping and, without moving or changing expression, yells at them to leave.

In another intimate scene, Vitalina is in the shower with her back to the camera. Viewed from outside the house, she is framed by a crudely constructed window opening covered with metal latticework. Turning toward the camera, she begins to shampoo her hair, which looks much longer and thicker than in the earlier bathroom scene. Suddenly, pieces of the roof rain down on her head, justifying her suspicious upward gaze in previous shots. Eyes closed with a pained expression, she presses her hands to the injured spot, lowering one hand to check for blood. She moves slightly forward and rests the side of her face against the edge of the window. Eyes narrowed, she stares out at something unseen, perhaps the ghost of Joaquim. Her look is deadly.

The roof is a recurring topic, a metaphor for a marriage damaged over time by Joaquim's failure to maintain it. "Couldn't you have fixed the roof?" she

On the leaking roof in a storm

whispers to his ghost, "You turned lazy . . . ran away." In one of the film's most powerful scenes, Vitalina appears on the tiled, busted rooftop on a stormy night; buffeted by high winds, she crouches while working her way to a large plastic tarp covering an opening. The tarp has come loose and is flapping wildly in the gale. This physically demanding, nearly two-minute shot, which required Vitalina to move carefully across the roof to rearrange large pieces of wood holding down the tarp, was actually filmed in a primitive studio constructed in the abandoned cinema that had been a set for the church. Costa used a huge fan and a green screen for the stormy sky in the background—an unusual special effect for his films. When Vitalina's task is completed, she stands, looks around at her work, and, in a pose reminiscent of frontier women in old Hollywood movies, raises her left hand with palm facing out to her forehead.

In a 2022 interview with Thomas Austin, Costa talked about this shot, which turned out to be less difficult than he had anticipated: "We didn't need that many takes. It was just because Vitalina had really performed those actions quite a few times in her real life: climbing to the roof on stormy nights, trying to stop the rain from falling in her kitchen or on her bed."[28] When Austin suggested the scene is perhaps the closest Costa has come to John Ford, Costa acknowledged Vitalina's Ford-like gesture with her hand turned out over her brow; in another interview, however, he said, "I never asked why she did that or what she was seeing. But it was because of this shot that I decided to go to Cape Verde to shoot the ending of the film. Who knows, maybe Vitalina is seeing herself on top of another roof, across the ocean."[29] He also suggested the greater importance of other directors to this scene:

> But for me, with this scene you could also think of some of the women in Mizoguchi's films, if only because John Ford was more manly. But it could also be Russian—it could be Dovzhenko. But of course if you have that, what can you do: you're surrounded by ghosts again. I'm not saying it's a shot or an image I remember from Mizoguchi. It's more a spirit of mothers, widows, running around the landscape in Japan, escaping soldiers, battling, searching for food, repairing, et cetera. But, I guess, more than Ford or Mizoguchi, I'm thinking of a filmmaker who was certainly important for this film: Mikio Naruse.[30]

Costa's reference to Japanese director Mikio Naruse, who is relatively little known to US audiences, is significant. He may have been thinking of Naruse when he made *Vitalina*—in fact, he mentioned his debt to critic Chris Fujiwara, whose writing on Naruse enables us to understand what probably interested Costa. Like Mizoguchi, Naruse (1905–1969) was a director of films about women and of a genre called *shomingeki*, dramas of poor people. Fujiwara points out that many of these films give major roles to widows: in Naruse's world, even when the man is alive, he is "necessarily dead . . . unable to fill the ideal of masculinity." And yet despite the loss and sadness in Naruse films, "the worldview they imply isn't tragic" because Naruse "puts so much weight on the ability of his heroines to change their minds about their problems. . . . A certain increased distance is always available to Naruse's women. Reflecting this possibility, most of the director's films contain moments when he suddenly withdraws his camera from a scene, putting us outside a window to peer in at the character."[31]

One thinks of the scene that views Vitalina through a window outside her bathroom; the roof falling on her head makes her angry, but the viewpoint momentarily distances her from the brooding she has done on the toilet. Her gesture when she stands on the roof may be reminiscent of Hollywood Westerns, suggesting a certain pioneering quality, but more importantly it shows her determination to overcome hardship and, as with Naruse's women, her ability to solve her problems. Vitalina's stance and far-off gaze are linked with a shot that occurs soon after. We see what may be a younger version of her at the home she helped construct in Cape Verde; it is as if time has fallen away, with her younger self standing outside the house in her black scarf, gazing at a point beyond the nearby mountains. (The shot is repeated with powerful effect at the end of *Vitalina*.)

Among mourners who come to the house in Cova de Moura are the young couple Ntoni (Manuel Tavares Almeida) and Marina (Marina Alves Domingues), who sit at Vitalina's kitchen table, where Ntoni eats a plate of food and compliments her cooking. Vitalina learns from Ntoni that they have been squatting in a train station and that he scavenges for food and other items outside a supermarket. Marina, who neither eats nor speaks, leaves the kitchen to smoke a cigarette at the open front door. Ntoni confides to Vitalina that Marina is not well. He recalls doing jail time with Joaquim, who was a prison cook and Ntoni his helper. He says: "We who drink, we who steal, we can be very deceitful. But we also know how to help our fellow men. He never forgot, always gave me a hand. Last time I saw him, he was sitting by the door, had put on weight, dreadlocks, sandals, full of himself. So many times he asked me to help him fix this house. He wanted more rooms, a new paint job, [fix] the walls, tile the floor. His head was full of dreams. He said: 'My wife must see this house all pretty.'"

Vitalina seems a bit unsettled, perhaps because the person Ntoni describes is at odds with the man who "didn't want [her] close to [him] even dying" and denied her the ritual of viewing his body before its burial. Toward the end of the film, Ntoni returns alone to Vitalina's house, bringing her jars of food and two partly empty perfume bottles, which he arranges on the table, where flowers are the only reminder of the altar for the dead. To these offerings, he adds a statuette of a black bird. This time, their conversation is intimate, almost confessional, as they take turns speaking of love and abandonment. Ntoni says that Marina has left him, triggering a memory of his father, who left his mother to return to Cape Verde and die. Despite their separation, Ntoni describes how his parents remained in love, regularly talking on the phone, calling one another "sweetheart." When the father's remorse for his decision overcame him, he came back to Lisbon and died in the same Amadora hospital as Joaquim.

Ntoni's story about love and his mention of Joaquim sets Vitalina talking about Joaquim's earlier relationship with a young woman in Cape Verde who, remarkably, was also called Vitalina. Although she took all his savings and left him, he held on to photographs of her. Vitalina turns from Ntoni and seems to gaze into the distance, delivering a monologue addressed to the departed Joaquim. She has a vision of her doppelgänger in Cape Verde, describing photographic images of her "laying on that bed, her arms stretched open . . . in the bathroom washing her hands . . . in the kitchen washing the dishes . . . [wearing] your lace shirt . . . in a tight little blue dress, her legs wide open [showing] her white undies." These images suggest a man besotted with a woman whose mundane activity captivated him as much as her erotic poses. Imprinted on Vitalina's mind, they may explain the identity of the woman in the photographs mourners burned at the beginning of the film. These pictures, unlike Vitalina's letters, which she fails to find in the house, Joaquim appears to have never thrown away. Or are the burned photos of a Cova da Moura lover, the mysterious woman at his burial ceremony? In either case, Vitalina has never been faithfully loved. As if reflecting on his own abandonment, Ntoni remarks: "Sometimes, even if there's love, things don't work out." Looking out a window that frames her like a painting, Vitalina replies softly, almost wistfully: "If there's love, things must work out . . . love is so important."

Joaquim was a sloppy worker and a womanizer, but Vitalina still feels the need to communicate with him: "The padre says I have to learn Portuguese to speak to you," she says in one of her monologues. "If I learn, will you say all you didn't say to me in Cape Verde?" We watch her slowly sound out words in an old Portuguese newspaper article tacked above the kitchen sink. But the priest's advice about language rings hollow, just as Joaquim's neglect cannot be explained by a linguistic barrier. In her desire to communicate with him, she reminds her dead husband that all her apparently discarded letters were written to him in Portuguese (perhaps translated by someone in Cape Verde).

The film circles back to a road alongside the cemetery at night, where Vitalina encounters Ntoni pushing a grocery cart with scavenged building materials. He tells her Marina has died from burns caused by a mattress set on fire by a candle. But in the next scene, the spooky, nocturnal cemetery from the beginning of the film takes on a totally different look. Vitalina and the priest appear in daylight, following a coffin rolled along a path between crypts festooned with colorful flowers. After the burial (perhaps of Marina), they join hands over the grave, located near a wall. As they turn and walk away, the cemetery's vastness comes into view, with numbered plots, small and large monuments, flower displays, and what looks like a housing project in the distance. If there is any conscious debt to John Ford, it is here, in a couple

Visiting the dead

of low-angle shots that emphasize the proximity of the dead to the billowy clouds above. Costa sets the camera at a low level so that the horizon runs across the bottom third of the image, creating an epic grandeur.

The procession and burial seem to provide Vitalina and the priest with a measure of purpose and peace. They wander among the burial plots, stopping to stand together over a recent grave with a mound of fresh earth, presumably where Joaquim lies. The film could have ended at this gravesite, suggesting a sense of closure with the man who left Vitalina for another life, if not an actual reconciliation. But Costa brings the story full circle with a close-up of Vitalina lying in her bed, experiencing lingering grief or concern. She hears off-screen sounds, and another close-up shows her bare feet, no longer marked as they were when she exited the aircraft on her arrival in Lisbon, stepping out her front door into the sunlight. She discovers three men, probably from the group of Joaquim's mourners, working on her roof, replacing old tiles with new ones, a sign that there is a hope for her in the new homeland. While two younger men work toward the back, the third, a well-dressed, middle-aged man in the foreground, turns his face in a three-quarter profile and stares into

A roof in Cape Verde

the distance. There is nothing to explain who this man is or what has captured his attention, but he is clearly helping Vitalina construct a solid home.

We cut to what might be a memory image or perhaps a view of Vitalina's daughter in the present day. We see Vitalina's house in Cape Verde and a young woman looking toward the horizon. She carries a cement block on her head and goes up to the roof, where a young man applies mortar with a brush. She squats and hugs him, and he playfully touches her face with the brush. Standing, she turns, lifts her hand to her brow, palm-side out, and stares at something far away. She is the mirror image of the Vitalina we saw on the stormy Cova da Moura rooftop. When we asked Costa about this shot, he told us that one could regard it as the past or the present; for him, its chief importance is to lighten the atmosphere by casting Vitalina's real-life children as the young couple.[32]

Notes

1. Jonathan Romney, "Film of the Week: Horse Money," *Film Comment* (blog), July 16, 2015, https://www.filmcomment.com/blog/film-of-the-week-horse-money/.
2. C. K. Stead, *The New Poetic* (New York: Harper Torchbooks, 1966), 151.

3. Jonathan Rosenbaum, "Pedro Costa's *Horse Money*," *Art Forum* 53, no. 10 (Summer 2015), www.artforum.com/print/201506/pedro-costa-s-horse-money-52252.

4. Neil Bahadur, "Interview: Pedro Costa," *Film Comment* (blog), July 22, 2015, https://www.filmcomment.com/blog/interview-pedro-costa/.

5. See Nuno Barradas Jorge, *Refocus: The Films of Pedro Costa* (Edinburgh: University of Edinburgh Press, 2021), 130.

6. Pedro Costa, *Film at Lincoln Center Podcast*, episode 41, "#41—Pedro Costa," Film Society of Lincoln Center, 2015, https://soundcloud.com/filmlinc/41-pedro-costa?utm_source=www.filmlinc.org&utm_campaign=wtshare&utm_medium=widget&utm_content=https%253A%252F%252Fsoundcloud.com%252Ffilmlinc%252F41-pedro-costa.

7. Costa, "#41—Pedro Costa."

8. Aaron Cutler, "*Horse Money*: An Interview," *Cineaste* XL, no. 3 (Summer 2015), https://www.cineaste.com/summer2015/horse-money-pedro-costa-aaron cutler.

9. For more about the disquiet after the revolution, see Raquel Varela and Joana Alcântara, "Social Conflicts in the Portuguese Revolution, 1974–1975," *Labour / Le travail* 74 (Fall 2014): 151–77.

10. Costa, "#41—Pedro Costa."

11. Cutler, "*Horse Money*."

12. Pedro Costa, "The Mystery of the Great Pyramid," trans. Ricardo Matos Cabo and Andy Rector, *Film Comment* (blog), July 15, 2016, https://www.filmcomment.com/blog/the-mystery-of-the-great-pyramid/.

13. Costa, "#41—Pedro Costa."

14. Rosenbaum, "Pedro Costa's *Horse Money*."

15. A military officer, António de Spínola helped Portugal transition to a democracy and was president of the republic from May to September in 1974, when he resigned.

16. Michael Guarneri, "Pedro Costa," *Bomb* 133 (September 1, 2015): 33.

17. Daniel Kasman, "Cinema Must Be a Ritual: Pedro Costa Discusses 'Vitalina Varela,'" *Notebook*, February 19, 2020, https://mubi.com/notebook/posts/cinema-must-be-a-ritual-pedro-costa-discusses-vitalina-varela?fbclid=IwAR3L1qWB2eVU_XHyH1zgwKe17QqoWtxbeYBHZ1U164S4eerdIX4G4Qr0OK4.

18. Pedro Costa, "A Conversation with Pedro Costa," Toronto Film Festival, September 2019, *Vitalina Varela*, DVD (New York: Grasshopper).

19. Costa, "A Conversation with Pedro Costa."

20. Quoted in Thomas Austin, "Bigger Than Life, or Stranger: Pedro Costa's *Vitalina Varela*: Part I," *Senses of Cinema* 100 (January 2022), https://www.sensesofcinema.com/2022/feature-articles/bigger-than-life-or-stranger-pedro-costas-vitalina-varela-part-i/.

21. Quoted in Haden Guest and Mark Peranson, "I See a Darkness: Pedro Costa on *Vitalina Varela*," *Cinema Scope* 80 (September 20, 2019), https://cinema-scope.com/cinema-scope-magazine/i-see-a-darkness-pedro-costa-on-vitalina-varela/.

22. See Michael Guarneri, "Pedro Costa," *Débordements*, November 11, 2019, https://www.debordements.fr/Pedro-Costa-2019.

23. Kasman, "Cinema Must Be a Ritual." https://mubi.com/notebook/posts/cinema-must-be-a-ritual-pedro-costa-discusses-vitalina-varela?fbclid=IwAR3L1qWB2eVU_XHyH1zgwKe17Qq0WtxbeYBHZ1U164S4eerdIX4G4Qr0OK4.

24. See Thomas Austin, "Bigger Than Life, or Stranger: Pedro Costa's *Vitalina Varela*: Part III," *Senses of Cinema* 102 (July 2022), https://mubi.com/notebook/posts/cinema-must-be-a-ritual-pedro-costa-discusses-vitalina-varela?fbclid=IwAR3L1qWB2eVU_XHyH1zgwKe17Qq0WtxbeYBHZ1U164S4eerdIX4G4Qr0OK4.

25. Guarneri, "Pedro Costa," *Débordements*.

26. Guest and Peranson, "I See a Darkness."

27. Lesley Stern, "Paths That Wind through the Thickets of Things," *Critical Inquiry* 28, no. 1 (2001): 324.

28. Quoted in Austin, "Bigger Than Life: Part III."

29. Quoted in Jordan Cronk, "House of the Spirits," *Film Comment*, January–February 2020, https://www.filmcomment.com/article/house-of-the-spirits-pedro-costa-interview-vitalina-varela/.

30. Quoted in Austin, "Bigger Than Life: Part III."

31. Chris Fujiwara, "Mikio Naruse: The Other Woman and the View from Outside," *Film Comment*, September–October 2005, https://www.filmcomment.com/article/mikio-naruse-the-other-women-and-the-view-from-the-outside/.

32. From our conversations with Pedro Costa in Lisbon in March 2024.

PART IV

Documentaries

Où gît votre sourire enfoui? (*Where Does Your Hidden Smile Lie?*, 2001)

Costa has often described *Where Does Your Hidden Smile Lie?* as his only love story and his only comedy—it is a love story because it pays tribute to the fifty-year marriage and creative partnership between filmmakers Jean-Marie Straub (1933–2022) and Danièle Huillet (1936–2006) and a comedy because it is filled with amusing moments of wisecracking and bickering between the two while they work at reediting a new version of their black-and-white film *Sicilia!* (1999), originally premiered at Cannes.

Costa's documentary was made during an interlude while he was editing *In Vanda's Room*, and it takes its title from a piece of German graffiti—*Wo liegt euer Lächeln begraben?*—used in the Straub and Huillet film *From Today until Tomorrow* (1997). Commissioned by the French ARTE TV series *Cineastes de notre temps* (Filmmakers of our time), the 103-minute documentary was shot mostly in the editing room at Le Fresnoy, home of a unit headed by Thierry Lounas at the National Studio for Contemporary Arts in northern France. "At first," Lounas said, "the Straubs did not want to do Costa's film," stating,

> They didn't want an official document . . . [and were concerned because] it seemed more lucrative for the television channel ARTE to produce a film about them than to support or buy their own films. Finally, the smallness of the editing room at Le Fresnoy created a problem for a film crew, even one reduced. I think there were two things that eased their minds: the reading of a review by Emmanuel Burdeau about the filming of *No Quarto da*

> *Vanda* with a small digital camera, and the fact that Jacques Rivette, whom the Straubs admired, very much liked Pedro Costa's films, which they, the Straubs, still did not know.[1]

Before discussing Costa's film, a brief commentary on Straub and Huillet is in order because their unique career and their film *Sicilia!* may be little known to readers. The two met at film school in Paris during a period when Straub had begun working as an assistant to directors Jacques Rivette, Jean Renoir, and Robert Bresson. Huillet had planned to be an ethnographic filmmaker, but when the Algerian War broke out, she moved with Straub to Germany so he could escape the draft. Their early films were made there, including their most successful full-length production, the remarkable musical *Chronicle of Anna Magdalena Bach* (1968), which features harpsichordist Gustave Leonhardt as Bach and Christine Lang as his second wife, Anna Magdalena. Its plot consists of chronological excerpts of Bach's music played by musicians in eighteenth-century costume, using eighteenth-century instruments. The performances are linked by a fictional diary read by Anna. Straub insisted on using direct sound recording, which, among other things, caused problems with backers. It took ten years to produce the film through what would today be described as crowdfunding. (Some of the funds came from Jean-Luc Godard.) Against all expectations, it was an art-house hit and firmly established Straub and Huillet's reputation.

Straub and Huillet's other films, made in Germany, Italy, and France, were adaptations of a sort, drawing on sources as various as Arnold Schoenberg, Friedrich Engels, Franz Kafka, Bertolt Brecht, Henrich Böll, Wassily Kandinsky, and Marguerite Duras. Straub, the more vocal of the pair, is often described as the director, but Huillet was a full creative partner: she produced, edited, and helped with writing, coaching actors, choosing locations, and creating costumes and designs while he was in charge of the *mise en scène*.

Their collaboration resulted from both love and politics. Straub and Huillet could be described as radical socialists, or perhaps as Marxists of an unusual kind, interested in older forms of collective society. When they were presented with a career award at the 2006 Venice Film Festival, they refused to attend the ceremony, and Straub caused a sensation by submitting a letter claiming that he supported terrorism against US capitalist imperialism. (Cameron Crowe, who was on the awards committee, tried unsuccessfully to have the award withdrawn.)

Publicity arising from the event did not help them with film distributors, and an additional barrier to appreciation of their work arose because they were closely studied by proponents of High Theory when France's *Cahiers du Cinéma* and Britain's *Screen* took a leftward turn. The Althusserian-Lacanian arguments of those and other journals attacked all forms of "illusionist" cinema: the Renaissance perspective of the camera, the "invisible" form of continuity editing, the conventions of realist acting, and even narrative itself, all supposedly designed to "interpellate" viewers as subjects of bourgeois ideology. Straub and Huillet appeared to suit the theorists' agenda perfectly. They were avowedly Brechtian and socialist, employed an unorthodox acting and editing style, and drew from left-wing and modernist sources. Theorists, however, seemed to ignore the fact that one of Straub's favorite filmmakers was the "illusionist" John Ford. They alienated potential viewers of Straub and Huillet, praising the films but making them seem doctrinaire, abstruse, and lacking in pleasure.

The best refutation of 1970s High Theory when applied to Straub and Huillet is a chapter on their *History Lessons* (1972) in Gilberto Perez's brilliant book *The Material Ghost*. The film is derived from an unfinished novel by Brecht and concerns a modern-day citizen of Rome who interviews different classes of ancient Romans, all dressed in the garb of their period. One of its aims is to show the persistence of the past in the present, and its costuming creates an "alienation effect." It nevertheless remains an engaging narrative. Perez reminds us that Brecht's "epic theater" was derived from Aristotle's use of the term *epic* to mean narrative rather than lyric or dramatic art. Brecht's general aim, Perez says, was to "show enough . . . for the spectator to see that art is work, not magic, but not show so much that the illusion of art breaks down altogether. How much to show in each case—enough to reveal the workings of art but not so much as to keep art from working—is the technique of the alienation effect. Lacanian-Althusserian theory fails to grasp this. . . . [I]t can only throw the baby out with the bath water."[2]

Costa has described Straub as "my master" and said that he especially admires the early Straub-Huillet picture *Not Reconciled: Only Violence Helps Where Violence Reigns* (1965), based on Henrich Böll's novel *Billiards at Half-Past Nine*. (The picture's subtitle comes from Brecht.) Costa has pointed out that the importance of the film lies in the way it shows how "something about the past should be something about the present."[3] Like *History Lessons* (1972) and *Sicilia!*, *Not Reconciled* is structured by a character who has conversations about the past with a variety of citizens—in this case, Germans in post–World War II Cologne. Using a complex arrangement of flashbacks, it deals with the way some Germans tried to repress the past even though it remained in the present.

Costa himself is clearly interested in the persistence of the past in the present, especially in *Horse Money*, which owes something to *Not Reconciled*. But his allegiance to Straub and Huillet also relates to their production methods. Like Costa, Straub and Huillet used minimal crews and equipment, rejecting the norms of the industry. They knew it is much easier to maintain artistic integrity by avoiding big-money producers, heavy mechanical apparatus, sets, drivers, caterers, and an army of production and postproduction workers. Their early films were shot on 16mm, and throughout their career they used small crews and mostly nonprofessional actors.

But no one would confuse the work of Straub and Huillet with that of Costa. Straub and Huillet used literary sources, insisted on direct sound, tended to work with particular technical experts (Renato Berta for camera and Louis Hochet for sound), and followed Brecht's rule that actors should speak as if quoting or reading lines. They occasionally used what came to be known as the *Straub shot*—a shot of long duration that conveys relatively little narrative information. In *Sicilia!*, for example, the camera lingers for a long time on a sign reading "CATANIA" at an empty railroad crossing. The city of Catania, the chief setting for the film, is the second largest in Sicily and an important cultural and industrial center in a picturesque setting near the volcanic Mount Etna. Straub and Huillet show us relatively little of Catania other than the railroad sign and a couple of nondescript shots out a train window. Later, in another Straub shot, the camera executes a long, slow, 180-degree pan across the empty landscape outside the city, showing distant vineyards and a few buildings on the horizon, followed by an equally slow pan back to the point where it began.

Sicilia! is loosely based on the much-admired Italian novelist Elio Vittorini's anti-fascist *Conversations in Sicily*, serialized and censored by the Italians in the late 1930s and first published in English translation in 1941. (One of its admirers was Ernest Hemingway, who wrote a foreword.) The novel concerns a young Italian who may or may not be living in New York, who receives a letter from his father and returns to visit his birthplace. During his journey, he converses with many people, including a poor man who sells oranges; a prosperous but unhappy landowner; a fascist policeman or enforcer; his mother, who takes him on a tour of the impoverished local populace; and an itinerant knife grinder who celebrates the dream of communal friendship. Much of the novel is ambiguous or dreamlike. Straub and Huillet strip it down to conversations with five characters, eliminate the father and his letter, and change some of the relationships.

In Costa's film about Straub and Huillet, we see bits of *Sicilia!* as Huillet edits a 35mm print on what appears to be a flatbed Steenbeck editing table with a large viewing screen. This kind of editing has been replaced in the digital age, but the aesthetics of editing remain the same. As Godard and others have remarked, Costa's film is the best picture ever made about the art of editing.

Huillet works from both standing and seated positions; we see Straub from a nearby open doorway leading to an outer hallway, usually with a small cigar in his mouth, pacing around, sometimes framed by the door à la Costa or Ford. He often enters the editing room, making pronouncements about cinema and kibitzing about the editing process. They speak French to one another, and the film they are working on is in Italian. She wears a sweater, her dark hair gathered in a ponytail; he wears a rumpled suit redolent of a proletarian intellectual. It may seem that he is obsessively (though quite interestingly) talkative, but many of his speeches are aimed at students observing from the back of the room. There would be no film without his talk, only the quiet work of Huillet at the editing table. He says many useful things about cinema, and some of the banter between him and Huillet has been compared to the comic battle between Tracy and Hepburn in *Adam's Rib* (1949).

Where Does Your Hidden Smile Lie? is another of Costa's films about a room. It begins with a wide-angle, establishing shot at a low level, with Huillet working in the light given off by a desk lamp and the bright silver of the editing screen. At the open door and hallway to her right, Straub wanders in and out, sometimes silhouetted, often standing in a pale, blue-gray light.

According to Thierry Lounas, "Filming began with a small crew: Pedro Costa with the small Panasonic camera he has used in *No Quarto da Vanda*, Jeanne Lapoirie with another digital camera, and finally the sound director Matthieu Imbert. The room is not large and the students occupy most of it. Costa decided to place himself behind [Huillet] while the other camera was placed . . . closer to the door so as not to disturb the students."[4]

Critic Patrick Tarrant has remarked that *Where Does Your Hidden Smile Lie?* creates a mise en abyme of montage, a film "made by a filmmaker editing filmmakers editing a film they have edited before."[5] We sometimes cut to an over-the-shoulder shot of Huillet as she works, and on one occasion we view her in profile while Straub takes a chair at her side and slightly behind to chat with her. There are a couple of shots of young men in the projection booth examining strips of 35mm film to be shown in a nearby auditorium. More often, we cut to Huillet's editing screen, where we see full-size excerpts from *Sicilia!* and hear conversation about it between Straub and Huillet. We also

Huillet and Straub prepare to work

occasionally see the couple in the shadowy theater where their films are being screened. They talk about their work in these scenes, but no audience is visible.

In an interview conducted by Thom Andersen, who once acted for Straub and Huillet, Costa explains that the editing room "was more or less a set, because we took out a lot of things. The students were right behind the camera. We changed the room a little bit." He also explains that Straub and Huillet's job at the time—artists in residence who gave lectures for students—was a means by which they could help support themselves: "They have this plan B, this escape plan, which is going to this school and in exchange for talking like this, about editing, about cinema, they can edit the films and they are given a print. One print." On day one, Costa says, "there were thirty students and on the last day there were three, one girl and two boys. And that's very sad because it's like a screening of one of their films. Everybody leaves."[6]

Costa tells Andersen, "I wanted to destroy a little bit . . . this common cliché, that Straub is intellectual, hermetic, or Communist, Marxist, Maoist, terrorist. . . . It's like saying, don't go see that. It creates indifference. . . . For them cinema is not disconnected: it has to do with a way of behaving every day." Andersen agrees, and has a memory of working with them: "[At the end of work everybody left for the day], all the actors and the whole crew, but they

At the editing table

stayed behind to clean up: they actually got down on their hands and knees and swabbed the floor of the location so the place would be left the way they found it. . . . They were doing the work that on any other movie would be done by the lowliest members of the crew."[7]

In Costa's film, we repeatedly see close views of shots or sequences from *Sicilia!* on the editing screen, where Huillet starts at the beginning of the film and goes through it scene by scene. There are just enough of these shots to give us a condensed version of the film and a sense of its aesthetics and politics. The opening shots involve a conversation with a seller of oranges; a close-up of him produces a testy but amusing exchange between Straub and Huillet about where the shot should begin. The editing involves fastidious, miniscule care with details that seldom concern ordinary filmmakers. When Straub complains about the way the performer pronounces an "n" in the phrase "non se ven dono" (don't sell yourself), Huillet asks, "Do you want my seat?" "No way," Straub says, but he keeps talking as Huillet works:

> STRAUB: It's . . .
> HUILLET: Shut up.
> STRAUB: He already has his mouth open.
> HUILLET: Better that way, just this once.

> STRAUB: You're serving stones in gravy. . . . It's where to cut. I don't trust . . .
> HUILLET: Fasten your seatbelt. It's better like this.
> STRAUB: A one frame difference. Don't spend one hundred years.
> HUILLET: I only need seventy.

The scene with the orange seller (Carmelo Maddio) was derived from Vittorini's novel but also inspired by a moment when Straub and Huillet were scouting locations for the film and found a huge number of oranges dumped in a river. In Brechtian fashion, Maddio speaks his lines as if reading rather than acting; he shouts the words like an orator at a public meeting, even though the leading character (Gianni Buscarino), a dark figure seen mostly from the back, is seated nearby on a quay, facing the water. Buscarino says he has been living in New York, where there are problems with employment. The orange seller says there are problems in Italy, too. His boss gives him oranges in lieu of wages for his labor, and he cannot sell the "accursed oranges" because there is a lack of olive oil and bread. A poor woman sits near him on the pavement, and when he offers her a free orange, she rejects it.

At this point, we cut to a disorienting shot of young men in the projection booth and hear Straub recalling an anecdote from Luis Buñuel's autobiography. Another cut takes us to the almost empty auditorium, where Straub enters and continues his speech while Huillet sits on the stage. He explains that when Buñuel first arrived in Hollywood for a brief career, he had dinner with Nicholas Ray. Ray said that when he first came to Hollywood, he was told that the only path to success in the industry was to make sure your second picture cost more than your first; in that way, there would be proper career "development." Straub and Huillet's films were of course made for a pittance, and Straub says the story about Ray is the worst thing he has ever heard about movies.

Back in the editing room, where Huillet is still working on the minute problem of an actor's mouth pronouncing the letter "n," Straub launches into a lecture as if talking to himself.

"You cannot expect form before the idea," he says. We cut to an empty white screen on the editing table:

> Things don't exist until they have found a rhythm, a form. In Aquinas, the form of the body gives birth to the soul. When someone says, "the form, the form, never mind the idea," it's a sellout. . . . First there is the idea, then the matter, then the form . . . That's what Eisenstein had when he organized his sequences. You can't [just] cut anywhere between [the matter]. I already

> explained that before coming into this joint. . . . The struggle with the matter gives rise to the form. . . . These are people who have no morals.

At this point on the editing screen, we see the Straub shot of the CATANIA sign near a railroad track. "Are you done?" Huillet says, "Are you calmed down?" Straub replies, "I'm always calm."

On the editing screen, we now see Buscarino has boarded a train to his former hometown and is having conversations with people sitting across from him in the train compartment. A large close-up shows a middle-aged man (Giovani Interlandi) who, despite being a prosperous landowner with two lovely daughters, is unhappy with his life: "I would give all that I own to feel more at peace with other men, as one who has nothing to cause self-reproach." A reverse shot gives a close-up of Buscarino, who asks, "Are you a professor?" The landowner replies that he believes in old values: "I am not a professor. I can read a book if I want to. I was with the Salesians as a child." (The Salesians were an Italian religious order noted for their culture and good works.)

The landowner suddenly complains of a "stink" and leaves as a fascist cop (Ignazio Trombello) enters the compartment. Another of Buscarino's traveling companions also exits because he senses that this newly arrived, mustachioed fellow belongs to the police and is disguising it. The fascist sits rigidly on his seat with his head thrown back, his hands on his knees, his mustache and large dark eyes giving him a pompous, theatrical quality. Crossing his legs, he holds his knee and says, "I was concerned about my luggage. You never know with these nasty fellows going around. I am an employee with the land registry."

Huillet stops the film and says, "Sound is better in the second shot. I thought it wouldn't work when we shot. It's better because one can feel the high frequencies of the train. I thought when shooting that we'd never edit with this shot. Even Durant [the sound man] said we should edit with a train track to blend with everything like a sauce." "The soup!" Straub says, and we cut to him as he paces around the small room. He is talking about the common practice of creating separate tracks of either ambient sound or nondiegetic music to seamlessly join shots: "There are lots of masterpieces in the cinema which hold together because of the soup—musical soup or sound soup. Nevertheless, we are restricted. If there's no music or soup, you need greater precision." This reminds him of a scene in Jacques Tati's *Mon Oncle* (1958), in which a laboring man is painting a stripe down the middle of a highway when a big Buick shoots past him ("I don't know much about cars," Straub says, "but

A fascist cop

it's a Buick!"). The laborer waves his paintbrush at the car and yells, "Would you like a little more?"

On the editing screen, the conversation with the fascist policeman resumes, and we again become aware of the Brechtian effect of the performances. Buscarino, subtly aware that he is speaking to a liar, compliments the policeman on his baritone voice and asks if he has ever been a singer. The policeman retains his posture but tosses his head back further, swelling with pride, recalling times when he has sung, speaking his lines almost operatically. The image freezes, and we hear Straub: "Some people have the impression that because we reject verisimilitude and TV-style cinema—even Woody Allen, Cassavetes, et cetera—that there is no psychology in our films. All this is psychology. There is no psychology in terms of the actor because there is a dramatic abstraction that goes deeper."

The image resumes, and we cut to Buscarino, who says, "Oh really?" The image stops, and we hear Straub. The issue at stake here is on what frame to cut from Buscarino to a reverse angle of the fascist. Straub says, "His reaction is 'Liar, I don't believe you,' and then he smiles to himself." Some viewers may think this point is trivial, but as Patrick Tarrant notes, Straub wants Buscarino's perception of a lie to be noticed so that the cut will make it "pass over" to the fascist, who does not seem to recognize it.[8] Straub argues that "in between the shots . . . it is extremely subtle psychology." This leads to another testy exchange:

> HUILLET: There's a smile lighting up his eyes.
> STRAUB: It would be better if we could keep it.
> HUILLET: Not easy.
> STRAUB: Go back to the clap. There.
> HUILLET: Don't start "There-ing" me. Because you keep interrupting me it keeps fucking up. You still don't have the discipline.
> STRAUB (humbly): I have something to say but I'll wait for your permission. [Pause.] I'll say it anyway.
> HUILLET: Spit it out.
> STRAUB: I don't want him to say "Gia" immediately. I don't want it to be an enthusiastic gesture.
> HUILLET: Tough luck. It works perfectly. When you see a continuity error in a good film, it's amusing.
> STRAUB: You can't turn your actors into statues . . . even if we have precisely defined positions, which they discover for themselves. [He pauses and looks at the edit.] I'm afraid you've won.
> HUILLET: Men!

We briefly go to the shadowy auditorium, where Straub and Huillet seem to be addressing students. "Peasants have no history," Straub says. "Workers have no history either. Charles Péguy, he said, 'Making a revolution also means reinstating old things.' Very old but forgotten. The myth, the unwritten story. That is the history of the peasants. Pavese also means a lot to us because he was an intellectual, an Italian petit bourgeois who didn't indulge in his own complacencies." These two writers have indirect importance for *Sicilia!* and for Straub and Huillet more generally. Charles Péguy, a late nineteenth-century French Dreyfusard, poet, and essayist, combined socialism with Christianity; Cesare Pavese, one of the most important Italian writers of the twentieth century, was a communist, poet, and novelist who also translated many English-language authors.

Back in the editing room, Huillet works on the crucial scene in which Buscarino visits his mother (Angela Nugara) in Catania, a meeting we watch on the editing screen. As the mother greets Buscarino with a formal embrace outside her doorway, the image freezes for a moment, and we see Huillet's finger pointing at something: "Did you see that? A butterfly." The mother then invites Buscarino into the house, which her father built with his own hands and where she has been living since Buscarino's father left with another woman. She cooks him a herring over an open fire, placing it on a small dining table, and they sit across from one another, their postures stiff and unchanging.

The postures and gestures in Straub and Huillet are always as Brechtian as the speeches: Buscarino has an elbow cocked and one hand on the table, and the mother is almost formally erect but with one arm bent. On the editing screen, *Sicilia!* cuts back and forth between them, keeping both in profile. The mother begins talking about her father, and we hear Straub saying that there were fourteen takes of the shot. We then cut briefly to the auditorium, where he talks about working with nonprofessional actors: "Actors had to work beginning at 5 or 6 a.m. We worked to get them interested . . . and develop trust. Straub meant nothing to them. We're not in the papers."

We do not see all of the revelatory scene with the mother, in which she talks about Buscarino's father and her own sexual history, but we do see a moment when a kind of quarrel breaks out. The mother reminisces about her father, who was not only a laborer and a socialist but also a great horseman who led religious parades in beautiful regalia. Buscarino is irritated because he thinks it is impossible to be both Catholic and socialist. We hear Straub expressing annoyance when Buscarino says *causa* (cause) because he is putting emphasis on the wrong word. The mother is insistent that there were no contradictions in her father's beliefs. She rises and goes to a window, looking out and recalling the splendid parades of long ago. Critic Richard Brody has eloquently described a quality of speech here and elsewhere in *Sicilia!*: "The dialogue is less spoken than declaimed; it's nearly sung." Moreover, he adds, Straub and Huillet's "images are a sort of visual music that sets the dialogue like a libretto and renders the performances operatic."[9] Not surprisingly, Straub and Huillet once made an impressive film based on Arnold Schoenberg's opera *Moses and Aaron* (1975). This scene is almost like a duo that breaks into an aria.

The mother is seen from the back as she looks out the window, the mountain scenery outside barely suggested. Straub recalls that he and Huillet once made scenes involving Mount Etna and Mont Sainte-Victoire: "One fine day you realize it's best to show as little as possible . . . and you realize it says more." The mother returns to the table and presents Buscarino with a fresh melon, which he savors as if recalling his childhood. The film stops on a shot of Buscarino, and Straub comments again: "This is the way everyone should be editing.

It is what I call part of cinematic rhetoric. . . . This is what Chaplin saw, without a Movieola. He'd use his bare eyes! He sees an open eyelid, a closed eyelid." He points his finger at the screen, indicating Buscarino's eye: "Movement is here." In a wide shot of the editing room, Straub's ever-present cigar makes him cough a bit, and he recalls something an actor said when Huillet complained about the cigar: "Every time you said I had been coughing for forty years, he would say, 'Well, the day he stops, that'll be the end of him.' I'll just have to go on." Huillet wryly replies, "Mercy on the rest of us."

Straub wants the next shot of Buscarino to start with the actor moving: "He moves like Bresson wanted actors to move . . . unconscious, mechanical gestures. . . . He has that meditative look." He recalls that one of the actors in *The Death of Empedocles* (1986) said to him, "One should recite verse while respecting it as verse. . . . He meant not linking every verse. In our films meter is meter and verse is verse. He realized that it had to be practiced, not done spontaneously." We cut to the auditorium, where Straub is talking to the unseen students about *Death of Empedocles* and its "old, precise kind of communist message." The screen goes dark; we hear a bit of violin while Straub says, "There are those who stick closely to reality but don't put their imagination there. . . . And there are those who distort reality for the sake of their so-called imagination. No patience. Genius is great patience. If you have patience it will be charged with contradiction."

Cut back to the screen at the editing table, where Straub complains because the actor moves too quickly after the clapper has signaled the beginning of a shot: "That's one of the most difficult things with actors, professional or not." On the editing screen, we see a shot of Buscarino and a barely visible palm tree frond waving in the wind at the top right of the screen. Huillet is annoyed by its appearance. The next shot shows Buscarino and a knife grinder (Vittorio Vigneri) at eye level, standing near the steps of a public building with the tree's fronds more prominent on the side. Straub says that the problem with a large crew is that one of the workers would undoubtedly have cut the palm fronds or tied them off. He also explains that the sequence "must be shot at level because it's about two characters who meet and are mistrustful but become brotherly. They're at the edge of an invisible abyss." As the friendship develops, Huillet worries because she can hear a car door out on the street slamming shut. She and Straub decide to leave it.

Huillet pauses on a different shot of the knife grinder, dressed in a shabby hat and plaid shirt. "Can I just point out," Straub's voice says as his finger points at the screen, "that it's my hat? I gave it to him. . . . I had to give him

Pointing at the shirt

that shirt and the trousers, too. I found that shirt in the rubbish in Rome." He compliments the Romans on laundering and wrapping the clothes they toss aside, but Huillet corrects him: "You're mixing up shirts. I bought that shirt. I didn't buy it, I stole it . . . from a supermarket in Rome. . . . The one you found had a cigarette burn in it."

In the auditorium, Straub talks about the problems he and Huillet had raising money for *Chronicle of Anna Magdalena Bach*. His original producers wanted the film to star Austrian conductor Herbert von Karajan or perhaps even movie star Curt Jurgens—ideas he felt were preposterous. He reads a bit from *Conversations in Sicily*, and we hear music from the Bach film. Back in the editing room, Straub says, "An artist is forever young"; he recalls for his unseen audience how he and Huillet met at film school (where he claims he was kicked out because he knew too much about Hitchcock). At some point he saw her from a distance in a lecture hall: "We weren't sitting that close to each other. . . . I was just watching her. . . . They must have noticed that I had fallen madly in love." He exits the room, and we cut to the closed red door of the auditorium, where Straub and Huillet peek through the door's two round windows to watch a film being screened. She goes up a stairway to exit, and he sits on the bottom step. The film ends as he puts his head in his hand, toys with a lighter, and waits patiently but wearily, moving his fingers to music.

In Thom Andersen's interview with Costa, Andersen says that he finds this ending sad. Costa disagrees: "This is not a sad movie, I think." Huillet had died before its release, but "I would hope that Jean-Marie sees the film on the screen and agrees with me that it's really, really close to what the Brecht guy would want."[10] As critic João Bénard da Costa has written, Costa conceived the film not only as a romance but also "as an 'ars poetica' and a reflection about what cinema means to the Straubs and himself."[11]

Costa's short film *6 Bagatelles* (2001) makes a nice addendum or footnote to *Where Does Your Hidden Smile Lie?* The eighteen-minute film is composed of six segments omitted from the longer film, each marked off by several seconds of black or white screen. A violin concerto by Webern is occasionally heard on the soundtrack. In the longest of two segments that directly concern editing, Huillet is editing a conversation between Buscarino and the mother. Straub remarks that he never says "action" and "cut" at the beginning and ending of a shot; he simply says "please" at the start and "thank you" when the actor stops. The second editing segment shows Huillet working as Straub tells her that the weather outside is nice. "A fat lot of good that does me shut up in here," she says.

The remaining segments are chiefly interesting for what they indicate about Straub and Huillet's politics. In one of them, Straub recalls a statement by Kafka that he thinks is from Kafka's diaries. He and Huillet made a film entitled *Klassenverhältnisse* (*Class Relations*, 1984) based on Kafka's unfinished novel *Amerika*, and one assumes they know a good deal about his work. Straub nevertheless claims he is no Kafka expert; he can only recall that Kafka once said something like, "In a contest between the individual and the world, bet on the world." Straub argues that commentators have misunderstood the statement, reading it as an expression of cynicism or despair over a system that always wins. It actually says, he tells us, that the individual needs the world and should commit or "bet" on becoming part of it.

The final segment of *6 Bagatelles* was shot outdoors on what seems a pleasant spring or summer day—a vivid relief from the dark editing room and shadowy auditorium where Straub and Huillet have been working. She sits at a picnic table, sewing a garment, while he leans back in a chair with a leg propped on the table and the ever-present cigar in his mouth. They are in conversation with people off-screen, one of whom is Thierry Lounas, who says something we cannot hear, prompting Straub to comment on socialism. Straub is critical of modern socialist states that promise utopia but ask for increasing sacrifice, regimentation, and conformism in the name of progress. Instead, he seems to prefer the "old, precise kind of communism" he spoke about in describing *Death of Empedocles* and in his recollection of Charles Péguy's idea that "making a revolution also means reinstating old things." Though he does not say so, his attitude has something in common with Walter Benjamin and Theodor Adorno, who were in different ways critics of instrumental rationality, whether in capitalist, national socialist, or communist states. (Benjamin's "angel of history," with its back to the future as it oversees wreckage, is perhaps relevant.)

At this point, Huillet finishes her sewing and rises. They prepare to leave and have a small domestic disagreement about their laundry, which has been left hanging out to dry on a clothesline. He thinks it might rain, and she says she is tired of dealing with the laundry; if it rains, the laundry can stay where it is and will eventually dry. They exit the shot, still bickering, and we hear a soft sound of distant thunder, probably added in postproduction. Straub and Huillet may be smiling, but if so, their smiles are hidden.

Ne change rien (*Change Nothing*, 2009)

Developed intermittently over a five-year period when he was also working on *Colossal Youth* and *Horse Money*, Costa's *Change Nothing* documents the performances, rehearsals, recording sessions, and voice training of French actress and chanteuse Jeanne Balibar, who, for much of the film, is accompanied by guitarist and composer Rodolphe Burger and two other musicians. (A short version, exhibited in 2005, showed some of its material and later became part of the complete film. Other footage was made into short films with the titles *A Safe Place*, *Tour du monde*, and *Les petits papiers*.) An outgrowth of Costa's youthful experience as a guitarist with long-standing interest in music, *Change Nothing* has been compared to Godard's Rolling Stones picture *One Plus One / Sympathy for the Devil* (1968) and Straub and Huillet's *Chronicle of Anna Magdalena Bach*. In our view, it more properly belongs in company with Costa's own *Where Does Your Hidden Smile Lie?*, which, as we have said, is the most instructive film ever made about the art of movie editing. Though entertaining and less didactic, *Change Nothing* is a companion because its chief subject is the meticulous work involved in artistic creation—in this case, of both recording and performing music.

Born in Paris, the multitalented Balibar is daughter of physicist Françoise Balibar and Marxist philosopher Étienne Balibar. As a girl, she wanted to be a dancer, and she retains the lithe body and expressive movement of someone with dance training. She became a singer and award-winning stage and screen actor with memorable performances in many excellent films, among them Jacques Rivette's *The Duchess of Langeais* (2007), Pawlet Pawlikoski's *Cold War* (2018), Apichatpong Weerasethakul's *Memoria* (2021), Xavier Giannoli's *Lost Illusions* (2021), and Olivier Assayas's miniseries *Irma Vep* (2022). In addition to acting, she is also a director/screenwriter for *Electra, for Instance* (2013) and *Wonders in the Suburbs* (2020).

Her colleague in this film, Rodolphe Burger, began as a professor of philosophy but turned to music, specializing in a vanguard style sometimes called techno-pop, with links to rock, blues, and jazz. Among his albums are *Par-amour* (2003) and *Slalom dame* (*Lady Slalom*, 2006), both produced with Balibar, who wrote many of the songs. Balibar has said of Burger, "His music is obstinate, stubborn, heady. . . . Rodolphe cannot be put into any musical category that exists today. He is a courageous guitarist."[12] Her own singing when she is working with Burger has been described by Dennis Lim as a "blend of poise and vulnerability. . . . Her sultry voice has a pearly ring to it but it's also a bit unsteady, and as a screen star in a world of pros she gives off a hint of diffidence."[13]

In a 2009 interview with James Hansen, Costa explained that he first met Balibar on the jury for a film festival in Marseilles:

> We spent all our time together . . . we immediately knew we shared more or less the same opinions. And, of course, I admired her as an actress. She's probably the European actress that I admire the most. During the festival, she told me she was going to record an album of songs she had composed with friends. She told me that she was getting a bit disappointed with film. . . . She asked me if I would do a music video for one of the songs. I never did the video but I didn't want to disappoint her. I came to see a concert she did in Paris and I liked it very much. I liked the music, I liked her voice. . . . I came to the next concert with a friend, Philippe Morel, who did the sound on the film, and I brought a small DV camera . . . one thing led to another. I came to see her rehearse and then by chance one of my films was opening in Tokyo and she was doing a concert in Japan at the same time. So, I organized some cameras very quickly, and that was it.[14]

In his liner notes for the DVD of the film, Costa adds: "I believe that as soon as [they] start looking, rehearsing, these musicians become characters in a work of fiction. . . . It's true that I like to look and discreetly be next to those who, like me, are looking for something . . . a tone or chord for Jeanne."[15]

The completed one-hundred-minute film, edited with Patrícia Saramago and supported by OPTEC Filmes in Portugal, Tokyo-based Cinematrix, and French Red Star Cinema, used multiple DV cameras and cost roughly 100,000 euros ($150,000). Locations included an attic space in the village of Sainte-Marie-aux-Mines in northeastern France and a café in Tokyo. Costa shot more than eighty hours of footage and shaped the feature in postproduction. Though he had many cameras, he opted as usual for long takes without camera movement, several from a low-angle, audience view, plus lengthy telephoto close-ups of Balibar singing. "There never was a music film that really inspired me," he told Hansen. "I had references, though: Godard and [Robert] Frank with the Rolling Stones, Warhol, and then some plain classical filming of two or three operas. . . . I thought perhaps we could do something a bit different about music, not the usual concert film or the usual documentary."[16]

The result is indeed unusual: no interviews, no biographies of the artists, and more emphasis on preparation and looks between musicians than performance. Dennis Lim has said of *Change Nothing* that "more than a music film, . . . it's a film that's musical in form."[17] Some have questioned whether it should be called a documentary, because it abandons the normal trappings of the form and has an elliptical, studied, stylized beauty.[18] Viewers of Costa's Fontaínhas trilogy have also argued over the documentary/fiction distinction, and at least one critic, Haden R. Guest, has described both the Fontaínhas trilogy and *Change Nothing* as "post-documentary"—a term, we confess, that baffles us.[19] Costa himself has hedged over how this film should be categorized. "There are so many people thinking about that issue," he told James Hansen. "It's difficult. For me, I feel it immediately when I go beyond a certain border [of reality]. . . . I don't know what to think. This film was a bit easier because the power of music is enormous, so I knew I could romanticize it a little bit and there was no danger [of betraying reality] . . . if there's fiction in this film, it's like a small B-picture, a Nick Ray movie."[20]

In our view, there is no reason to argue that *Ne change rien* is anything but a documentary. Those who think otherwise are perhaps unfamiliar with the history of the documentary mode, a baggy category that, from its earliest manifestations, has mixed visible evidence with artifice. (Costa's observations about the Lumières in his Tokyo lectures make exactly this point.) But whatever one wants to call it, *Change Nothing* is a gorgeously stylized, wide-screen, black-and-white film—one of the best formats for movies ever invented, though seldom seen in today's movie industry. Costa uses available light, augmenting illumination with cleverly placed lamps so that almost everything is darkly and seductively shadowed. In a review of the film, critic Matt Zoller Seitz compares the opening shot to "a monochrome silkscreen by a printmaker obsessed with old Blue Note album covers. Acres of coal black are etched by slivers of white light bouncing off instruments and musicians' clothes and skin . . . nearly half the frame is occupied by the ceiling over the musicians' heads, an inky canvas dotted by spotlights that might as well be stars."[21]

But the film was not planned to look that way. As Costa explained to Hansen, everything was first shot in color:

> Every filmmaker has this dream of doing a film in black-and-white, but it's less and less possible each day. . . . [*Change Nothing*] was shot in color since it's video. It was edited more or less in color. And then, one day, watching the long, nine-minute shot of the opera rehearsal [Balibar] does with her teacher, the editor and I . . . we just kept feeling something. It was a shot where Jeanne moved a lot, her neck and her mouth. Just by chance, I don't know what it was, but we turned off the color button on the monitor and something appeared that was not there in color—it was more sensual, more physical. Even her skin began to show things. So we thought this is great in black-and-white. You can feel it.[22]

Relatively little of the film involves public performances, although it opens with a precredit shot of the closing song of one of Balibar's Tokyo concerts—a rendition of Kris Jensen's "Torture." (Almost every song in the film has cinematic associations; "Torture" was memorably used in Kenneth Anger's *Scorpio Rising*, 1964.) Balibar is barely visible in a low-angle view from what might be a front row or an orchestra pit, wearing a long satin dress that reveals her shoulders and slender back. Lit from above by the starry lights of the totally dark ceiling, her face cannot be seen. Costa has said that he dislikes the gaudy light shows that accompany even the best pop bands, and he knows how to make darkness fascinating. Balibar ends the song by walking away into complete darkness as the audience applauds.

After the credits, we see the face that was denied us. An almost totally dark image shows light reflected on a pair of guitars propped on a stand: a still life, like many in Costa's previous films. We hear the squeak of a mic being adjusted, and Balibar says, "I need lyrics." We cut to a close-up—a dark-eyed beauty made-up for performance, lit by a rim light that outlines her high

Jeanne Balibar

cheekbones and long neck against total blackness. Her mouth is very close to the mic, and she begins softly singing "Peine perdue" ("Lost Cause" or, literally, "Pain in Vain"), a masochistic love ballad partly written and played by Burger, who is off-screen at the guitar. (Again, there is a cinematic connection; *Peine perdue* is the title of a legendary, never completed film by Jean Eustache.)

Balibar looks like she might be at a concert, but we soon discover this is a recording session. Enjoying the song, she raises an eyebrow and smiles a bit as she sings, then stops. "Did you screw up?" an off-screen voice in the studio says, adding, "Focus on continuity." There is a brief discussion of tempo, which Burger thinks should be slower. Balibar sings a bit, purses her lips, and says, "That's nice, otherwise it can get boring." We cut to Burger, who is sitting nearby with his guitar, assisted by band members Hervé Loos, Arnaud Dieterlen, and Joël Theux. At one point, he starts and stops the song, unable to suppress his laughter; his sound man tells him to "Keep the faith." They finish the song but are dissatisfied. From off-screen, Balibar says, "We should try to really bring out the silences. When I'm relaxed and in tempo, it works." A phone rings, and the film cuts to another still life of a desk lamp near a recording instrument, where Balibar, now seated in the distance near the back of the room, talks to someone on the phone. The music starts, and Balibar announces that Antoine (her son) is on the phone and that she wants to sing him the song. The sound of percussion becomes louder, and after confirming that her son can hear her on the phone, she sings, "I hurt myself, it comes so handy, that's how I get your full attention." After a few more verses she asks Antoine if he likes it. The scene ends with her seated and talking to him in the light of the desk lamp, followed by a still life of a keyboard, a microphone on a stand, and a VOX speaker immersed in darkness.

Costa keeps things shrouded in romantic mystery, cutting from musicians to objects and, as in his other films, never giving the viewer expository information or indicating changes of time or setting. He simply lets images and music exert their appeal, giving a sampling of performances and long periods of work on songs. Jonathan Rosenbaum, who dislikes most of the music in the film, feels that Costa's technique nevertheless makes it work: "When Costa combines the flickering flames of a furnace in the dark recording studio with disconnected phrases of Balibar and Burger noodling, how much this music is being recorded or performed or explored or questioned is secondary to the dance of the flames and notes or faces that accompany this process, which we're asked to join . . . so it's small wonder that when we see Balibar and her pals performing 'Johnny Guitar' in a club, it's the romance of the idea and the atmosphere as much as the story itself that carries us along."[23]

The technique is often disorienting. For example, after the twelve-minute "Peine perdue" sequence, we see a low-angle view of a dark stage with light falling on a piano keyboard at the far right. Two off-screen voices, one of them Balibar's, speak lines about sex, love, and marriage from Jacques Offenbach's nineteenth-century opéra bouffe *La Périchole* (of which we later hear more). Out of nowhere, a group of men come on stage. Where are we, and who are these men, who do not seem to be musicians? Later, Costa creates similar disorientation with an enormous close-up of a cat's face shot from so close it seems to be a monster. Eventually we realize it is a pet who roams the recording studio.

The scene shifts again; music begins, and we see an even more intense close-up of Balibar, who holds a mic almost against her mouth and sings "Ne change rien," a song written by her, Burger, and Yves Dormay, which she renders in near parlando style, backed by heavy percussion. The song's title, which also provides the title of the film, seems ironic in this context—the film as a whole is very much about small revisions and a process of stopping and restarting. The title might be an echo of a statement by Godard in his *Histoire(s) du cinéma*

(1988–1998): "Ne change rien pour que tout soit différent" (Don't change anything so that everything is different). The image is again very dark, Balibar's face visible only in the upper right quarter of the screen with a rim light making her hair look almost blond. We fade to black as the music continues and then fade into another close-up in smoky darkness that emphasizes her black hair and profile.

The next scene, one of the longest in the film, begins with Burger seated in a chair in preparation for a recording session, wearing a long white shirt over dark pants and holding an electric guitar in his lap. The room has two small lamps and a variety of equipment. Burger listens to a replay of music and begins strumming as Balibar enters, sans makeup and hair in a bun, and sits in the foreground. Holding a sheet of lyrics for a song, she lights a cigarette and begins humming the music as Burger counts out tempo. This shot lasts over six minutes; we progressively realize that Balibar is rehearsing a cover of Curtis Mayfield's title song from Gordon Park's *Superfly* (1972). She closes her eyes, continues humming without singing the words, and taps her hand in time to the beat of Burger's arrangement.

Costa has said that when the film was shown at festivals, audiences sometimes began filtering out at this point because of the length of the shot and the emphasis on work, but long takes in *Change Nothing* never seem especially long because of the music, which affects the sense of duration. "You've got it," Burger says. But Balibar is obviously ill at ease. "It feels a bit fragile," she says, "I feel tangled up in this thing. I'd need to hear 1, 2, 3, 4 for five minutes nonstop. . . . I'm caught up in this syncopating thing." Burger turns a dial near him, and we hear a guitar and bongos as she hums and taps with her hand. He claps to the rhythm. "I left out a note on purpose," she says. "I'm dragging." She keeps tapping.

We cut to another still life of a guitar on a stand. "Fuck," Balibar says from off-screen. A cut to a closer view of her shows her still seated, looking weary and bogged down. She has one hand over her closed eyes and the other still tapping the rhythm. Burger counts and looks at her encouragingly, but she is uneasy. "Wait," she says, "I'll just try something else." Burger steps out, and she spends another couple minutes beating out the tempo. We cut to Burger's empty chair. He returns, dressed in a sweater and with a drink. Sitting down, he prepares to play and says, "From the top?" We hear a guitar, bongos, and a snare drum with Balibar singing the lyrics off-screen.

We cut to another close-up of Balibar at a mic, made-up and singing in darkness, her face lit from the right. During pauses in the song, she takes deep drags on a cigarette. (She occasionally reminds us of Vanda Duarte in *In Vanda's Room*: she has the same thin body, dark hair, and hunger for a cigarette.) A couple of times, she inhales deeply, then draws smoke back up through her nostrils. When the song ends, Burger says off-screen, "That started off well," and she gives the band a charming smile. "Sure did," someone says. Feeling reassured, she lifts her chin and tilts her head back, stretching her neck to relieve tension. "Just have fun," someone says, and she replies with a laugh, "Like they say on movie sets." Burger says, "We'll have to hear it again, but it sounds good. So it goes like E, G, E, G, F, E, F, E, F." We fade out.

And now for something completely different. To the sound of a piano, we see another close-up of Balibar in dark surroundings, lit by a single light from the left. She is in period costume, hair gathered atop her head, wearing a necklace. We gradually realize that she is preparing for her role in an upcoming performance of Offenbach's *La Périchole*. Singing in French, she works with a female voice coach, who plays piano off-screen and is heard giving instruction. This close-up lasts almost ten minutes and is remarkable not only for the unexpected quality of Balibar's voice but also for her patience and effort. We have been accustomed to thin, breathy, close-mic renditions of torch songs; now, she performs in full-out operatic style, her eyes and mouth open wide, her voice and emotions projected.

Offenbach was a popular composer in the nineteenth century, and *La Périchole* is a light opera. Nonetheless, it requires great attention to accent, elocution, and detail. "Listen, peoples of America, of Spain and of Peru. . . . Listen, we only charge a dime for the perfectly genuine ('veridique') story," Balibar sings, swaying with the waltz rhythm of her aria. Suddenly the piano stops, and we hear the off-screen voice of her coach: "The 'v' isn't perfect," the coach says. "The tone's right, mind you, but for now I need you to put it at rest, and just follow your little path as usual." Like a weary athlete, Balibar, who has apparently been singing for a while, bows her head almost grimly and nods. For the rest of the shot, she is constantly interrupted by a gentle, encouraging, exhausting concern with small things. The length of the shot is important because it makes us intensely aware of her effort and constant revision. Signs of strain and even aging can be seen on her face—not a flattering close-up, but this was the shot that made Costa decide to change the film from color to black and white because it seemed "more sensual, more physical" and made Balibar's skin "begin to show things."

"Listen," she sings, "we only charge a dime, to the perfectly genuine story, of the two unfortunate lovers who lived happily ever afterwards." Again, the piano stops, and the coach speaks: "Here you mustn't go mellow. You can still

Being coached for an opera

add nuance without slowing down. That was great. . . . You have a wonderful ability to lighten things up." Balibar tilts her head back and chews on her bead necklace to relieve tension. "'We only charge a dime' was perfect," the voice says, "but don't slow down when you're not supposed to. . . . It's about precision. . . . You can do it. Just put the Creole accent aside." Balibar sings again and is repeatedly stopped for correction. When she reaches the phrase, "who could play the bassoon," her voice goes deep to imitate the instrument. Again, she is stopped. "Good but it could sound even sharper. . . . The low notes are beautiful," the coach says. "Now do it again but cut it. Stay on this wonderous, dreamy side. Offenbach is punchy. . . . Think of the continuity."

The coach begins playing the piano again. "Now," she says to Balibar, "as if we were in a cheesy melodrama." Balibar stretches her neck from the tension and quietly says, "Fuck." Her singing resumes, but the stopping and starting continues, her off-screen coach noting various details: "I'd like more energy on 'coups' and a little less on 'genoux,' a bit more like a Western." Balibar yawns to loosen up. More instructions are given: "Don't put your arm back. You need your consonants to be lighter, it's not an elegy. 'Genoux' doesn't have

Listening to a playback

three *n*'s. There's not enough breath support . . . you must carry on without getting weak." Finally, at the point where we become concerned for Balibar's stamina, the session stops. "Bravo!" the coach says, "We made it." Balibar asks, "We leave it here, then?" "Yes," the coach says. Balibar turns in the darkness, saying, "I'm just thinking, we didn't buy anything for lunch. I'll look in the fridge, but . . ." The film cuts to the cat's face in close-up.

The next sequence shows a low-angle profile of Balibar sitting at a recording studio mic in front of what looks like a film screen, wearing dark clothes and lit from the left. She has returned to the recording of "Peine perdue," and we hear the sounds of a guitar and bongos. This scene was shot with two cameras and required artful work on sound not only by the recording studio technicians but also by Costa and his sound editor; it has the same self-reflexive quality as his Straub and Huillet film, which documents editing while employing editing—in this case, the art is sound editing. Hands pressed to the top of her head, Balibar turns to the light, fingers tapping to the beat. An off-screen voice asks, "Is it not working?" An arm appears in the frame and adjusts the mic; she slips on a pair of earphones and waits a while in silence.

"I'm lost," she says, and sings a few lines. We cut to a soundboard where an engineer and Burger make adjustments as she sings, then back to Balibar, now viewed from the right side of the studio. We realize that the light in the previous shot of her came from a window at the left, which now makes her a silhouette. She hears music in the earphones and begins to sing, but we hear only her voice. Costa leaves us outside the creation of an illusion, laying bare the technical shaping of an arrangement. Balibar stops in frustration. "I'm so focused on the tempo, you know," she says. She begins singing again and makes a graceful gesture with her hand. "Great!" Burger's voice says when she stops, "Let's put some drums on top." We cut to a later point in time and another shot that feels noir-like: Burger sits alone in the dark studio, listening to the track with soft drums and cymbals as the studio cat wanders around.

Costa then shows us a couple of performances shot in Japan, where Balibar and Burger appeared in clubs and an auditorium. He never tells us the location (or that any part of the film was shot in Japan), and one specific shot has baffled some viewers. We see two Japanese women smoking cigarettes and sitting side by side at a café table. A clock on the wall reads four eighteen o'clock, and a semi-opaque window in a door to the right bears a sign in English reading "Coffee." The reflection of street traffic appears in the glass of a framed picture on a wall behind the women, and we hear piano music, to which the two silent, inexpressive ladies listen and sometime nod in rhythm. When one of them finishes her cigarette and rises, we realize she is wearing an apron. They appear to be workers on break in an empty café near a performance. Whatever the location, the shot is Costa's small tribute to the working class; it recalls brief scenes in the Fontaínhas films in which we see glimpses of unidentified workers going about their activities apart from the central action. (While in Japan, Costa visited the grave of Japanese director Mikio Naruse, who used a similar technique in his films.)

We next see a performance that may or may not be in proximity to the two workers: an eye-level shot shows Balibar, Burger, and two other musicians on stage in a cabaret with a battery of lights above them. Balibar wears a blouse and low-cut jeans and plays a bit on a keyboard as she sings into a microphone and moves to the tune. Then we suddenly cut to a brightly lit scene in a large, white room, possibly a backstage area where Balibar, her hair wrapped in a scarf, sits at a table, holding a bottle of water and listening to music from outside. This is one of two shots in the film without darkness and shadow. She appears to be resting after a job, and the shot links her as a worker to the two Japanese women.

In a wing of the theater

The scene changes to Balibar's performance in *La Périchole*, which Costa films from backstage, without onstage action or operatic spectacle. "For the opera," Costa told James Hansen, "We saw the rehearsal and the complete opera, but what you see is a third representation . . . completely intentional."[24] This third representation is consistent with the film's emphasis on work: a costumed pianist plays lively music at the rear of a theater stage as actors and workers move in and out through doors at the left. Choral music emanates from the unseen stage area at the right. Balibar enters from the right, costumed in an elaborate, floor-length satin dress, and stands in front of the piano, joining in the song of the chorus; her back is slightly turned to us, and when her song ends, she gracefully exits through one of the doors, apparently waiting for a later entrance on the stage proper. "I'm Offenbach's biggest fan now," Costa said to Hansen. "It was a miracle. I don't know how this kind of thing happens. I think Offenbach works perfectly with the pop songs. And then Jeanne told me that this opera is the source for a film I love, *The Golden Coach* by Jean Renoir. . . . A magnificent film in color. It reassured me about using black-and-white so that I wouldn't be repeating *The Golden Coach* in color."[25]

The next sequence shot, apparently from the small Japanese club we saw earlier, provides an amusing confirmation of Costa's remark that "if there's fiction in this film, it's like a small B-picture, a Nick Ray movie." Balibar and the band perform Peggy Lee and Victor Young's "Johnny Guitar," the title song of Nicholas Ray's celebrated 1954 Western, which is loved by every auteurist. Balibar is in jeans and an off-shoulder sweater. At one point, she drinks from a bottle of water, and she and Burger seem to be having fun with the number.

From public performance, Costa returns to the recording studio, where Balibar, Burger, and the band are at work on "Ton double," a song written by Burger and Pierre Alfieri. In an unmoving sequence shot that lasts roughly fifteen minutes, Costa shows the group aiming to complete a recording of the song with a few touches involving electric guitar. He shoots the scene with a wide-angle lens and slightly canted camera; as usual, he keeps much of the room in deep shadow. Burger wears a white shirt and dark pants and is seated at screen right, illuminated by a single light. Balibar, dressed in black, stands at a mic toward the left, in front of a bright movie screen that makes her a silhouette. A recording engineer is visible in the dark foreground, and everyone wears earphones. "Straight from here," someone says. Balibar turns to Burger and asks, "Do I look at you?" Burger says, "The demo didn't sound bad. It's the straight version."

As in the earlier scenes of recording "Peine perdue," this one involves unheard melodies and reveals the mechanics of sound recording and editing. Burger, listening through his earphones, begins snapping his fingers, stomping his foot, twisting, almost dancing in his chair. Balibar begins moving to music we only vaguely sense, raising her arm with a sexy expressiveness. She sings everything in parlando style; from our sonic perspective, she might as well be reciting a poem in a rhythmic, insinuating tone. Viewers of the film are denied the backing track, but Balibar's unamplified words and movement make the scene fascinating. "I laugh at your jokes," Balibar sings, "sleep near you at night, / stick with you everywhere. / Can you guess who I am? . . . / I envy what you are, / delight in what you say. / Can you guess who I am? / Your devil. / Your swaying shadow. / Your embarrassing double."

After more lyrics, her singing ends and someone says, "Now that's what I call a song!" Balibar turns to Burger and says, "Rodolphe, maybe it could be nice, I could try to bond with your voice, just follow through right after you." We now realize that "Ton double" is (appropriately) a duet and that Balibar has been singing along with Burger's voice, recorded on the track she heard in her earphones. "You prefer this backing?" someone asks, and after an unheard

Performing "Rose"

playback, Burger says, "There's still some patchwork to do. It can be interesting but there's still some work to do." Everyone starts moving around in the shadows, laughing and looking for some wine to celebrate the occasion. Balibar's voice says, "We've got a good bottle. I can open it. I was a waitress for a year!"

Costa returns to *La Périchole* and the offstage shot we saw earlier of the pianist, now leaning his chin on one hand and playing with the other. As he begins to play with both hands, we hear Balibar's voice from the stage, singing a lovely Offenbach aria filled with pathos: "How can we be tender to each other, when we are always in want of bread? . . . I am weak, for I am a woman, and someday, my dear one, I shall have breathed my last sigh, believing I was giving you only a sigh of love . . . I sign, La Périchole, who loves you but cannot go on." As she reaches the end of the aria, a costumed member of the opera company enters from the backstage doorway at the left, crosses behind the piano player, and exits right, nibbling on a slice of melon.

For the charming conclusion of the film, Costa takes us back to the dressing room we saw earlier, with its white walls, bright light, and no trace of shadow or glamour. In a wide-angle shot, Balibar is wearing a scarf wrapped around her hair and leaning over a long table that holds a couple of water bottles. She looks somber and weary. Burger enters in the foreground and sits on the table near the camera at the extreme right. Holding his guitar, he looks at Balibar and says, "Shall we start with four or eight—let's do four." He begins strumming the guitar while the sound engineer sits and taps out a rhythm on a water bottle. Now leaning with her back against the wall, Balibar begins softly singing "Rose," a song written by her and Burger: "Rose is in love, wants happy love songs, turns grey into bright night. / I love every inch of you, she says, your eyes, your voice, your fingertips. / English makes you say silly things. . . . Everybody knows, Rose c'est la vie. / Rose says, if I was an actress, a luscious dancer, a seductress. / Rose is in love. From her newfound love song, Rose waters will flow. / Rose is a rose, is a rose." At the end of the song, she leans one hand on the table and covers her mouth with the other. Her eyes are smiling at Burger, who nods in approval. It is as if they have performed this song just for Costa.

Notes

1. Thierry Lounas, "Notas sobre *Onde jaz o teu sorriso?*," in *Onde jaz o teu sorriso? Diálogos*, ed. Pedro Costa, Jean-Marie Straub, and Danièle Huillet (Lisbon: Assírio & Alvim), 2004, 110.

2. Gilberto Perez, *The Material Ghost: Films and Their Medium* (Baltimore: John Hopkins Press, 1998), 292.

3. Thom Andersen, "No Secrets Just Lessons: A Dialogue between Pedro Costa and Thom Andersen on Danièle Huillet and Jean-Marie Straub," *Cinema Scope* 29 (Winter 2007): 40–41.

4. Lounas, "Notas sobre *Onde jaz o teu sorriso?*," 114.

5. Patrick Tarrant, "Montage in the Portrait Film: Where Does the Hidden Time Lie?," *Alphaville: Journal of Film and Screen Media* 5 (Summer 2013), https://www.alphavillejournal.com/Issue5/HTML/ArticleTarrant.html.

6. Quoted in Andersen, "No Secrets Just Lessons," 41.

7. Quoted in Andersen, "No Secrets Just Lessons," 44.

8. Tarrant, "Montage in the Portrait Film," 6.

9. Richard Brody, "What to Stream: *Sicilia!*," *New Yorker*, September 5, 2020, https://www.newyorker.com/culture/the-front-row/what-to-stream-sicilia.

10. Andersen, "No Secrets Just Lessons," 41.

11. João Bénard da Costa, "De sorrisos ocultos," in Costa et al., *Onde jaz o teu sorriso?*, 145.

12. Quoted in Carolin Overhoff Ferreira, "High and Low: Popular Music in Portuguese Cinema and Pedro Costa's *Ne change rien*," *Music and the Moving Image* 9, no. 1 (Spring 2016): 28.

13. Dennis Lim, "The Sound of Music: Pedro Costa's *Ne change rien*," *Artforum* 49, no. 3 (November 3, 2010), https://www.artforum.com/columns/dennis-lim-on-pedro-costas-ne-change-rien-195951.

14. James Hansen, "Interview with Pedro Costa," *Film Quarterly* 63, no. 2 (Winter 2009): 54.

15. Pedro Costa, *Ne change rien*, DVD liner notes (New York: Cinema Guild, 2011).

16. Hansen, "Interview with Pedro Costa," 54.

17. Lim, "The Sound of Music," 2.

18. See Ferreira, 27–28 and her quote of Chris Fujiwara.

19. See Ryan J. Meehan, "Pedro Costa's Post-documentary," *Harvard Crimson*, November 11, 2010, www.thecrimson.com/article/2010/11/2/costa-ne-change-rien.

20. Quoted in Hansen, "Interview with Pedro Costa," 56.

21. Matt Zoller Seitz, "Light and Shadow, and Music on the Wondrous Dreamy Side," *New York Times*, November 2, 2010, www.nytimes.com/2010/03/movies/03nechange/html.

22. Quoted in Hansen, "Interview with Pedro Costa," 55.

23. Jonathan Rosenbaum, "Finding Oneself in the Dark: Costa's *Ne change rien*," March 7, 2023, https://jonathanrosenbaum.net/2023/03/ne-change-rien/. Costa told Rosenbaum that the black and white made the veins in Balibar's neck visible as she sang.

24. Quoted in Hansen, "Interview with Pedro Costa," 55.

25. Quoted in Hansen, "Interview with Pedro Costa," 55–56.

PART V

Exhibitions, Short Films, and a Work in Progress

Exhibitions

This section of our book returns to a question we raised at the beginning: What is cinema? If a short clip from a movie is shown on the wall of a museum space alongside paintings, is it still cinema? At a recent exhibit on modernism at the Museum of Modern Art in New York, for example, high-resolution video projections of clips from the works of Charles Chaplin and Oscar Micheaux were shown on the same walls as canonical modernist paintings.

Film is watched today not only in museums but also at home, on airplanes, on laptop computers, and on iPhones. This is the age of expanded cinema. Where museum art is concerned, avant-garde and experimental filmmakers have long found a home in the museum environment. Andy Warhol's lengthy 16mm films of the early 1960s—*Sleep, Blow Job, Empire,* and *Eat,* all of which involve a minimum of movement—have been shown in museums, galleries, and underground venues. Douglas Gordon's *24-Hour Psycho* (1993), an appropriation of Hitchcock's film projected in video at two frames per second and lasting a full day, was originally a museum installation. Several distinguished contemporary directors have made video installations, among them Chantel Akerman, Victor Erice, Jean-Luc Godard, Abbas Kiarostami, Raúl Ruiz, and Apichatpong Weerasethakul. As Nuno Barradas Jorge points out in his discussion of Pedro Costa's exhibitions, the question has become not so much what is cinema but where is cinema.[1]

Given his emphasis on the shot rather than the sequence and the "painterly" quality of his images, one might think that Costa would have always been interested in cinema for museums. But in interviews, he has spoken of

The End of a Love Affair

his reluctant attitude toward video installations, remarking that on occasion, the sight of one has been enough to make him run in the opposite direction. He complained that films in museums "do not have the power they do in a theater. . . . They lose light."[2] Beginning in the early 2000s, however, he accepted a few invitations. One of his first was a sixteen-minute digital film called *The End of a Love Affair* (2003), which appeared not only in museums but also at the Festival Temps d'Image in France and the Cinemateca Portuguesa and Centro Cultural de Belém outside Lisbon.

The film is set in a no-frills bedroom in a Lisbon *pensão,* partially lit by a window. Standing in medium-shot profile is a man (Gustavo Sumpta) holding the back of a chair as he gazes out the window. (Sumpta went on to play Vanda's husband in *Colossal Youth.*) The shot never changes, and in typical Costa fashion, there are no clues as to who the man is or the nature of his circumstances. Dressed in an orange T-shirt and plaid pants, he occasionally leans to the side or moves the chair. All the while, his eyes are focused somewhere beyond a pair of gauzy curtains that hang straight or fill with puffs of air, billowing toward him. The only sounds are muted outside noises of traffic and passersby.

Suddenly, nondiegetic music begins to play, and the scene takes on a different mood. The slow-paced instrumental has delicate flute lines that soar and retreat like the rising and falling curtains. The room's drabness and man's despondency seem strangely compatible with, even enhanced by, the dreamy, romantic melody, which comes to an end and is replaced by the sound of children's distant play. Some viewers may recognize the music as a recording of "The End of a Love Affair," famously sung by Billie Holiday, but Costa waits to reveal its title—also the film's title—until the end.

Costa subsequently used this installation in master classes about cinema's ability to make us see and hear in a more reflective or contemplative way. His use of this particular example is significant not only in terms of the meditative quality of this and many of his feature films but also because most people do not watch museum installations in the same way they watch movies in a theater. A few museum viewers will sit on a bench for a long while to contemplate a painting or video, but most wander from one object to another, giving their full attention for only a few minutes. Sometimes, a darkened room with a bit of seating—a black box theater, as it were—is provided for showing a video, but people usually wander in and out. Costa is aware of this phenomenon and uses it in his museum work, which varies in length and screen size.

In 2005, two years after *The End of a Love Affair,* Costa and sculptor Rui Chafes exhibited works at the Serralves Museum in Oporto, Portugal. The exhibition ran from October 2005 to January 2006 and was followed by the publication of a bilingual (English/Portuguese) volume titled *Fora! / Out!* (2006) with conversations involving Costa, Chafes, and museum staff, along with illustrations of their works. Costa mounted four installations: *Casal da Boba,* an eight-hour color video; *Benfica, Colina do Sol e Pontinha,* an eleven-minute color video on two screens; *Minino macho, minino fêmea* (*Little Boy Male, Little Girl Female*), a thirty-seven-minute color video on two screens; and *Fontaínhas,* a four-and-a-half-minute color video. He explained that most of these works, including the eight-hour video, which consisted of outtakes of conversations between Ventura and Vanda in a white-walled bedroom, came from *Colossal Youth,* the film he was making at the time: "I've been filming almost every day for around two years. What I brought to the exhibition is basically fresh material that belongs to this work. I still haven't decided whether or not it will be part of the film. The double projection is in the intermediate room (*Minino macho, minino fêmea*) between Rui's 'bed' (*Não tenho mais nada* [I have nothing else]) and the 'parlatory' (*Vê como tremo* [See how I tremble]), is a variation of that which I previously produced for Witte de

With in Rotterdam at [curator] Catherine's [David] wish."[3] Costa went on to describe his idea for *Casal da Boba*:

> From the moment we decided to work in this large room I immediately thought about a large-scale projection, on an old-fashioned screen, measuring over 7 meters, equivalent to the size of the old monumental cinemas.... The idea was to transform this white room into something spectacular... only by adding white to white. Finally, I thought about the eight hours of continuous projection and how this very extended period of time could re-dimension and condense the physical space of this projection room....
>
> *Casal da Boba* is the raw material that we filmed over four months in Vanda's room and contains not only several fictionalized scenes but also the work involved and pauses that occurred parallel to it.... It is not a question of representing things in a "true to life" manner, a day in the life of these two people [Vanda and Ventura]. It is a work about the work involved in filming one second in the day of these two people. It is about the eight hours that these two people need in order to narrate a single second.[4]

Nothing much happens in *Casal da Boba*. Vanda and Ventura speak to one another, fall silent, watch TV, sleep, and eat. The video is in some ways an homage to Warhol, whom Costa admired, in the sense that the exceptional duration of scenes in which almost nothing happens is a challenge to the spectator. It was also an intriguing use of museum space. The white walls of the room where it was exhibited matched the barren white walls of Vanda's bedroom in Casal da Boba, and the white-on-white effect, combined with the size of the screen, was a subtle affront, a challenge or critical merging of cinema and museum. It gave the effect of melding the museum spectator with Vanda and Ventura, putting everything in the same white room.

When asked by an interviewer how he felt about showing a work spectators were unlikely to view in its totality, Costa replied: "I think the best response to your question is to say that this film is dedicated to the security guards of the Serralves Museum who open the room in the morning and close at night."[5] His aim, he said, was to avoid the basic desires of the museumgoer: "Just another Sunday of aesthetic exaltation."[6]

While *Casal da Boba*'s presentation is closer to conventional film projection, *Fontaínhas* requires the viewer to walk through a darkened, tunnel-like corridor to hear words spoken by Ventura, who appears on a tiny screen. In a barely perceptible voice, the text of his speech is the "100 thousand cigarettes" love letter inspired by Robert Desnos. When asked about the unusual staging, Costa replied: "I felt it was necessary to ensure that this tunnel was spatially concrete and physical—thus obliging the visitor to advance through the darkness, attracted by the call of a distant voice. Or perhaps, this corridor simply represents my encounter with Ventura—the three years that we lived and filmed together, the famous 'long road that I journeyed in order to reach him.'"[7] (The work also anticipates the long dark tunnels traversed by the zombie-like, hallucinating Ventura in *Horse Money.*)

Years after the Serralves exhibit, Costa commented on his attraction as a filmmaker to narrow, dark spaces: "I think I am a better filmmaker inside enclosed spaces, corridors, and alleys: I need them in order to think, to work. The community of Fontaínhas also taught me this practice. In the end, all the films we have been making together are simply films about housing problems, quests for homes: our lost house, our possible future, desired home in all its forms, concrete and imaginary. They're about the fear of losing that house, the roof, our home, the fear of losing this center."[8]

Derived from *In Vanda's Room, Little Boy Male, Little Girl Female* shows the dismantling of the lives of Cape Verdeans, whose community in Fontaínhas, with its humble structures and narrow passageways, is slowly being demolished. Costa made the soundtrack of the teardown as loud as possible to disturb and provoke visitors in the museum's large space. On a pair of screens are images of residents in private spaces on the right and in public spaces on the left. Long sequences on each screen change at different intervals. An interactive component allowed viewers to manipulate the images into different combinations, making their own "edit."

Those familiar with *In Vanda's Room* and *Colossal Youth* will recognize a few individuals and settings in this exhibit. They include Zita and Vanda smoking heroin in a bedroom; Zita holding her brother Diogo, who wields a small plastic ruler; two boys doing drugs in an abandoned home; Ventura sitting in darkness beside Bete; and a toddler standing in a doorway with a bike, looking in at an older woman. Costa includes a grim shot of a boy injecting another in the neck in the light of a doorway where they are hiding out. Not all the private domestic scenes show people. In a shot of different colored glass bottles arrayed on a table, the liquid in two partially full receptacles moves in time to the trembling caused by the demolition outside.

The exterior images on the left screen are mostly shot in a narrow passageway showing the comings and goings of men, women, and children. Occasionally piercing the loud noise of bulldozers are the shouts of children. We see a man sweeping ruined pavement strewn with debris; a wood fire blazing on the ground, over which a woman heats a large pan of food; a few dogs weaving around pedestrians; and young men selling and buying drugs. Several passersby walk away from the camera to observe the ongoing demolition, suggested by puffs of dust and debris in the distance. Although the left screen consists primarily of exteriors, one extended take focuses on an exposed room in ruins with an ironing board still standing. The lighting blinks, as if to suggest that time for the place and its people is running out.

In *Benfica, Colina do Sol e Pontinha*, the double screen shows two different scenes from *Colossal Youth* involving conversations between Ventura and Paulo. One takes place in the hospital where Ventura visits Paulo, who is recovering from a bullet wound in his leg. The other is in an empty apartment in Casal da Boba where Paulo, now on crutches, talks to Ventura about a conman's scheme to dupe residents into donating to a funeral; he has just returned from a painful trip up several flights of stairs where, instead of money, a woman gave him some yogurt.

One of the most striking of Costa's exhibitions, largely because of its setting, was the four-minute *As filhas do Fogo* (*The Daughters of Fire*, 2013). First used in a more conventional museum environment in the 2005 Oporto collaboration with Chafes, it was later mounted on large screens inside the São Roque Church in Lisbon, which is adjacent to the Museum of São Roque. The spectacular baroque church, filled with religious art and artifacts, provided a background or shared space for huge videos of the close-ups of young Cape Verdean women featured at the beginning of *Down to Earth*. The church gave those barely moving images a spiritual quality, and the images made an implicit comment on their surroundings. (The title of the installation seems to have inspired a powerful short film discussed below.)

An elaborate multimedia Costa exhibition, *Canción de Pedro Costa* (*Song of Pedro Costa*) was arranged in Barcelona at La Virreina Centre de la Imatge from October 2022 until April 2023. Nearly all the items in the exhibit were related to music, an art form used in various ways in Costa's films and with which he grew increasingly preoccupied as he began planning a new film. Among the exhibit items were a video, "Songbook of Fogo," which uses the scrapbook he compiled while making *Down to Earth*; an excerpt from *Change Nothing* featuring Balibar at work on a song; an excerpt from *Horse Money* entitled "Ventura's Song," which shows Ventura singing "Alto Cutelo"; a recording of the verses of "Our Voices Will Sing No More" from a stage production Costa directed in Portugal and used for his most recent short film (for more about both the stage production and film, see below), accompanied by five frame enlargements from *Down to Earth, Colossal Youth,* and *Horse Money;* "Morna of Shadows," consisting of five projections on suspended screens surrounded by music of the morna composed by violinist Bassoé (Raul Andrade) for *Down to Earth;* and two independent video works by Costa, "Songs to Avoid Suicide" and "To the Little Radio," with lyrics by Bertolt Brecht and music by Hanns Eisler, the two video screens mounted to face one another. In November 2023, the exhibition moved for a four month stay at La Fundación Luis Seoane in A Coruña, a city in Galicia in northwest Spain.

Short Films

Costa has occasionally created short films excerpted from features or later incorporated into them. *Change Nothing,* for example, was released as a twelve-minute short in 2005, and in 2009 it became part of the documentary feature. The short film *6 Bagatelles* consists of outtakes from *Where Does Your Hidden Smile Lie?,* and the harrowing elevator sequence in *Horse Money* began as a short called *Sweet Exorcism,* reedited for later use in the feature (minus opening and closing shots that gave the original a narrative context). By the same token, the following three short films involve repurposing or rearrangement—they are thematically related and share much of the same footage.

Tarrafal (2007), *A caça ao coelho com pau* (*The Rabbit Hunters,* 2007), and *O nosso homem* (*Our Man,* 2010)

In 2006, Costa participated in a Calouste Gulbenkian Foundation project with five other directors—Chantal Akerman, Vicente Ferraz, Wang Bing, Aiysha Abraham, and Apichatpong Weerasethakul—for an omnibus titled *O estado do mundo* (*The State of the World,* 2007) to celebrate the Gulbenkian's fiftieth anniversary. Costa's sixteen-minute short was titled *Tarrafal,* the name of the town on Santiago Island in Cape Verde where the infamous concentration camp was operated by the Salazar dictatorship between 1936 and 1974. (Tarrafal was also home to some of the actors who appeared in Costa's films.) Around the same time, Costa was invited with directors Harun

Farocki and Eugene Green to make shorts for an omnibus called *Memories*, sponsored by South Korea's Jeonju Festival Digital Project. The requirements stipulated that the films be digitally shot, run less than thirty minutes, and have modest budgets. Costa's contribution was a twenty-two-minute color film with the somewhat unusual title *A caça ao coelho com pau* (literally translated "the rabbit hunt with club"). These two shorts share footage and were reedited and combined in the twenty-three-minute *O nosso homem* (*Our Man*) in 2010.

The shorts portray a group of Cape Verdeans who live on the periphery of Lisbon near the densely wooded area used in *Horse Money* and near a rambling tin shack from where, in the distance from atop a hill, we see the Casal da Boba housing project. With little action and plot, the shorts depend on characters' conversations about their past and memories of what they once had and have lost. Although the sun is shining brightly, they wear winter hats and jackets to keep warm. Ventura appears in all these shorts, mostly as a walking companion and sounding board for an old friend (Alfredo Mendes), a former bricklayer whose name, like that of Ventura and the other characters in the films, is never mentioned. Ventura also crosses paths with a younger Cape Verdean (José Alberto Silva), who has a prison record and is facing deportation to Tarrafal in Cape Verde. Despite the films' obvious similarities, they differ in their approach. Viewed together, they enlarge on the struggles and injustices suffered by the Cape Verdean community.

Costa has said that he made the first of the films, *Tarrafal*, as a way to raise awareness of the government's action against José Alberto, who was, in fact, being deported. It begins with a scene between José Alberto and his mother (Lucinda Cardoso), sitting close together near a table in their shack and talking about places where their relatives, now mostly deceased, once lived in Cape Verde. The light is dim in the room, and the mother's blue sweater, red and white headscarf, and patterned jacket give the only touches of color to the grim interior. She tells her son, who occasionally smiles, looking down at the table and playing with a knife, that she would never return to her home in Cape Verde—a place without water or electricity—except "to rest her bones" after death. José Alberto asks about a house she owns there and suggests that they could move, as he has a friend in Tarrafal who was deported because he has a prison record. At this point, we have no knowledge of José Alberto's deportation notice or the significance of his mother's comment that the only person who would return to Cape Verde is "perhaps some poor bastard who's sent back there." The somber emotional tenor in the shack momentarily lifts

José Alberto and his mother

when a woman outside calls to another. Smiling, the mother nods and says, "Just like Cape Verde."

Costa spent many days on this long sequence shot, which was intended to show the son bidding his mother goodbye. But the two (who play themselves) refused to broach the topic of the son's imminent deportation, perhaps wanting to avoid facing it.[9] Instead, the conversation shifts away from family matters, and the son asks his mother to explain island lore involving a trickster. He looks at her in childlike fashion, as if asking for a bedtime story. According to legend, she says, this trickster would plant letters on unsuspecting adults, who would follow him to some remote spot where he would ask for the paper he had addressed to them. Casting a demonic spell, he would bore a hole in his victims' heads and suck out all the blood. As she recounts this tale, giving many examples of people who were tricked, her son, who has been cleaning his fingernails with his knife, begins to suck on and bite his nails. He seems to feel that the government's deportation notice is not unlike the demon trickster's cursed letter.

Costa has said that the demon in *Tarrafal,* also implied in the other two short films, reminded him of Jacques Tourneur's late-career masterpiece

Ventura and José Alberto

Night of the Demon (1957), which concerns a magician who has the power to kill his victims by passing them letter-sized parchments containing runic symbols.[10] By means of these missives, the magician empowers a monstrous demon to do his bidding. Tourneur wanted the supernatural beast to be only suggested, but his producer ordered scenes of it seizing its victims; apart from that revision, the film has the subtly haunted atmosphere characteristic of most of Tourneur's work, which several of Costa's shorts and features share.

In the next scene, José Alberto is sitting on a board outside the shack smoking a cigarette and playing with his knife. He rises to walk away, and we cut to a low-level view of Ventura, seated near a tree and looking at something off screen. We cut to an even lower-level view of a small man in the nearby woods who is holding a wooden club raised over his head in a dramatic, statuesque pose. The film shifts back to Ventura, who says to himself, "Life nowadays is a funny thing," and muses about losing his job and being thrown out of his home by his wife. We see José Alberto walking by, a yellow flower in his mouth, preoccupied by a letter he is holding. Ventura offers his condolences, the reason for which has yet to be revealed. A conversation between the two ensues as they watch the small man in the woods. José Alberto remarks that the fellow will never catch a rabbit that way. As José Alberto continues reading the piece of paper, Ventura states that José Alberto's father was a friend of his. José Alberto says he was in jail when his father died, although he was able to help bury him.

We cut to nighttime. Ventura and the small man with the club are sitting and talking in what appears to be the shack from the first scene. The unidentified man tells Ventura about a fall he once had when working, after which he wandered dazed into a restaurant and was arrested for eating a meal for which he could not pay. After being taken to the police station, he was dumped near railroad tracks in the woods. Ventura asks if they killed him. He replies that he does not know. We gradually realize that this is a conversation with a dead man, like the ones Ventura has in *Colossal Youth* and *Horse Money*.

The two men next appear in a wide shot, their backs to the camera, sitting side by side in daylight with cats wandering around the nearby shack. The small man recalls a time when all this was unpopulated. He spies a rabbit somewhere in the distance, remembers how he once hunted for game to feed his family, and gives Ventura the ingredients for a recipe. After a period of silence, Ventura says his friend's gold tooth was missing when he was buried and speculates that it was used to pay for his funeral. He adds that his friend's face was beaten. The small man says that the housing project that appears in the distance did not exist when he lived here and that white people beat up anyone walking where they were now sitting. The film ends with a close-up of José Alberto's deportation notice—the demonic letter, its official seal at the top—pinned against a wall with José Alberto's knife. When *Tarrafal* appeared as part of *The State of the World* omnibus at Cannes in 2007, Costa described it as a horror story. José Alberto will be deported; his widowed mother will lose her son; and the rabbit hunter, beaten, discarded by the authorities, and missing his gold tooth, now wanders like a ghost.

Costa omitted the *Tarrafal* scene of the mother and son from *The Rabbit Hunters*, giving greater attention to the rabbit hunter's stories about his plight and Ventura's encounter with José Alberto, who talks about learning to catch rabbits in prison and attending his father's burial. Several scenes are identical to those in *Tarrafal*, but the film begins with a close-up of the old rabbit hunter sleeping on the ground near a wall painted with graffiti that reads "Death to cops." He rises, makes a few feeble moves to gain his balance, and calls out to Ventura, who is stretched out nearby in front of a building. Both appear to be homeless, although Ventura leads the rabbit hunter into the building,

The deportation notice

which looks like Casal da Boba. As they peer between large slats open to the outside, the old man talks of being mistreated by children here. Hunger is a central theme. The old man recalls his sister rejecting a sick rabbit and dove he caught to eat. The continued wanderings of the two take them to a school kitchen in the housing complex, where the cook (António Semedo) serves them broth in small cups, explaining that the stew meat is for the children, whose voices can be heard outside. Ventura remarks to the cook that "a lot of departed spirits walk with me."

Back outdoors, the little old man recalls signing a paper after his wife threw him out of their house, not realizing the paper was for a divorce. Shortly after, Ventura crosses paths again with José Alberto, holding the yellow flower in his mouth and reading the deportation notice. Various shots of the old man moving through the woods with a raised club are followed by José Alberto's memories of prison and of hunting and catching rabbits to feed his family. Ventura refers to José Alberto's father as a good bricklayer. For the first time, we realize that the aged rabbit hunter, a "departed spirit," is José Alberto's father. The film ends with the same shot as *Tarrafal* of the deportation notice pierced with a knife.

In 2010, Costa followed this film with a twenty-three-minute color short called *Our Man,* which draws from both *Tarrafal* and *The Rabbit Hunters,* although largely from the latter. It shows Ventura and the old man wandering through a building and stopping by the school kitchen. They sit in the same tin shack featured at the beginning of *Tarrafal,* and the old man again tells Ventura about the fall that left him dazed and his arrest and mistreatment for not paying in a restaurant. Again, the film ends with the knife and the deportation notice.

The focus of the three shorts on poverty, homelessness, and zombie-like wanderings condenses primary issues treated in Costa's feature films. In all three shorts, Ventura sings a snippet of verses about being fired, abandoned by his wife, and left to wander, which is also true of the unfortunate rabbit hunter. All three films are about memories: the mother's remembrances of her homeland and the legend of a trickster; the old man's recollections of hunger, mistreatment, and possible death; Ventura's memory of the old man's beaten face and funeral; and José Alberto's evocations of prison and hunting rabbits. The knife featured at the end of each film suggests not only brutality but also an aggression unapparent in José Alberto or any of the other characters. Significantly, knives of different types are prominent in Costa's subsequent feature, *Horse Money,* in which memory becomes undistinguishable from hallucination.

As filhas do Fogo (*The Daughters of Fire,* 2023)

This nine-minute film should not be confused with Costa's video installation of the same title exhibited at the São Roque Church and Museum in Lisbon and at Japan's Hara Museum in 2013 (discussed above). It originated instead in a one-hour multimedia event Costa directed in Lisbon in 2021 in collaboration with the early music ensemble Os Músicos do Tejo. The music, film, and theater portrayed three sisters from Cape Verde who arrive as immigrants to Europe and are guided by a jester as they travel day and night through a maze of urban slums, ultimately joining the working class as cleaning women.

The roles of the three sisters were sung by Selma Uamusse, Karyna Gomes, and Elizabeth Pinard. A character identified as "man with the radio" was sung by Miguel Sermão, and three other characters were shown in film clips: "woman in the green room" (Selma Uamusse), "man in damp room" (Costa Neto), and "junky" (Fernando Guimarães). The music and words came from a rich variety of sources: Henry Purcell, John Dowland, Claudio Monteverdi, Franz Schubert, J. W. Goethe, Luca Marenzio, György Kurtág, Hanns Eisler, Bertolt Brecht, Johann Sebastian Bach, Giovanni Battista Pergolesi, Gil Scott-Heron, Brian Jackson, William Lawes, Marc Antoine Charpentier, Biago Marini, and Anton Chekhov.

The short *The Daughters of Fire*, which may have been used in that event, was exhibited at Cannes in 2023 alongside shorts by Wang Bing and Jean-Luc Godard; the three shorts have since been distributed in a video release. Most people will see this film in a DVD or Blu-ray form, but in a theater, its effect must be overwhelming. Chris Fujiwara saw it at the Yamagata International Documentary Film Festival in Japan and commented on the experience:

> Watching *The Daughters of Fire*, one is struck at first by the scale of the film. The screen takes on something of the character of an installation that one relates to in a real space. We become aware of it in its physical presence. The size and the spread of the image are grand, overpowering. An impression that the music, when it is fully present in an auditorium, as it was just a few minutes ago, can only strengthen. It is still a film that, like normal films, is received in a single look. Since it is, however, a composite image, our look is also divided.[11]

The Daughters of Fire is a beautifully shot three-screen triptych, not unlike those painted long ago for churches and altarpieces. At the left, in a low-angle close-up, a young woman, her eyes raised, walks along a dark wall speckled with the still-molten fire of a volcano. At the right, in close-up, a young woman peers around a post or open doorway, looking toward us. At the center, a young woman lies on a beach of dark volcanic rock beside the ocean and rises to stand, looking toward the land. The three women (Elizabeth Pinard, Alice Costa, and Karyna Gomes) sing an oratorio in Creole derived from Biagio Marini's *Passacaglia*, op. 22 (1655), with lyrics based on an old Ukrainian folk song. The music is played by a string quartet consisting of two violins, a viola, and a cello. The verses speak of fatigue, loneliness, suffering, a struggle to live, and the mystery of life:

> What a terrible day. . . . I'm tired, we'll be alone, begin again all alone. . . . We must live, there will come a time when we know why we suffer. We must work and the mystery will end. We'll be alone, we'll be gone forever. We

The Daughters of Fire

> must live, we must work, only work, rain or cold we must work and the mystery will end. We'll be alone, we'll be gone forever.... They will forget our faces.... Suffering, our voices will sing no more.... No one will remember how many of us there were.

The film ends with footage from the 1951 documentary by Portuguese geographer and anthropologist Orlando Ribeiro, part of which Costa used at the beginning of *Down to Earth*. We see majestic landscape shots of the island of Fogo, which has the largest volcanic mountain in the archipelago. (For those who know Costa's work, the sight of this mountain may recall a quote used by Straub and Huillet in one of their films: it comes from Cézanne, who, while showing one of his several paintings of the volcanic Mont Sainte-Victoire, said, "See this mountain, once it was fire.") From the same documentary, we see footage of some of the island's inhabitants, emerging naked or barely clothed from a tiny house of lava.

A Work in Progress

The Daughters of Fire marks a return to the island where Costa's almost career-long devotion to Cape Verdeans began. It also portends his future work. When it was shown at Cannes, Costa said it provided a seed for a feature he was planning. This would be a musical, but one unlike his 2009 documentary *Change Nothing,* "which had a lot of music in it, but it wasn't a musical film." He commented on the kind of music he planned to use:

> The music I'm using for [*The Daughters of Fire*] is ancient music, Western baroque. For the longer film, I think I will use ancient European music as well as popular folk music, mainly from Cape Verde . . . a more prosaic, profane way of looking at things. The paintings I prefer are those of the Dutch Golden Age, which are very documentary. The Dutch painters started painting people at work—Vermeer, Rembrandt, they all began painting regular, everyday life. In this sense [the experience with *The Daughters of Fire*] was serendipitous. Music was this way of concentrating things. I think music does this better than film. The pop song is a good example, or the folk song, which is a way of concentrating big stories, sagas.[12]

Costa's origins as an artist were as an adolescent guitarist in a band, and he seems to know as much about the history of music as he does about the history of cinema. Most of his films contain snippets of music he loves; two of his museum exhibits are about music as much as images, and one of his features was originally planned as a rap musical. The film he is making as we write is a culmination of this interest in musical cinema. Essentially an oratorio, it expands the narrative suggested in *The Daughters of Fire,* telling the story of three women entirely through song.

When we discussed the film with Costa in March 2024, he explained that it involves three stories of women who live in different locales and time periods: New Bedford, Massachusetts, in the 1920s; Rotterdam in the 1970s; and Lisbon in the present day. The film will interweave these three stories, moving back and forth in time. Costa was searching for specific locations for the filming; he had originally planned to find a New Bedford factory site, but shooting there was impractical. He hoped to find a place in Hamburg to "play" New Bedford, but at the time we spoke, he said he might have found a good spot closer to home. The completed film will be entirely musical, with the same kind of wide-ranging sources as the libretto in *The Daughters of Fire* stage presentation, plus added lyrics by Costa himself.

This film in progress is an ambitious outgrowth of the remarkable career we have described in this book, in some ways unexpected but in other ways entirely logical. Costa's cinema has been unified in purpose and innovative in style. Those familiar with his work cannot fail to anticipate it eagerly.

Notes

1. See Nuno Barradas Jorge, *Refocus: The Films of Pedro Costa* (Edinburgh: University of Edinburgh Press, 2021), 90–109.

2. Pedro Costa and Rui Chafes, *Fora! / Out!* (Oporto: Fundação Serralves, 2007), 68.

3. Costa and Chafes, *Fora! / Out!*, 74.

4. Costa and Chafes, *Fora! / Out!*, 84, 86.

5. Costa and Chafes, *Fora! / Out!*, 88.

6. Costa and Chafes, *Fora! / Out!*, 90.

7. Costa and Chafes, *Fora! / Out!*, 104.

8. Costa in Guarneri, "Documentary, Realism, and Life on the Margins."

9. See Michael Guillén, "Pedro Costa (and Others) on *Casa de lava* and *Tarrafal*," *Evening Class* (blog), March 12, 2008, https://theeveningclass.blogspot.com/2008/03/pedro-costa-and-others-on-casa-de-lava_12.html.

10. Guillén, "Pedro Costa."

11. Chris Fujiwara, untitled talk sent by the author to James Naremore on *The Daughters of Fire*, Yamagata International Documentary Film Festival, October 9, 2023.

12. Quoted in Giovanni Marchini Camia, "Pedro Costa and Wang Bing, Music and Reality," *Cinema Scope* 95 (September 2023): 49, 51.

FILMOGRAPHY

***O sangue* (*Blood*, 1989)**
Portugal
Production: Trópico Filmes
Direction: Pedro Costa
Screenplay: Pedro Costa
Photography: Martin Schäfer
Editing: Manuela Viegas
Sound: Pedro Caldas
Music: The The; Igor Stravinsky
Cast: Pedro Hestnes, Nuno Ferreira, Inês de Medeiros, Luís Miguel Cintra, Canto e Castro, Isabel de Castro, Henrique Viana, Luís Santos, Manuel João Vieira, Sara Breia, José Eduardo, Ana Otero, Pedro Miguel, Miguel Fernandes
Black and white, 35mm
95 minutes

***Casa de lava* (*Down to Earth*, 1994)**
Portugal, France, and Germany
Production: Madragoa Filmes with Gemini Films and Pandora Film
Direction: Pedro Costa
Screenplay: Pedro Costa
Photography: Emmanuel Machuel
Editing: Dominique Auvray
Sound: Henri Kaikoff
Music: Raul Andrade, Travadinha, Finaçon, Prince, Nico M'Barka, Paul Hindemith

Cast: Inês de Medeiros, Isaach de Bankolé, Edith Scob, Pedro Hestnes, Sandra do Canto Brandão, Cristiano Andrade Alves, Raul Andrade, João Medina, João Gomes de Pina, Amália Tavares, Clotilde Montrond, António Andrade, Manuel Andrade, Daniel Andrade, António Lopes, Sidónio Pais, Joaquim Antunes, Joaquim Carvalho, Mónica Calle, Luís Miguel Cintra, Isabel de Castro
Color, 35mm
110 minutes

***Ossos* (*Bones*, 1997)**
Portugal, France, and Denmark
Production: Madragoa Filmes with Gemini Films and Zentropa Productions
Direction: Pedro Costa
Screenplay: Pedro Costa
Photography: Emmanuel Machuel
Editing: Jackie Bastide
Music: Wire, Os Sabura
Cast: Vanda Duarte, Nuno Vaz, Maria Lipkina, Isabel Ruth, Inês de Medeiros, Miguel Sermão, Berta Susana Teixeira, Clotilde Montrond, Zita Duarte, Beatriz Lopes, Luísa Carvalho, Aresta, Ana Marta, Iuran, Ricardo Tavares, Carolina Eira
Color, 35mm
94 minutes

***No quarto da Vanda* (*In Vanda's Room*, 2000)**
Portugal, Germany, and Switzerland
Production: Contracosta Produções with Pandora Film, Ventura Film
Direction: Pedro Costa
Screenplay: Pedro Costa
Editing: Dominique Auvray, Patrícia Saramago
Music: György Kurtág
Cast: Vanda Duarte, Zita Duarte, Lena Duarte, Manuel Gomes Miranda, Diogo Pires Miranda, Evangelina Nelas, Miquelina Barros, António Semedo, Paulo Nunes, Paulo Jorge Gonçalves, Pedro Lanban, Fernando José Paixão, Julião, Geny
Color, HD DV
178 minutes

***Où gît votre souriree enfoui?* (*Where Does Your Hidden Smile Lie?*, 2001)**
Portugal and France
Production: ARTE France, AMIP, Contracosta Produções
Direction: Pedro Costa

Photography: Pedro Costa, Jeanne Lapoirie
Editing: Dominique Auvray, Patrícia Saramago
Cast: Danièle Huillet, Jean-Marie Straub
Color, HD DV
104 minutes

6 Bagatelas (***6 Bagatelles*, 2001**)
Portugal and France
Production: ARTE France, AMIP, Contracosta Produções
Direction: Pedro Costa
Photography: Pedro Costa, Leanne Lapoirie
Editing: Patrícia Saramago
Music: Anton Webern
Cast: Danièle Huillet, Jean-Marie Straub
Color, HD DV
18 minutes

Juventude em marcha (***Colossal Youth*, 2006**)
Portugal, France, and Switzerland
Production: Contracosta Produções, Les Filmes de l'Étranger, Unlimited Film, Ventura Film
Direction: Pedro Costa
Photography: Pedro Costa, Leonardo Simões
Editing: Pedro Marques
Music: Os Tubarões, György Kurtág
Cast: Ventura, Vanda Duarte, Beatriz Duarte, Gustavo Sumpta, Cila Cardoso, Isabel Cardoso, Alberto Barros "Lento," António Semedo, Paulo Nunes, José Maria Pina, André Semedo, Alexandre Silva "Xana," Paula Barrulas
Color, HD DV
154 minutes

Tarrafal (***Tarrafal*, 2007**)
Portugal
Production: LX Filmes, Fundação Calouste Gulbenkian
Direction: Pedro Costa
Photography: Pedro Costa
Editing: Patrícia Saramago
Cast: José Alberto Silva, Lucinda Tavares, Ventura, Alfredo Mendes
Color, HD DV
16 minutes

***A caça ao coelho com pau* (*The Rabbit Hunters*, 2007)**
Portugal
Production: Pedro Costa, Jeonju International Film Festival-Jeonju Digital project
Direction: Pedro Costa
Photography: Pedro Costa
Editing: Cláudia Oliveira
Cast: Alfredo Mendes, Ventura, José Alberto Silva, Isabel Cardoso, Arlindo Semedo, António Semedo
Color, HD DV
22 minutes

***Ne change rien* (*Change Nothing*, 2009)**
Portugal and France
Production: Sociedade Óptica Técnica
Direction: Pedro Costa
Photography: Pedro Costa
Editing: Patrícia Saramago
Cast: Jeanne Balibar, Rodolphe Burger, Herbé Loos, Arnaud Dieterlen, Joël Theux
Black and white, HD DV
100 minutes
[Expanded from a 2005 short film titled *Ne change rien*]

***O nosso homem* (*Our Man*, 2010)**
Portugal
Production: LX Filmes, Fundação Calouste Gulbenkian, Jeonju Digital Project, Sociedade Óptica Técnica
Direction: Pedro Costa
Photography: Pedro Costa
Editing: Patrícia Saramago
Cast: José Alberto Silva, Lucinda Tavares Silva, Ventura, Alfredo Mendes, António Semedo
Color, HD DV
24 minutes

***Sweet Exorcism* (2012)**
Portugal
Production: Sociedade Óptica Técnica
Direction: Pedro Costa
Photography: Leonardo Simões
Editing: João Dias

Cast: Ventura, António Santos
Color, HD DV
30 minutes

***Cavalo dinheiro* (*Horse Money*, 2014)**
Portugal
Production: Sociedade Óptica Técnica
Direction: Pedro Costa
Photography: Leonardo Simões
Editing: João Dias
Cast: Ventura, Vitalina Varela, Tito Furtado, Benvindo Tavares, António Santos, Alberto Barros, Pedro Tavares, Isabel Cardoso, António Semedo, Luís Mendonça, Arlindo Pina, José António Veiga, João Gomes, Maurício Fernandes, Joel Santos, Maria dos Reis Pina, Alfredo Mendes, Zulmira Varela, Katelly Varela, António "Teacher" Leite, Gustavo Sumpta, José Alberto Silva, Maria Silva, António Silva, António Cruz, Tei Varela, Armando da Graça, José Tavares, Eunice Adão, Aliu Baldé, João Fortes, Eugênio Pedro, Martinho da Veiga, Luzia Tavares, Joaquim Tavares, Manuel Semedo, Miro Monteiro, Pires Duarte, Joyce Worm, Emanuel Lima, José Delgado, Vyachevslav Zhupik, Paulo Mota, Cristina Torres, Bubaka Embaló, Neusa Silva
Color, HD DV
104 minutes

***Vitalina Varela* (2019)**
Portugal and Cape Verde
Production: Sociedade Óptica Técnica
Direction: Pedro Costa
Screenplay: Pedro Costa, Vitalina Varela
Photography: Leonardo Simões
Editing: João Dias, Vítor Carvalho
Cast: Vitalina Varela, Ventura, Manuel Tavares Almeida, Francisco Brito, Marina Alves Domingues, Nilsa Fortes, Lisa Lopi, Bruno Brito Varela, Imídio Landim Monteiro, João Baptista Fortes, João Raimundo Monteiro, Benvinda Mendes
Color, HD DV
124 minutes

***As filhas do Fogo* (*Daughters of Fire*, 2023)**
Portugal
Production: Clarão Companhia
Direction: Pedro Costa

Screenplay: Pedro Costa
Photography: Leonardo Simões
Editing: Vítor Carvalho
Music: Biagio Marini, Os Músicos do Tejo
Cast: Alice Costa, Karyna Gomes, Elizabeth Pinard
Color, HD DV
9 minutes

BIBLIOGRAPHY

Andersen, Thom. "A Band of Outsiders." In *Letters from Fontaínhas: Three Films by Pedro Costa*, 26–29. New York: Criterion Collection, 2010.

———. "No Secrets Just Lessons: A Dialogue between Pedro Costa and Thom Andersen on Danièle Huillet and Jean-Marie Straub." *Cinema Scope* 29 (Winter 2007): 40–45.

Austin, Thomas. "Bigger Than Life, or Stranger: Pedro Costa's *Vitalina Varela*: Part I." *Senses of Cinema* 100 (January 2022). https://www.sensesofcinema.com/2022/feature-articles/bigger-than-life-or-stranger-pedro-costas-vitalina-varela-part-i/.

———. "Bigger Than Life, or Stranger: Pedro Costa's *Vitalina Varela*: Part III." *Senses of Cinema* 102 (July 2022). http://www.sensesofcinema.com/2022/feature-articles/bigger-than-life-or-stranger-pedro-costas-vitalina-varela-part-iii/.

Bahadur, Neil. "Interview: Pedro Costa." *Film Comment* (blog). July 21, 2015. https://www.filmcomment.com/blog/interview-pedro-costa/.

Barradas Jorge, Nuno. *Refocus: The Films of Pedro Costa*. Edinburgh: University of Edinburgh Press, 2021.

Batalha, Luís. "Cape Verdeans in Portugal." In *Transnational Archipelago: Perspectives on Cape Verdean Migration and Diaspora*, edited by Luís Batalha and Jorgen Carling, 62–73. Amsterdam: Amsterdam University Press, 2008.

Bazin, André. *What Is Cinema?* Translated by Hugh Gray. Berkeley: University of California Press, 1967.

Bértolo, José. "Alone in the Marriage Portrait: Pedro Costa's *Vitalina Varela*." *Forma de vida*. Accessed March 2024. https://formadevida.org/jbertolofdv23.

Bresson, Robert. *Notes on the Cinematograph*. New York: NYRB Classics, 2016.

Brody, Richard. "What to Stream: *Sicilia!*" *New Yorker*, September 5, 2020. https://www.newyorker.com/culture/the-front-row/what-to-stream-sicilia.

Cachado, Rita Ávila. "O plano especial de realojamento: Ambiente histórico, político e social." *Análise social* 206, no. 48, 1 (2013): 134–52.

Camia, Giovanni Marchini. "Pedro Costa and Wang Bing, Music and Reality." *Cinema Scope* 95 (Summer 2023): 46–51.

Codesal, Javier. *Canción de Pedro Costa*. Barcelona: Joaquín Gallego Editor and Ajuntament de Barcelona, Institut de Cultura, La Virreina Centre de la Imatge, 2022.

Costa, João Bénard da. "De sorrisos ocultos." In *Onde jaz o teu sorriso? Diálogos*, edited by Pedro Costa, Jean-Marie Straub, and Danièle Huillet, 142–50. Lisbon: Assírio & Alvim, 2004.

———. "O negro é uma cor ou o cinema de Pedro Costa." In *Cem mil cigarros: Os filmes de Pedro Costa*, edited by Ricardo Matos Cabo, 15–27. Lisbon: Orfeu Negro, 2009.

Costa, Pedro. *Casa de lava – Caderno*. Lisbon: Pierre von Kleist, 2013.

———. "A Closed Door That Leaves Us Guessing." Tokyo Film School lecture. *Rouge* 10 (2007). http://www.rouge.com.au/10/costa_seminar.html.

———. "A Conversation with Pedro Costa." Interview, Toronto Film Festival, September 7, 2019. *Vitalina Varela*. DVD. New York: Grasshopper.

———. *Film at Lincoln Center Podcast*. Episode 41, "#41—Pedro Costa." Film Society of Lincoln Center. 2015. https://soundcloud.com/filmlinc/41-pedro-costa?utm_source=clipboard&utm_medium=text&utm_campaign=social_sharing.

———. "I Have to Risk Each Shot." Interview by Michael Guillén. April 5, 2008. http://pedrocosta-heroi.blogspot.com/2008/04/i-have-to-risk-each-shot.html.

———. "The Mystery of the Great Pyramid." Translated by Ricardo Matos Cabo and Andy Rector. *Film Comment* (blog), July 15, 2016. https://www.filmcomment.com/blog/the-mystery-of-the-great-pyramid/.

———. *Ne change rien*. DVD liner notes. New York: Cinema Guild, 2011.

Costa, Pedro, and Rui Chafes. *Fora! / Out!* Oporto: Fundação Serralves, 2007.

Costa, Pedro, and Jean-Pierre Gorin. *No quarto da Vanda*. Audio commentary. DVD. New York: Criterion Collection, 2010.

Costa, Pedro, Cyril Neyrat, and Andy Rector. *Um melro dourado, um ramo de flores, uma colher de prata: No quarto da Vanda, Conversa com Pedro Costa*. Lisbon: Midas Filmes and Orfeu Negro, 2012.

Cronk, Jordan. "House of the Spirits." *Film Comment*, January–February 2020. https://www.filmcomment.com/article/house-of-the-spirits-pedro-costa-interview-vitalina-varela/.

Cutler, Aaron. "*Horse Money*: An Interview with Pedro Costa." *Cineaste* XL, no. 3 (Summer 2015). https://www.cineaste.com/summer2015/horse-money-pedro-costa-aaron-cutler.

Fajgenbaum, Emma. "Cinema as Disquiet: The Ghostly Realism of Pedro Costa." *New Left Review* 116–17 (March/June 2019): 137–59.

Fernández, Horacio Muñoz, and Iván Villarmea Álvarez. "Aesthetic Tendencies in Contemporary Portuguese Cinema." *Cinema Comparat/ive Cinema* III, no. 6 (2015): 39–45.

Ferreira, Carlos Melo. *Pedro Costa*. Oporto: Edições Afrontamento, 2018.

Ferreira, Carolin Overhoff. "High and Low: Popular Music in Portuguese Cinema and Pedro Costa's *Ne change rien*." *Music and the Moving Image* 9, no. 1 (Spring 2016): 23–37.

Fujiwara, Chris. "Mikio Naruse: The Other Woman and the View from Outside." *Film Comment*, September–October 2005. https://www.filmcomment.com/article/mikio-naruse-the-other-women-and-the-view-from-the-outside/.

———. Untitled talk sent by the author to James Naremore on *The Daughters of Fire*. Yamagata Documentary Film Festival. October 9, 2023.

Gerbault, Aurélien. "All Blossoms Again." In *Supplements: Letters from Fontaínhas: Three Films by Pedro Costa*. DVD. New York: Criterion Collection, 2010.

Godard, Jean-Luc. *Godard on Godard*. Edited by Jean Narboni and Tom Milne. New York: Viking Press, 1972.

Goffman, Erving. *Frame Analysis*. New York: Harper, 1974.

Guarneri, Michael. "Documentary, Realism, and Life on the Margins," interview with Pedro Costa, *BOMB* 133 (Fall 2015). https://bombmagazine.org/articles/2015/07/16/pedro-costa/.

———. "Pedro Costa." *Débordements*, November 11, 2019. https://www.debordements.fr/Pedro-Costa-2019.

Guest, Haden, and Mark Peranson. "I See a Darkness: Pedro Costa on *Vitalina Varela*." *Cinema Scope* 80 (September 20, 2019). https://cinema-scope.com/cinema-scope-magazine/i-see-a-darkness-pedro-costa-on-vitalina-varela/.

Guillén, Michael. "Pedro Costa (and Others) on *Casa de lava* and *Tarrafal*." *Evening Class* (blog), March 12, 2008. https://theeveningclass.blogspot.com/2008/03/pedro-costa-and-others-on-casa-de-lava_12.html.

———. "Pedro Costa and Others on *O Sangue* (*The Blood*, 1989)." Cinematheque Ontario program notes. March 7, 2008. https://theeveningclass.blogspot.com/2008/03/pedro-costa-and-others-on-o-sangue.html.

Hansen, James. "Interview with Pedro Costa." *Film Quarterly* 63, no. 2 (Winter 2009): 54–56.

Hasumi, Shiguéhiko. "Aventura: Um ensaio sobre Pedro Costa." In *Cem mil cigarros: Os filmes de Pedro Costa*, edited by Ricardo Matos Cabo, 133–8. Lisbon: Orfeu Negro, 2009.

Jenkins, David. "Some Violence Is Required: A Conversation with Pedro Costa." *Notebook*, March 11, 2013. https://mubi.com/notebook/posts/some-violence-is-required-a-conversation-with-pedro-costa.

Kasman, Daniel. "Cinema Must Be a Ritual: Pedro Costa Discusses 'Vitalina Varela.'" *Notebook,* February 19, 2020. https://mubi.com/notebook/posts/cinema-must-be-a-ritual-pedro-costa-discusses-vitalina-varela.

Lash, Dominic. *The Cinema of Disorientation: Inviting Confusions.* Edinburgh: Edinburgh University Press, 2020.

Lim, Dennis. "António Reis and Margarida Cordeiro," *Artforum* 5, no. 10 (Summer 2012). https://www.artforum.com/columns/antonio-reis-and-margarida-cordeiro-200235/.

———. "The Sound of Music: Pedro Costa's *Ne change rien.*" *Artforum* 49, no. 3 (November 2010). https://www.artforum.com/columns/dennis-lim-on-pedro-costas-ne-change-rien-195951/.

Lopes, José Vicente Lopes. *Tarrafal-Chão Bom: Memórias e verdades.* Vol 1. Praia: Instituto da Investigação e do Património Cultural, 2010.

Lounas, Thierry. "Notas sobre *Onde jaz o teu sorriso?*" In *Onde jaz o teu sorriso? Diálogos,* edited by Pedro Costa, Jean-Marie Straub, and Danièle Huillet, 109–16. Lisbon: Assírio & Alvim, 2004.

Martin, Adrian. "A vida interior de um filme." In *Cem mil cigarros: Os filmes de Pedro Costa,* edited by Ricardo Matos Cabo, 91–96. Lisbon: Orfeu Negro, 2009.

———. *Blood.* Liner notes. DVD. New York: Criterion Collection, 2009.

———. "Reviews: *Blood:* The Inner Life of a Film." *Film Critic: Adrian Martin* (blog). Accessed December 15, 2022. https://www.adrianmartinfilmcritic.com/reviews/b/blood.html.

McGilligan, Patrick. "Letters from Fontaínhas: Interview with Pedro Costa." *Film International* 8, no. 3 (2010): 82–90.

Meehan, Ryan J. "Pedro Costa's Post-documentary." *Harvard Crimson,* November 11, 2010. www.thecrimson.com/article/2010/11/2/costa-ne-change-rien.

Moutinho, Anabela, and Maria da Graça Lobo. "Conversation with Pedro Costa: The Encounter with António Reis." *Cinema Comparat/ive Cinema* III, no. 6 (2015): 17–22.

Oliveira, Ana Balona de. "Rooms of Colossal Bones: Pedro Costa's Trilogy." *Mute,* June 26, 2008. https://www.metamute.org/editorial/articles/rooms-colossal-bones-pedro-costas-trilogy.

Pantenburg, Volker. "Realism, Not Reality: Pedro Costa's Digital Testimonies." *Afterall* 24 (2010): 54–61.

Peranson, Mark. "Pedro Costa: An Introduction." *Cinema Scope* 27 (Summer 2006): 6–15.

Perez, Gilberto. *The Material Ghost: Films and Their Medium.* Baltimore: John Hopkins Press, 1998.

Rancière, Jacques. *The Emancipated Spectator.* Translated by Gregory Elliott. New York: Verso, 2009.

———. *Pedro Costa: Os quartos do cineasta*. Lisbon: Relógio d'Água, 2003.

———. "Política de Pedro Costa." In *Cem mil cigarros: Os filmes de Pedro Costa*, edited by Ricardo Matos Cabo, 53–67. Lisbon: Orfeu Negro, 2009.

Romney, Jonathan. "Film of the Week: Horse Money." *Film Comment* (blog), July 16, 2015. https://www.filmcomment.com/blog/film-of-the-week-horse-money/.

Rosenbaum, Jonathan. "Films of the Future (on Pedro Costa)." February 1, 2024. https://jonathanrosenbaum.net/2024/02/cinema-of-the-future/.

———. "Finding Oneself in the Dark: Costa's *Ne change rien*." March 7, 2023. https://jonathanrosenbaum.net/2023/03/ne-change-rien/.

———. "Pedro Costa's *Horse Money*." *Art Forum* 53, no. 10 (Summer 2015). www.artforum.com/print/201506/pedro-costa-s-horse-money-52252.

Sadlier, Darlene J. *The Portuguese-Speaking Diaspora: Seven Centuries of Literature and the Arts*. Austin: University of Texas Press, 2016.

Seitz, Matt Zoller. "Light and Shadow, and Music on the Wondrous Dreamy Side." *New York Times*, November 2, 2010. https://www.nytimes.com/2010/11/03/movies/03nechange.html.

Stead, C. K. *The New Poetic*. New York: Harper Torchbooks, 1966.

Stern, Lesley. "Paths That Wind through the Thickets of Things." *Critical Inquiry* 28, no. 1 (Fall 2001): 317–54.

Tarrant, Patrick. "Montage in the Portrait Film: Where Does the Hidden Time Lie?" *Alphaville: Journal of Film and Screen Media* 5 (Summer 2013). https://www.alphavillejournal.com/Issue5/HTML/ArticleTarrant.html.

Varela, Raquel, and Joana Alcântara. "Social Conflicts in the Portuguese Revolution, 1974–1975." *Labour / Le travail* 74 (Fall 2014): 151–77.

Vieira, Estela. "Pedro Costa's Cinematic Walls." *Journal of Lusophone Studies* 2, no. 1 (2017): 165–80.

Virillo, Paul. *The Vision Machine*. Translated by Julie Rose. London: BFI, 1994.

INDEX

JAMES NAREMORE is Chancellors' Professor Emeritus of English, Comparative Literature, and The Media School at Indiana University Bloomington. Among his books are *More Than Night: Film Noir in Its Contexts, The Magic World of Orson Welles, Charles Burnett: A Cinema of Symbolic Knowledge,* and *On Kubrick*. He is editor (with Patrick M. Brantlinger) of *Modernity and Mass Culture.*

DARLENE J. SADLIER is Professor Emerita of Spanish and Portuguese at Indiana University Bloomington. Her most recent books are *Memories of Underdevelopment, A Century of Brazilian Documentary Film: From Nationalism to Protest,* and *The Lilly Library from A to Z: Intriguing Objects in a World-Class Collection*. She is editor and translator of *One Hundred Years after Tomorrow: Brazilian Women's Fiction in the Twentieth Century.*

For Indiana University Press

Sabrina Black, Editorial Assistant

Tony Brewer, Artist and Book Designer

Allison Chaplin, Acquisitions Editor

Anna Garnai, Production Coordinator

Sophia Hebert, Assistant Acquisitions Editor

Samantha Heffner, Marketing and Publicity Manager

Katie Huggins, Production Manager

Nancy Lightfoot, Project Manager/Editor

Dan Pyle, Online Publishing Manager

Michael Regoli, Director of Publishing Operations

Pamela Rude, Senior Artist and Book Designer

Stephen Williams, Assistant Director of Marketing